The Nuremberg Medical Trial

Studies in Modern European History

Frank J. Coppa
General Editor

Vol. 53

PETER LANG
New York • Washington, D.C./Baltimore • Bern
Frankfurt am Main • Berlin • Brussels • Vienna • Oxford

Horst H. Freyhofer

The Nuremberg Medical Trial

The Holocaust and the Origin of the Nuremberg Medical Code

PETER LANG
New York • Washington, D.C./Baltimore • Bern
Frankfurt am Main • Berlin • Brussels • Vienna • Oxford

Library of Congress Cataloging-in-Publication Data

Freyhofer, Horst H.
The Nuremberg medical trial: the Holocaust
and the origin of the Nuremberg medical code / Horst H. Freyhofer.
p. cm. — (Studies in modern European history; vol. 53)
Includes bibliographical references and index.
1. Nuremberg Medical Trial, Nuremberg, Germany, 1946–1947. 2. War
crime trials—Germany. 3. Human experimentation in medicine—Law and
legislation—Criminal provisions. 4. Human experimentation in
medicine—Europe—History. I. Title. II. Studies in
modern European history; v. 53.
KZ1178.F74   341.6'9—dc21   2003005573
ISBN 0-8204-6797-9
ISSN 0893-6897

Bibliographic information published by **Die Deutsche Bibliothek**.
Die Deutsche Bibliothek lists this publication in the "Deutsche
Nationalbibliografie"; detailed bibliographic data is available
on the Internet at http://dnb.ddb.de/.

The paper in this book meets the guidelines for permanence and durability
of the Committee on Production Guidelines for Book Longevity
of the Council of Library Resources.

© 2004 Peter Lang Publishing, Inc., New York
275 Seventh Avenue, 28th Floor, New York, NY 10001
www.peterlangusa.com

Printed in The United States of America

Acknowledgments

THE IDEA TO PUBLISH a book on the Nuremberg Medical Trial occurred to me years ago when I taught History of Science at Florida Institute of Technology. An assigned research project revealed that, with the exception of Alexander Mitcherlich's and Fred Mielke's 1949 classic *Doctors of Infamy*, my students were unable to find a single work that presented a comprehensive overview of the trial. I have since presented three papers dealing with different aspects of the trial at the annual meetings of the German Studies Association. These papers form the basis for the three chapters of this book. They include many helpful comments and ideas generated during discussion sections following paper presentations. I would like to thank all of my colleagues for their sustained interest in this subject.

I would also like to thank the many colleagues in the legal and medical professions who have given me their professional advice on the subject in their areas of expertise. My wife, C. Sue Freyhofer, M.D., was unrelenting in her criticism of many of my presentations when they needed focus, particularly with respect to the relationship between medicine and law. Without her help, this book would not have been possible.

The cardiologist Vid Valdmanis, M.D. assisted me in placing complex medical questions in the context of larger philosophic and bioethical developments.

I am indebted to Middlebury College for its generous Research Fellowship that gave me the time and resources needed for a comprehensive investigation of the documents of the entire trial. It took two years. I am equally indebted to Plymouth State University for the sabbatical that allowed me to compose the book. Fleur Laslocky and Hans Raum of Middlebury's Starr Library and Gary McCool of Plymouth's Lamson Library have provided invaluable assistance in my research. Donald Singer from the National Archives in Washington, D.C. has been generous with his time helping me locate the photographic material contained in this work.

Michael Carr's footwork in organizing the documentary material of this manuscript has been invaluable. So was Marie-Therese Gardner's help in translating French documents. No words can justify my gratitude to Rick Agran for his timely assistance in editing the manuscript, especially during the last stages of its completion. He may have succeeded in eliminating most of my "Germanisms" from the text.

All remaining shortcomings of the work are, of course, my own responsibility. If anything, I would hope that they might help encourage more debates and scholarly dialogues on a subject that certainly deserves a fuller treatment than it has received thus far.

Table of Contents

Approaches to Representing the Subject

FOLLOWING WORLD WAR II, the victorious Allies in Europe-under the leadership of the United States, the Soviet Union, Great Britain, and France-created military tribunals to bring to justice the individuals who held major responsibility for the atrocities committed under the Hitler regime. To that purpose, the Allies created laws and set up tribunals, the first of which was the International Military Tribunal in the City of Nuremberg. Here the Allies tried the highest available Nazi leaders for conspiracy to wage war, war crimes, and crimes against humanity. Of the twenty-three defendants in the dock, nineteen were founds guilty. Eleven received the death penalty. Seven received sentences ranging from ten years to life in prison.

Following this Major Trial, the United States set up the American Military Tribunal in an effort to try other high ranking Nazi officials. These officials were grouped by profession or area of responsibility, such as jurisprudence or medical service. The first group to be tried consisted of twenty-three physicians and medical administrators. On November 21, 1946, they were indicted for subjecting inmates of Nazi concentration camps to torturous and fatal medical experiments, acts that met the definition of war crimes and crimes against humanity as interpreted in the Major Trial. Some of the defendants were also charged with conspiracy to commit crimes and membership in organizations found to be criminal in the Major Trial, such as the Gestapo (Secret Police) or the SS (Schutzstaffeln, or Protective Guards). But most of the tribunal's focus remained on the charges pertaining to the medical experiments.

The Medical Trial, better known as the Doctors Trial, lasted nine months. On August 20, 1947, sixteen of the defendants were found guilty. Seven received the death penalty, the rest sentences ranging from ten years to life in prison. After exhausting all appeals, the capital defendants were executed on June 2, 1948. Josef Mengele, the most notorious of the medical experimentors, was not among them. He, like many others, had gone into hiding before the trial. Others had escaped justice by committing suicide.

The Nuremberg Medical Trial revealed what may have been one of the most gruesome chapters in the Holocaust. The defendants were brought to account for the torturous murder and mutilation of thousands of human test subjects. Yet they tried to convince the court that these acts had been legally correct, medically necessary, and morally right. This was all the more disturbing as the court came to realize that many of the defendants could not be dismissed as secondary minds with a penchant for sadism, as one might have assumed. On the contrary, some of them were outstanding scholars and recognized leaders in their fields. They advanced their arguments with unwavering conviction and submitted an overwhelming amount of evidence in their support. They attempted to prove that: (1) no universal standards of human research ethics existed when they performed their experiments; (2) they had acted in accordance with existing law; (3) the use of prison inmates as research subjects was generally accepted practice pioneered and still practiced in the penitentiaries of the accusing nation, the United States; and (4) the torturous conditions under which the medical experiments were performed were primarily the effect the horrendously destructive war had on nearly everybody who was touched by it, especially in Germany. Although their arguments were firmly dismissed by the tribunal, reading the court records provides little comfort for anyone who would like to believe that the case had left no unanswered questions.

Chapter I of the book describes the experiments on human subjects for which the physicians and administrators were indicted against the historic background and medical tradition that made them possible. It concludes with a discussion of experimental results and their utilization. Chapter II describes the trial itself and concludes with a legal analysis of the case, its outcome, and implications for the future. It describes the origin of the Nuremberg Medical Code, perhaps the most enduring legacy of the entire trial. It is the most globally recognized guide for the treatment of human medical subjects. Chapter III offers a debate on the ethical dimension of the trial, not only for the field of medicine, but modern society in general. The material presented is based primarily on the trial records, which contain the arguments made by the prosecution, the replies offered by the defendants, the evidence produced by both sides, and the deliberations and conclusions drawn by the court.

Discussions about such matters are not without their challenges. Giving a voice to the defendants, letting them present a rationale for their ghastly deeds, may diminish the dignity of their victims. It may be argued that therefore no perpetrator of the Holocaust should ever receive a "fair hearing". At the very least, any explanation of their motives should always be acceptable to the memory of the victims. It may also be argued that observing this noble principle may limit people's ability to learn the lessons needed to prevent history from repeating itself. One way of facing the dilemma is to deny it.

When staring at the sun for too long, Hegel wrote in his *Philosophy of History*, the eyes begin to see dark spots emerging like protective shields against a burning truth. Nietzsche reversed the metaphor in his *Birth of Tragedy,* writing that bright spots will emerge before the eyes that stare too long into the abyss of human nature. Apparently, humans find unveiled truth and unmasked horror equally unbearable. They will try to cover both with soothing images, either offered by their culture or produced by themselves. But efforts to remove these images never seem very successful.

Claude Lanzmann provides a case in point. He stated that when making his film *Shoah,* which exposes Adolf Hitler's genocide of Jews, he "was trying to look straight into this black sun which is the Holocaust" and concluded that " the only way to cope with this blinding reality is to blind one's self to all kinds of explanation. To refuse the explanation. It is the only way."[1] In other words, the only way to see and cope with the full horror of the Holocaust is to refuse to accept any explanation and to resist the temptation of covering the horror with soothing images offered by answers to the question *why.* Lanzmann believes explanation is not only soothing, but exonerating. This is a truly unbearable thought for many. Therefore only description, an exhaustive account of the *how* of the horror, is tolerable. This is what he attempted to do in his *Shoah.*

The critic Ron Rosenbaum, who interviewed Lanzmann several years after the release of the film in 1985, argues that Lanzmann, as much as he tried, had not been able to live up to his own intentions.[2] In this interview Lanzmann indicated that he did acknowledge the acceptability of some form of explanation after all.

Indeed, trying to provide an exhaustive factual account of the Holocaust without *some* form of explanation should agonize even the most patient individual. No such account could ever be complete. The gruesome facts are too many. What facts should be included and what facts should be omitted depends on the selection of the form of representation. And the reasons for the selection provide an explanation for the *how.* Different selections lead to different, often irreconcilable, explanations. This inescapable conclusion leads to the disturbing realization that every representation of historical phenomena to some degree is a result of human choice. The choice could always be different.

Lanzmann, a former secretary of Jean-Paul Sartre, was well aware of this dilemma and apparently tried to escape its obvious implication for the representation of the Holocaust by keeping his gaze on the "black sun", hoping perhaps that the blindness it would cause would make him a clairvoyant. And how else could a victim or anyone who identifies with the victims of the Holocaust approach this subject? Indeed, many have opted for silence, finding solace in the words of George Steiner that "the world of Auschwitz lies outside speech as it lies outside reason."[3]

The question regarding the proper representation of the Holocaust has been a matter of particular concern in the country of its origin, Germany, especially since the fall of the Berlin Wall in 1989. A general debate ensued with respect to finding an appropriate form for a Holocaust memorial in the center of the newly renovated capital. Many designs were proposed in open competition and their respective merits debated by the public. The German parliament ultimately adopted and funded the design of the American architect Peter Eisenman, but not after much heated controversy. The original design showed about 3,000 tombstone-like barren, rectangular steles assembled closely together. Visitors wandering between them had little choice but to ponder the immensity of the exhibit in relative silence. Given the original design, there would be no place to obtain information, gather for discussions, organize workshops, or engage in any of the many activities requiring dialogue. A majority of the public and parliament, seeing a need for such dialogue, argued for the inclusion of such a place, and the final redesign combines approximately 2,700 steles with a small documentation center attached to one side.

It should not be surprising that the land of the perpetrators contains some loud dissenting voices disapproving of the entire project. But what should be surprising is that some of those voices come from the political left. For instance, Martin Walser, in his acceptance speech of the Peace Prize of the German Book Trade in Frankfurt in October of 1998, refocused the entire debate on how to think about and represent the Holocaust appropriately in Germany by Germans. He confessed that at 71 years old, he was no longer able to gaze into Lanzmann's "black sun," at least not as represented by the mass media. He questioned the wisdom of the many intellectuals who, as he saw it, had arrogated to themselves the right to shame the German public for their own purposes. He remarked:

> Everyone knows our historic burden, the everlasting shame. No day goes by without being confronted by it. Could it be that the intellectuals, by confronting us with our shame and by dutifully working for the preservation of the gruesome memories, may succumb to the illusion, if only for a moment, to be exempted [from guilt] and to be closer to the victims than the perpetuators? A momentary easing of the inexorable opposition of perpetrators and victims. I have never thought it possible to leave the ranks of the accused. At times, when I cannot look anywhere anymore without being attacked by an accusation, to find relief, I have to tell myself that the media have turned

> accusation into a routine. I have turned away at least twenty times already when the
> worst filmclips of concentration camps were shown.[4]

And turning "the center of Berlin into a football-sized nightmare made of concrete," he added, only demonstrates to future generations what ill work people can do who feel responsible for the conscience of others. Conscience is an individual matter, he proclaimed in contradiction to his Marxist roots, and that is where the matter should rest. His speech did not encourage dialogue, but it stirred up controversy.

Ignatz Bubis, the head of the Central Council of Jews in Germany, immediately accused Walser of "mental arson." Again, a public debate ensued that drew comments from nearly every person of stature in Germany, including President Roman Herzog and Chancellor Gerhard Schroeder. If anything, the debate confirmed the continuing difficulty of finding proper ways to represent the Holocaust in any context. It reminded everyone of the continuing suspicion that exists between people who see their natural place on the side of the victims and those who feel it is their responsibility to accept the legacy of the perpetrators, albeit grudgingly.

The well-known legal philosopher and novelist Bernhard Schlinck, in an article commemorating the 56th anniversary of Germany's capitulation, has argued that both sides have to deal with the trauma they inherited from World War II and the Holocaust separately, at least for now. But the descendants of the victims and the descendants of the perpetrators have to realize that efforts to come to terms with the trauma by confronting the past will ultimately succeed only if they succeed on both sides. And neither side can prescribe to the other how to proceed.[5]

It should not be surprising that those who try to preserve the dignity of the victims should look with suspicion upon efforts to make acts such as committed by Nazi physicians subjects of understanding. But it seems inconceivable that anything that may be said about them could make them less than condemnable, medically, legally, and particularly morally, Lanzmann's warning not withstanding. But condemnation is not enough, as the well known bioethicist Arthur Caplan has pointed out. He writes,

> Ironically, the scale of immorality is one of the reasons why the moral reasoning of health
> care professionals and biomedical scientists during the Nazi era has received little
> attention from contemporary bioethics scholars. It is clear that what Nazi doctors, biologists, and public health officials did was immoral. The indisputable occurrence of
> wrongdoing suggests that there is little for the ethicist to say except to join others in
> condemnation of what happened. But condemnation is not sufficient.[6]

Trying to understand what motivated German physicians such as Josef Mengele to pursue their bloody work the way they did is still a controversial undertaking. Some explanations have been offered by scholars such as Robert

Proctor, Benno Mueller-Hill, George Annas and others. But so far there has only been one author who has written a major work focusing exclusively on this question. Robert Jay Lifton's *The Nazi Doctors*, published in 1986, leaves no doubt that most of the camp physicians committed the most condemnable atrocities imaginable.[7] But he offers an explanation. He argues that they were able to do so only by separating the humanitarian side of their personality from its demonic side, thereby living a double existence. He bases this Jekyll and Hyde explanation on personal interviews he had with surviving camp physicians, many of them members of the SS. The book was well received by the general public, but it generated some sharp criticism from a number of scholars in the field.

Norman Ravitch, an expert on the subject, rejects the possibility of such "doubling." To him, the categorical distinction between the humanitarian principles that sustain the medical profession and the totalitarian principles that sustain such fascist views as espoused by the Nazis are irreconcilable under any circumstances. He is particularly disturbed by Lifton's argument that there were indeed some camp physicians who had managed to remain decent human beings. Referring to such a physician named in Lifton's book, Ravitch concludes that "the only failure of Dr. Lifton's method and analysis lies in his inability to convince us how this SS doctor could be at the same time a humane medical man and a true believer in the Nazi program."[8]

Thomas Kohut, also an expert on the subject, agrees that this combination is indeed an objective impossibility. But he also thinks it was possible for Nazi doctors to somehow skirt the issue of morality, mainly by dismissing it altogether. Kohut believes that Lifton's analysis is weak on a number of points. "Lifton's model of doubling," he writes, "fails to comprehend the motives of the Nazi doctors; it does not explain the psychological attraction of the Nazi ideology or why doctors and others committed to that ideology participated enthusiastically in the extermination of millions of helpless people."[9] Kohut further warns that the idea of "doubling" can be used to justify unconscionable acts retroactively. Also, he argues, understanding Nazi physicians requires one to have a certain measure of empathy, if not sympathy, for them. Lifton seems to show some empathy, but not enough for the task. While Kohut finds this refreshing, it also means that he thinks Lifton's study is seriously flawed because it is not objective.

On the other hand, Bruno Bettelheim, a renowned writer and camp survivor, gives much credit to Lifton's efforts to gain a better understanding of the minds of Nazi physicians. But in his review of Lifton's *The Nazi Doctors* he restates an often heard fear. "I restricted myself to trying to understand the psychology of the prisoners and shied away from trying to understand the psychology of the SS," Bettelheim writes, "because of the ever present danger that understanding fully may come close to forgiveness."[10]

Lifton defended his approach of analyzing Nazi physicians and particularly the idea of "doubling" against his critics in a subsequent article.[11] He notes that Kohut's charge of empathy and even sympathy for Nazi physicians with some irritation, having left no doubt about his Jewish identity and feelings for the victims in his *The Nazi Doctors*. Heeding Kohut's warning would indeed confine the study of Nazi physicians and other Holocaust perpetrators to little more than open-ended chronicles of atrocities, as envisioned by Claude Lanzmann and as provided to some degree by such scholars as Michael Kater and Ernst Klee.

Producing chronicles of atrocities may indeed be a more reassuring guarantor for all those who share the hope that such atrocities must happen "never again" than any inquiry into the minds of those who committed the atrocities ever could. But human history casts a long shadow on this hope. Chronicles of atrocities have often led to counter-chronicles and further atrocities, as such recent crises observed in the Balkans, the Middle East, and Africa remind us again. Analyses of the perpetrators' thoughts and motives that include perspectives of the perepetrators themselves may not be the most effective step toward breaking such vicious cycles, but it is reasonable to suppose that the potential benefit of such analyses outweighs their potential harm.

Lifton's *The Nazi Doctors* probably represents the only major attempt so far to gain some understanding of the perpetrators' deeds by invoking the perpetrators' own perspectives on them. Benno Mueller-Hill with his book *Murderous Science* has done something similar with respect to geneticists and anthropologists who committed or contributed to atrocities during the Nazi regime as well.[12] Other studies, such as George Annas' and Michael Grodin's *The Nazi Doctors and the Nuremberg Code*, Angelika Ebbinghaus' and Klaus Doerner's *Vernichten und Heilen*, and Francis Nicosia's and Jonathan Huener's *Medicine and Medical Ethics in Nazi Germany* have added valuable comments to these efforts.[13] But the small volume of studies on the subject do not match the enormity of the crimes, crimes committed by people who largely thought they were doing no wrong. We should wonder why they thought that way. In the words of Arthur Caplan, "[t]he puzzle of how it came to be that physicians and scientists who committed so many crimes and caused so much suffering and death did so in the belief that they were morally right cries out for analysis, discussion, and debate."[14] This book is meant to offer some assistance in dealing with this puzzle.

CHAPTER 1

The Road to Nuremberg

None of us is allowed to make the apologetic suggestion that man is irrevocably evil.
—Alexander Mitscherlich and Fred Mielke in the preface of
their *Das Diktat der Menschenverachtung*

Not turning away, but facing the trauma liberates the soul.
—Theodor Litt, cited in Ernst Klee's *Was Sie Taten—Was Sie Wurden*

I would probably do everything just the way I did it then.
—Defendant Hans Romberg at the Medical Trial when asked how he would act
under circumstances similar to those that prevailed during the Hitler regime

I might have been no different from Eppinger, and that is a reason to repeat his story.
—Howard M. Spiro, Professor of Internal Medicine and Gastroenterology
at Yale University, trying to explain Hans Eppinger's role in torturous
experiments on inmates at Dachau Concentration Camp

The Nuremberg Medical Trial: A Symbol of Broken Trust

IN 1852, A GERMAN medical journal reported on an experiment performed to
determine the contagiousness of secondary syphilis. A physician injected the
discharge of a syphilitic woman into eleven uninfected hospitalized patients,
men and women ranging in age from 17 to 28, who all contracted the disease.
The patients were kept ignorant of the potentially fatal experiment performed
on them, and the readers were informed that all was done "without infring-
ing the laws of humanity."[1] At the time, such experiments were not uncommon in Western countries and their publication evoked little concern for the
welfare of the human subjects, among either physicians or the unaware pub-

lic. When ethical concerns were raised at all, it usually was to demonstrate the supposed integrity of the researcher, not to deplore the plight of the subject.

The situation did not change much until atrocious abuses by physicians who had conducted experiments on concentration camp inmates during World War II became public knowledge in the years following the war. Twenty-three German physicians and administrators were indicted for war crimes and crimes against humanity before an American Military Tribunal in Nuremberg. The defendants tried to convince the judges that those experiments had not crucially exceeded conventional standards for medical experimentation on human subjects, and their exceptional callousness was not as much a sign of individual human failure as it was a testimony to the brutalizing effect of the war.

To the judges, those arguments demonstrated an urgent need for clear and binding standards capable of protecting human subjects from further abuse and an institutional framework capable of safeguarding these standards. In the past, physicians defined these standards largely for themselves. They had managed to keep matters dealing with their proper observance of these standards in the hands of their own professional organizations. The Nuremberg Medical Trial had made it obvious to many observers that this self-regulatory Hippocratic tradition had failed miserably during the Hitler regime and that the time had come to impose external constraints on the medical profession and on the political system in which it operates. Consequently in their verdict, the judges introduced a set of medical principles which researchers working with human subjects must observe to assure their subjects' welfare. The principles are generally known as the Nuremberg Code. It stipulates that no one may be part of a medical experiment without competent informed consent and the right to withdraw this consent at any point during the experiment.

Outside Germany, the code was largely viewed as a means to restrain German barbarians from practicing inhumane medicine, but it was deemed unnecessary for physicians elsewhere. Many, in fact, regarded it as an instrument created by the Allies to force the German medical profession back into the Hippocratic tradition they had abandoned. Inside Germany it was seen more as an instrument to purge the medical profession of a small group of supposedly atypical physicians whose ethical principles of "doing no harm" (primum non cocere) had been depraved by the doctrines of National Socialism. Few physicians anywhere, inside or outside of Germany, felt that the Nuremberg Code had a direct bearing on their work. Some even continued dangerous experiments with unsuspecting subjects, in some cases with fatal results, such as the syphilis experiments on African-Americans at the Tuskegee Institute in Alabama.[2]

By the mid-century, such experiments had become rare, and the decades following World War II saw a growing challenge to the largely paternalistic role physicians had played in the past. Increasingly, patients challenged this role in medical offices, hospitals, legislatures, and the courts. To be sure, their growing demand for more information about, and greater control over the treatment of, their own illness, as well as matters of communal health and medical research were not raised in the "Spirit of Nuremberg." Few people knew anything specific about the trial, and most Germans frantically concentrated on rebuilding their country while trying to forget their embarrassing past as fast as possible. But a general awareness that some physicians had been convicted in Nuremberg of the most heinous abuses imaginable, and that the court had established guidelines to prevent further abuses in the future, gave added justification to the public's questioning attitude. The fact that the guidelines were drawn up chiefly to prevent abuses of human subjects in medical experiments rather than to regulate medical treatment of patients apparently did not change its largely symbolic meaning.

It may be argued that the Nuremberg Medical Trial symbolizes a break, not so much with the image physicians have of themselves, but with the image patients have of themselves. People everywhere have given notice of their new found suspicion that the supposed fiduciary healer may not always have their best interest in mind, indeed, given the proper circumstances, may turn out to be a killer, as the trial demonstrated. The traditional assumption of trust between physician and patient was questioned not by the physician but by the patient. The Medical Trial may not have contributed much to the erosion of this trust, a trust that had always empowered the physician much more than the patient. But if this erosion needed a symbol, Nuremberg provided it, at least in Germany.

The Hippocratic Tradition and Its Modern Challenges

FOR PHYSICIANS, THE TRUST that patients increasingly questioned after the Nuremberg Medical Trial had always been part of a set of basic medical principles whose origins are commonly traced back to the writings of Hippocrates. For centuries, they defined the practice of medicine as a proper application of medical skills and ethics within the organizational framework of a self-regulating profession. Skills and ethics were seen as inseparable tools acquired through proper medical training. However, the skills, if not the ethics, had already come under attack long before the Medical Trial. The Hippocratic science on which they rested was revolutionized by such questioning minds as Andreas Vesalius and William Harvey in the sixteenth and seventeenth centuries, before finally being overthrown in the nineteenth century by such pioneers as Louis Pasteur and Paul Ehrlich.

Hippocrates subscribed to a theory of disease that dominated medical practice for more than two millennia. Accordingly, four basic organic substances with opposing qualities, the humors, formed a harmonious synthesis in the constitution and function of the human body, called homeostasis. Illness occurred when, through flawed interaction between parts of the body or the body and its environment, this homeostasis developed discords, or humeral imbalances. The physician's cure, following proper diagnosis of type and degree of humeral imbalance, consisted primarily in restoring the homeostasis through changes in the patient's external and internal environment, e.g., through dietary prescriptions, bleeding, sweating, visits to spas, etc. By removing traditional supernatural elements from his humeral pathology as much as possible and grounding it in logically verifiable observational data, Hippocrates and his followers laid the foundation for the first scientific medical tradition in Western civilization.

They also organized physicians into a guild system under strict codes regulating the conduct of members with each other and with their patients. These codes guaranteed patients the full benefit of the physician's skills, regardless of social station, and protection from certain abuses, but they did not promise full disclosure of diagnosis and prognosis. Given the social stratification of the Greek city-state, with its institution of slavery, such a suggestion would have been met with general astonishment. How much of a patient's disposition a physician would disclose was left to his discretion and apparently corresponded closely to the patient's ranking in society, a practice that largely remained in effect until fairly recent times and has by no means disappeared from our society altogether.

Hippocrates' humeral pathology provided the basis for medical theory and practice until the early part of the nineteenth century, when, primarily through the introduction of more efficient microscopes, researchers detected the cell as the essential building block of life and its method of replication by division. The step from humoral to cellular pathology did not take long.

The contributions of researchers like Robert Virchow, Louis Pasteur, and Paul Ehrlich to the subsequent theory explaining disease as an invasion of cells, called germs, which destroy its host organism through continuous replication, fill many pages of most medical textbooks. According to cellular pathology, or the germ theory of disease, the body must be viewed as a battlefield, where invading germs fight with armies of defenders, produced by the organism's response system. Because germs generally spread between hosts, whole groups of organism are subjects of contagion. The consequences of the new theory were far-reaching and changed the physician's role in society considerably.

Since the new germ theory of disease did not allow physicians to distinguish between the well-being of the individual and that of the community as clearly as the humoral theory had, their traditional responsibility for the health of the individual diminished in favor of an increased responsibility for the community. Instead of aiding nature's healing power by restoring individual humoral balances, their role now consisted in eliminating a crippling and often deadly swarm of invisible soldiers from as many infected human bodies as possible. Much of this struggle shifted from the doctor's office to newly created research laboratories and hospitals, where the search for "antibodies" and "magic bullets" produced new drugs and vaccines designed to protect whole populations from real or potential epidemics.

Most of the epidemic research was performed on animals, but eventually the more promising findings had to be tested on human beings. These tests posed considerable risk to the individual subjects initially testing a new medication. Serious and lasting harm, if not death, could result. Faced with this responsibility, the researching physician had to reassess his traditional role as healer. Should the physician betray the trust of a seriously ill, possibly moribund patient by concealing the dangers of an experimental drug if the patient's ignorance would help maintain necessary hope and strength for recovery? More seriously, should patients be subjected to a certain risk in exchange for an uncertain benefit for the larger population? Some physicians not only answered in the affirmative but saw in this question less a dilemma than a chance for medical progress. Those physicians were likely to seek service in the larger hospitals, where many needy patients came to be viewed as potential subjects for medical experiments.

Frequently the physicians were the first subjects of their own experiments. When they decided to involve others, they often did so with much agony, as demonstrated by Pasteur's account of his celebrated first inoculation of a boy who had contracted rabies with a vaccine so far tested only on animals:

> I had reached a total of fifty dogs, of all ages and breeds, proved to be absolutely immune, when on July 6, 1885; three persons from Alsace arrived unexpectedly at my laboratory. One of the three was Joseph Meister, aged nine years, who had been cruelly bitten by a mad dog on July 4th. . . . The death of this child seemed inevitable. On the advice of Professors Vulpian and Grancher, I decided, not without keen and cruel uneasiness, to try out on Meister the method which I had constantly found successful with the dogs.[3]

The well-known result of the experiment initiated the conquest of rabies, saving countless numbers of people from certain death. But the new treatment was not without its risks either. Some people died of the inoculation. For a disease that was considered 100 percent fatal, these failures were overshadowed by the treatment's overall success. Similar contributions to public health included Robert Koch's inoculational treatment of tuberculosis and cholera and Paul Ehrlich's treatment of syphilis. They too required inoculations of infected patients with experimental vaccines, ultimately to their benefit.

Not all medical research was therapeutic, i.e., designed first to help the subjects on whom experiments were performed, and then others who shared the same symptoms. An increasing number of physicians argued that the continued success of such therapeutic research required more basic non-therapeutic research to determine the conditions under which some diseases emerge, the stages through which they pass, and the means by which they travel between hosts. Such information can be obtained through animal experiments and diligent observations of patients. But during the century preceding the Nuremberg trials, many physicians and public leaders felt such an approach was too time-consuming, especially in view of the increasing problems of rapid industrialization.

Urban crowding and growing poverty increased the likelihood of runaway epidemics. Increasing industrialization also fostered national rivalries, as leading entrepreneurs urged their respective governments to provide political and military protection in the scramble for greater access to worldwide resources and markets. Such rivalries, and the boost they gave to the potential for war, called for healthy and industrious populations at home. Fears of losing the competitive edge in this struggle intensified when Herbert Spencer predicted the probable extinction of societies unfit to prevail in a world of perpetual scarcity and deadly struggle for survival.

The message was clear. Fitness, both physical and mental, was essential for individual and national survival. Unfitness was a liability no society could afford for long. The message did not fail to make its impression on the medical profession, in particular on physicians eager to advance their careers through services the community would find valuable. Spencer's widely accepted message also provided a rationale for using the unfit to enhance the survival chances of the fit. Accordingly, an indigent hospital patient could be of service to the community as a subject for non-therapeutic research of the kind recounted in the opening paragraph of this chapter. The subject's resistance could be circumvented through concealment and misinformation, a practice apparently common at the time.

The rapid industrialization of the Western world and its supporting gospel of progress through fierce competition spurred medical research to find faster cures for debilitating diseases, even at the cost of dehumanizing individuals as research subjects. Many physicians undoubtedly saw industrialization itself as an illness from which the population had to be shielded to preserve health.

The concept of health usually conjures up images of natural organic processes that seem antithetical to the manufactured existence of industrial life. For many observers, healthy rural communities were increasingly threatened by an ailing mechanized society. But whether their aim was to preserve public health in more traditional settings or to strengthen popular health for a more industrial existence, many physicians by the middle of the nineteenth century felt that medical research had to provide more of the needed tools to do their work. Some obviously felt that obtaining those tools required the performance of risky non-therapeutic experiments on human beings

Human Experimentation Before the Outbreak of Global War

PERHAPS THE MOST COMPREHENSIVE list of human experiments performed during the latter part of the nineteenth century was compiled by the German physician Albert Moll. This list was published in 1901 as part of his generally recognized authoritative work *Aerztliche Ethik*. He admitted that his survey of the respective literature was by no means complete, mainly because many experiments were not a matter of record. But the work contains references to most areas of medical research involving human subjects at the time. Of the approximately 600 such cases discussed, the following excerpts typify aims and methods used by the researchers:

> Two German scholars experimented with vaccines to protect men from abdominal typhus. They injected cultures from lymph swellings, whose bacilli had been killed at a temperature of 56 degrees Celsius, into the back skin of healthy individuals. The reaction was violent: shivering, dizziness, pain, temperature increase and disturbed sleep. . . . Dangerous and most irresponsible inoculations have been performed in the United States of America against scarlet fever. Trying to find a protective vaccine, one hospital physician injected mucous particles from the throat and mouth of a scarlet-inflicted patient into the skin of ten children, who were either mildly ill or healthy. They all contracted scarlet and did not recover without showing some very serious symptoms.[4]

Moll's report on the most recent smallpox research includes this note:

> A northern scholar had already researched the possibility of inducing artificial immunity with protective vaccination. He tried to determine whether the body's absorption of protective substances would prevent reaction to later inoculations. He injected sterilized lymphs under the skin of orphans. The children, fourteen in all, were inoculated in this way for many days. These often cited tests are especially noteworthy because of the researcher's comment that, "perhaps I should have first tried those tests on animals. But because of the high cost of those most suited for the task, calfs [sic], I, with the permission of the chief physician X, started my experiments on orphans in the orphanage Y, hoping eventually to conduct animal experiments as well." These words give the impression that the researcher in question must have removed his feelings [for helpless children] considerably from that of a normal person. A different, now deceased scholar pondered the question "whether it is possible to induce small pox with excretions (saliva, urine, bronchial mucus, feces)" and recommended continued research on the matter.[5]

Moll noted further:

> This aberration does not seem to recognize national and political boundaries. The cases which I have surveyed in the literature of the field during the past several years come from many different countries, of which I would like to mention Germany, Austria, Switzerland, France, Italy, England, Russia, Norway, Sweden, Denmark, Romania, and the United States of America.[6]

Moll felt the apparent impression of many Europeans that aberrations were more prevalent in the United States than elsewhere needed correction. Taking issue with a report in the *Berliner Zeitung*, he wrote:

> The English physician Dr. Berdoe informs the press in a note that American physicians perform poison experiments on insane people. According to the Bulletin of Johns Hopkins University in Baltimore, this is indeed the case, and it happens fairly often. Eight insane people from Baltimore's city asylum recently were selected for some medical experiments. According to the physicians making the selections, these people had been in the asylum for such a long time that a cure seemed out of the question. They received thyroid extract until they showed loss of weight, weakening of pulse and other dangerous symptoms. Two of these unfortunate people became raving mad. One died before the frenzy stopped. The researcher drew the conclusion from this "that such treatment is not without danger for the health and life of the patient." This obviously is correct. In other countries, such physicians would simply be turned over to the courts. Their verdict might also not be without danger for the health, and perhaps life, of the experimenting physicians.
>
> The author of this informative note, which so strongly faults America, apparently is oblivious to the fact that in Europe too, in Germany and Austria, for example, similarly scandalous experiments have been performed.[7]

Moll concluded:

> When I think about all the experiments performed on human beings, inside and outside the hospitals, it becomes evident that their therapeutic benefit, on the whole, does not amount to much. It seems to me that it stands in no relation to the tortures to which so many human subjects were subjected.[8]

To stop such exploitation, Moll enthusiastically endorsed a recent directive by the Prussian State that made experiments on minors and impaired persons illegal and required a signed affidavit of informed consent from medical subjects.[9] The 1900 directive in part was a response to public complaints about a research professor in Breslau, Albert Neisser, who in 1892 injected seven unsuspecting healthy children and adolescents with serum from syphilis patients to find means of immunization against the disease. So far, the restraints researchers had placed on their experiments had largely been a matter of custom and individual discretion. Now they had become a governmental requirement, apparently the first of its kind in Western countries.

Vulnerable populations at home were not the only source of human subjects. Many researchers found large populations of potential subjects for their experiments in other parts of the world, parts that were under Western control and where westerners were struck by unfamiliar diseases. Better-known examples include the non-therapeutic experiments of Walter Reed on Cuban residents to study the spread of yellow fever and Richard Strong's experiments on Filipino prisoners to contain plague and beriberi during the first years of the 20th century.

Reed, a surgeon in the U.S. Army, built a research station in Cuba in 1900 and found the volunteers he needed for experiments to determine the cause of the malaria epidemic with the help of some monetary enticement, $100 in gold for participating and an additional $100 for contracting the disease.[10] Most volunteers were local residents, but a few were Americans. As members of Reed's staff, some did not accept monetary rewards. Of the more than 20 subjects who contracted yellow fever, no one died, although a few people died in experiments at the research station conducted by others.[11]

Richard Strong, also a member of the U.S. Army, tried to develop vaccines against a number of epidemic diseases. He also seems to have been the first researcher to have used prisoners as human subjects on a larger scale. Working in Manila in 1905, he inoculated prisoners condemned to death with attenuated cultures of plague organisms.[12] There is no indication regarding their voluntary status or compensation. Of the 42 subjects injected, no one died. During the same year, he inoculated a little over half of the 1,838 inmates of Bilibid Prison outside Manila with cholera vaccine and found that the cholera death rate was higher among those inoculated.[13] A few years later, he convinced 29 prisoners condemned to death to participate in an experiment to find the causes of beriberi for "an abundance of cigarettes of any kind that they wished and also cigars if they desired them."[14]

Eventually, medical experiments were also performed on prison inmates in the U.S. In 1915, Joseph Goldberger, a physician with the U. S. Public Health Service, conducted experiments at the Rankin Prison Farm near Jackson, Mississippi, to determine the causes of pellagra, an often-fatal disease that had taken on epidemic proportions especially in the South. He found 12 volunteers, including six who were serving life terms for murder. All were promised and received pardons for their participation.[15] Goldberger induced pellagra in six of the subjects and proved that the disease had a dietary origin. Later he would show that the intake especially of yeast would be preventive and curative. These findings dramatically improved the life of poorer populations in the South at little cost and no lasting harm to the prison subjects. As a result, the idea of using prisoners for similar experiments gained more acceptance.

The only group to voice organized resistance to such practices was the anti-vivisectionists, which had monitored and condemned experiments on animals for nearly half a century. They suspected that the researchers' insistence that humans, unlike animals, volunteered to be non-therapeutic subjects merely mis-represented the conditions under which prisoners gave their consent.

The general acceptance of the germ theory of disease brought about a race among researchers to identify and study the behavior of a seemingly inex-haustible variety of germs. It was soon discovered that several animal species, among them homo sapiens, played host to identical sets of germs and had shown similar or identical responses. Hence, the effects of those germs on humans could be studied reliably in certain animals. The subsequent prolifer-ation of such studies, especially on rats, rabbits, monkeys, and guinea pigs, led to a substantial public concern for animal welfare and a movement to protect them from cruel medical research.

While the concern was more for helpless animals than for the more self-protective humans, antivivisectionists left no doubt about their feeling that "the man who vivisected in the morning . . . too often appeared in the operating theaters of the hospitals in the afternoon," where he would "look upon patients, especially charity patients in hospitals, as so much experimental mate-rial."[16] Antivivisectionists did not even exempt Claude Bernard, who, in his *Introduction to Experimental Medicine* in 1865, described rigorous ethical safeguards for medical experiments on animals and human beings and pro-scribed any kind of non-therapeutic research on people. Though the antivivi-sectionist movement appeared to be strongest around the turn of the nineteenth century, promoting a number of legislative animal protection mea-sures, it remained viable for much of the early twentieth century and was the only organized public movement to address questions of human research.

Collective Versus Individual Health After World War I: The Primacy of Ideology

WITH THE OUTBREAK OF World War I, the focus of much of the world shifted from various concerns at home to the battlefields. The events there provided different national, social, and economic groups with conflicting sets of evidence regarding the war's origin and purpose. Many economic and political leaders found confirmation that the escalating Darwinian struggle for greater markets and more resources had finally erupted into all-out military confrontation. This view was shared by a majority of the rural population and members of the mid-dle class. The traditional life style of craftsmen, small business owners, physi-cians, civil servants and others seemed threatened by an all-consuming march of industrialization. They usually identified the real culprit as the insatiable appetites of other nations. Many members of the growing urban population, particularly industrial workers, saw the events of World War I as a confirmation of Marx's prediction that the law of diminishing return on capital investment would heat up the struggle for shrinking profits between the major owners of capital and cause a breakdown of the whole capitalist structure.

The subsequent call for workers everywhere to abstain from this carnage for profit and to prepare for the expected overthrow of all capitalist regimes solidified a growing split between revolutionary (orthodox) and evolutionary (revisionist) minded adherents of Marx's socialist theory. In most European countries, the latter group comprised the majority, whose members complied, with some reluctance, with the various war measures of their respective governments, notably general conscription and military procurements.

In Russia the revolutionary contingent of organized socialists, the Bolsheviks, were in the majority. The evolutionary contingent, the Mensheviks, made up the minority. Both had been declared illegal by the tsarist regime and many of their leaders were driven into exile. Both assumed a principal role in the overthrow of their country's autocratic regime during the war, but the Bolsheviks obtained near dictatorial control over most of Imperial Russia by the end of 1917.[17] Their subsequent encouragement of revolutionary socialist parties in other countries, particularly Germany, to obtain dictatorial control too generated a growing fear of Bolshevik-style rule among many of these countries' citizens. An increasing number of them responded by endorsing extreme measures, such as outlawing all socialist parties, to stop this threat.

A further key element in shaping these events was the U.S. declaration that its late entry into the war on the side of the Entente was prompted not by national self-interest but by ideology, namely, "to make the world safe for democracy." Given the U.S.'s imperialist posture reaching back to the Mexican-American War, many people in the Alliance, particularly in Germany, Austria, and Turkey, had many reasons to suspect that the American declaration was little more than a political ploy to dismantle their own empires and open their markets and resources to the commercial influence of the Entente countries. The German and Austrian rural middle class in particular felt that such development would further uproot their traditional lifestyles already challenged by socialism. Increasingly, they would develop an extreme reactionary stance against a perceived threat of socialism on the one hand and laissez-faire liberalism on the other. And the number of such "reactionaries" eventually would swell dramatically.

The end of World War I, particularly the Bolshevik call for world revolution and the U.S. message to spread democracy abroad, was characterized by a sharp escalation in ideological rhetoric. It would strengthen existing divisions between most countries of the Western world, and increasingly also between their various classes, cutting across national divisions. As a result, advocates of all three major ideological groups: liberals (mainly of the laissez-faire variety), socialists (especially in the orthodox camp), and reactionaries (commonly referred to as fascists after the formation of Italy's fascist movement in 1919), vigorously mobilized support among their respective constituencies in anticipation of a major showdown.

Each group portrayed the showdown as an epic conflict between two sides, viewing both of the other groups as one foe with two faces. Liberals saw themselves as champions of freedom, fighting the twin evils of totalitarianism. Socialists saw themselves as champions of equality, fighting the twin evils of inequality. Fascists saw themselves as champions of idealism, fighting the twin evils of materialism. All saw themselves justified by, and acted in accordance with, the different lessons they drew from the war. Liberals of the losing countries agreed to contain mass aggression more effectively in the future; those of the victorious countries vowed never to give in to it in the first place. Socialists everywhere found that they needed more preparation to prevail in their global class struggle and were determined to work harder to raise their organizational and material readiness for the coming "final battle." Fascists called for a heightened commitment of individuals to make sacrifices for the threatened values of their communities.

All were opposed by a small number of pacifists. Erich Maria Remarque, for instance, in his autobiographical novel, *All Quiet on the Western Front*, insisted that no ideology or cause was worth the slaughter and mutilation of millions of young men, even children, in the most brutal trench warfare in human memory. A whole generation of French and German high school students had been decimated. There may perhaps be no clearer testimony to this fact than the recollection of the playwright Carl Zuckmayer as he stood with his friends amidst a large crowd and listened to the German Emperor's mobilization order:

> We had linked arms and formed a chain in order not to lose touch with one another in the crowd. To this day I remember the names of everyone who was with me then: Karl Gelius, Franz Klum, Leopold Wagner, Heinz Roemheld, Geo Hamm, Richard Schuster, Ferdinand Pertzborn, Fritz Hahn. I see their seventeen-year-old faces as they were then, young and fresh. There is no other way I can see them, for they never aged. Everyone I have mentioned here is dead, killed in the war.[18]

The Darwinian consequences of the disappearance of so many of the brightest and healthiest youngsters from European society hardly escaped notice. Georg Friedrich Nicolai, the German physician who together with Albert Einstein openly condemned the war in a pamphlet called *Appeal to the Europeans*, expressed dismay not only over the slaughter on the battlefields but

also over the adverse impact it had on the European population and the survival of its culture. The war, Nicolai wrote, protects

> the blind, the deaf mutes, the idiots, the hunchbacks, the scrofulous, the insane, the
> impotent, the paralyzed, the epileptic, the dwarfed, the deformed. All this refuse and
> waste of the human race can rest peacefully. No bullets will fly by their ears. And while
> the young, the brave, and the strong rot on the battlefield, they can sit at home and
> lick their sores.[19]

With millions of maimed veterans to care for, their disabilities living proof
of their sacrifice for the community, individuals with different disabilities who
"sat it out at home" increasingly came to be viewed as a burden society could
ill afford, not only by the reactionary minded, but by people of every part of
society. Low birthrates and lingering economic problems added to a growing
fear that Western society was losing its survival fitness, unless drastic counter-
steps were taken.

In an anticipation of a progressively intensifying Darwinian struggle for survival, spokesmen of all major ideological groups advocated, even before the war,
for comprehensive public health measures that would drastically reduce the
propagation of genetic defects, advocating sterilization and institutionalization
of those designated unfit.

Such concerns eventually led to the formation of various interest groups,
collectively referred to as the eugenics movement, whose origins have been
traced to the works of Francis Galton, a cousin of Darwin. Since different ideological groups interpret the term fitness differently, the proposed eugenic measures have varied accordingly. For liberals, fitness meant the ability to thrive in
a supply-and-demand economy, an economy whose rules are the product of
majority consent. For socialists it meant chiefly an ability to live by the dictates
of class struggle, whose victorious outcome is determined by recognizable laws
of history. For reactionaries it meant chiefly the ability to assume one's natural place in a living community, whose life flows from a transcendental source.
In time of need, this place may be on the battlefield, where many individuals
could face their ultimate fitness test.

The various prescribed eugenic measures to improve the fitness of the general population have differed accordingly. Liberals for the most part have
advocated "benign neglect," hoping that Darwin's law of natural selection
would cause sufficient social attrition to contain any wider spread of inherited or acquired traits of unfitness. Such a view opposes active eugenic measures,
such as confinement or sterilization. Active measures were advocated, however, by many liberals after World War I to stop a perceived counter-selection.

Socialists have usually argued that, with the exception of physically evident
genetic defects, most individual impairments are socially induced, and that the
most effective eugenic measure consists in a general overhaul of the entire social

structure in which individuals are forced to live. They consider liberal measures as mere temporary, if often necessary, patchwork. To the degree that the desired overhaul is expected to improve the fitness of all citizens, the entire revolutionary socialist program may be considered a positive eugenic measure.

Reactionaries generally blame physical as well as so-called social impairments on genetic defects. Reduction and elimination of such defects becomes a high priority. If medical measures fail, carrier of defects are often subject to institutional confinement, sterilization, abandonment, and in some cases, especially when there is an assumed great danger to the larger society, forced euthanasia. During the Hitler regime, this led to large-scale extermination of people with a variety of impairments, some of them very minor. Since reactionaries as a rule feel strong affinities with transcendental powers, which traditionally, as in the case of Christianity, have guaranteed the sanctity of individual life, such measures have met much resistance. Supporting such measures often served as a litmus test for determining who is a true reactionary, e.g., National Socialist, and who is not.

Unlike liberals and socialists, reactionaries recognize no commonly applicable principle that could subsume and explain general historic processes by way of quantification, such as Adam Smith's law of supply and demand or Marx's law of dialectical materialism. Perceived threats to the survival and identity of the community typically initiate a reach for guidance from the past, with a selective eye toward legends of grandeur, greatness, and gods, revealing non-quantifiable values that differ from community to community. The greater the threat to the community, the greater the espousal of those values.

The Italian Fascisti found their identity in the glory that was Rome, the Spanish Falange in the spirit of the crusaders, and the German National Socialists in the heroism of the Nordic race. Such heroism ultimately was invoked to awaken all Nordic people, particularly those living within the confining borders of the German state, to the dangers to their race and their intrinsic powers to overcome them. The dangers were identified as the excessive commercial spirit of liberalism, which reduced all values to the prize they would bring at the market, and the leveling egalitarian spirit of socialism, which reduced all values to material processes. Of the two, reactionaries found socialism to be the most threatening, especially in the form of Russian Bolshevism.

The most virulent of all the reactionaries of the twentieth century, the National Socialists, likened the Nordic race to an organic body and identified liberals and socialists of all colors as poisonous cells that had infiltrated the body to destroy it. They had nearly succeeded in doing so during World War I. Unless some drastic cure was forthcoming shortly, those cells would finish off their work in a short time. With this message, the National Socialists prevailed in national elections and assumed power in January 1933.

Rudolf Hess's statement that National Socialism is applied biology found immediate application. The interchangeability of political and medical language, characteristic of much of reactionary ideology, now marked public policy. Two of the regime's first decrees read like medical prescriptions. One ordered the removal of the ideologically opposed and another of the physically and mentally handicapped from the ailing German body.

In April 1933, the regime announced the "Law for the Restoration of the Professional Civil Service," and in July of the same year the "Law for the Prevention of Progeny with Hereditary Defects." The first decree initiated a purge of the civil service to oust outspoken socialists and liberals and was aimed primarily at Jews, who by definition belonged to either one group or the other. Unlike non-Jewish socialists and liberals, Jews were deemed genetically incapable of converting to a National Socialism based on racial purity, hence seemed the safest target for any purge right from the start.

The eugenic "Law for the Prevention of Progeny with Hereditary Defects" allowed for immediate compulsory sterilization of people with "congenital mental defects, schizophrenia, manic-depressive psychosis, hereditary epilepsy . . . and severe alcoholism."[20] In addition, opposition parties and labor unions' activities were declared subversive and were outlawed. Special camps were built to house the thousands, and eventually millions, who were subsequently accused of violating the legislation, often on mere suspicion, without formal charges, right of counsel, appeal, or court hearing.

The National Socialists had little reason to suspect their measures would arouse much criticism abroad. They had admired the ruthless means with which the Italian fascists crushed their opposition after their ascent to power in 1922. At the time, fighting socialism, if not liberalism, received approving nods from many quarters in other Western countries. And anti-Semitism had a long-standing tradition throughout Western Civilization.

The National Socialists were aware of the fact that forced sterilization of social undesirables had long been introduced in many states of the United States. None other than Chief Justice Oliver Wendell had upheld those laws in a Supreme Court decision with the following words: "It is better for all the world, if instead of waiting to execute degenerate offspring for crime, or to let them starve for their imbecility, society can prevent those who are manifestly unfit from continuing their kind."[21]

Whether Holmes's reference to "all the world" was to be understood literally or not, his opinion did express a prevailing, if not always admitted, sentiment among many citizens of the Western nations at the time. No one acted on this sentiment as radically as the National Socialists in Germany did. As one scholar observed: "The triumph of eugenic sterilization programs in the United States during the 1930s influenced other nations. Canada, Germany, Sweden, Norway, Finland, France, and Japan enacted sterilization laws. In

England, sterilization was ultimately rejected, but in Germany the Nazis sterilized more than 50,000 'unfit' persons within one year after enacting a eugenics law."[22]

The National Socialists wasted little time in their professed goal to reclaim territory, population, economic strength, and military power lost as a result of defeat in World War I. They pursued their goal with the desperate energy of a people doubtful whether their patient, the German nation, would recuperate in time to meet the challenge of greater conquests. Parts of German territory in Prussia had been given to Poland and needed to be reannexed. Parts of the dismantled Austrian Empire with a strong German population had been given to newly created Czechoslovakia and needed to be integrated into their own newly created Third Reich, the National Socialists argued. Between 1936 and 1939, Germany prepared for military confrontation with a pace unmatched in history. The professed confidence of the victorious nations of World War I, particularly France and Britain, to contain Germany and maintain the status quo in Europe is short of breathtaking. Eventual concessions by France and Britain with Czech border regions did not stop the German occupation of most of Czechoslovak territory and the "liberation" of West Prussia and Danzig with modern tanks and fighter planes a year later. What the National Socialists saw as a reannexation of German land, the Poles saw as an attack on their sovereign territory. When German forces crossed over Polish borders on September 1, 1939, Germany provoked a war that eventually would touch the affairs of most parts of the world.

German Medicine After the Outbreak of World War II

WITH THE BEGINNING OF the war, the National Socialists stepped up their eugenic "invigoration" of the German national body. By decree of Chancellor Hitler, dated September 1, 1939, the day of Germany's attack on Poland, the sterilization program was extended to comprise extensive euthanasia measures. Individuals with incurable diseases could be given "mercy death" at the advice of empowered physicians. During the two years of its official enforcement, as many as 300,000 individuals with various kinds of impairments, some of them not too serious, may have been killed, mostly with phenol injection and carbon monoxide gas poisoning. The measure drastically reduced the number of inmates in many hospitals and asylums, making their beds available for the coming waves of war casualties.

The killings were performed by the medical staff of a few designated asylums with newly built gas chambers into which the doomed people were transferred suddenly and killed unawares. Relatives typically received notice that the handicapped member of their family had died of natural causes, usually from sudden and unexplained heart failure. Despite the strict secrecy with which the euthanasia measures were executed, the truth could not be concealed indefinitely. While inquisitive individuals searching for the true fate of their deceased and missing relatives found little cooperation from state authorities, their plight was recognized by some church leaders, who protested vehemently in letters to Hitler's Chancellery and the Ministry of Justice, and eventually publicly in their church services. These efforts pressured Hitler to order a stop to the euthanasia killings within Germany in August 1941. By that time, German troops had penetrated into the U.S.S.R., and the killings would expand on a much wider scale on conquered soil in the East.

While Germany's attack on the U.S.S.R. in June 1941 may have been a strategic blunder, it was quite consistent with the National Socialists' crusade against Bolshevism, the ultimate disease in the ailing body of Western culture, which had to be eradicated lest the body die. Just a year earlier, the Darwinian etiologist and later Nobel laureate Konrad Lorenz had reminded an attentive audience that, "if the elimination of the diseased elements fails, they will penetrate the national body [Volkskoerper] with means and causes biologically analogous to the way cells of a malignant tumor penetrate a healthy body and eventually destroy it along with themselves."[23]

Given the literal understanding of language so characteristic of reactionary minds, most National Socialists saw in such words from the scientific community a confirmation that the struggle against Bolshevism was a matter of life and death, with no mercy for the losers. If Bolshevism in all its manifestations were not eradicated soon, it would indeed destroy all of European society.

Such prospects raised the anxiety of many Germans and the attack of German troops on Soviet territory signaled a renewed determination of National Socialists to fight their main foe, not only on the battlefields, but behind the front lines as well. Anyone living under the Hitler regime and suspected of undermining German victory in the slightest was at the mercy of its arbitrary totalitarian power. Past or present socialist affiliations, support of liberal causes, or simple doubt in Germany's ability to prevail in its struggle was sufficient cause for incarceration in one of the many concentration camps, including those newly built in the East. Jews in particular suffered the wrath of the system. Given National Socialist ideology, they were the creators and chief propagators of Bolshevism and had to be treated accordingly, first by removal from society with the possible prospect of resettlement in the East or elsewhere. When that proved unworkable, the treatment became mass extermination. This monstrous plan had been formed as early as mid-1941, but was officially sealed by the regime's leaders at the infamous Wannsee Conference in January 1942. Jews constituted the great majority of concentration camp inmates who were exterminated as the cancerous cells Lorenz had warned about, chiefly in gas chambers dismantled in the German asylums and rebuilt on a larger scale in the camps of the East. As before with the physically and mentally handicapped, those classified "socially handicapped" were led into the death chambers largely unaware of their fate. Millions of civilian victims, women carrying babies, elderly supporting each other, took those last steps without return. The National Socialists' insistence on pursuing this "healing of society" and "triumph over the Jewish-Bolshevist beast" without remorse worked with a routine perhaps never to be understood by anyone.

The call for personal sacrifice also was heeded to perhaps an unprecedented degree. The war in the East raged unabated, with casualties ranging in the millions, including not only soldiers but civilians as well. Many fell victim to spreading epidemics such as typhus, dysentery, and tuberculosis, fostered by starvation and cold. To spare fighting men such a fate, some German military leaders and physicians initiated research programs designed to develop greater protection from and cures for war-related injuries and diseases. And to keep the diminishing prospects of ultimate victory alive, they soon extended the scope of their research to include the development of offensive bacteriological weapons as well.

As entry of the United States into the war on the side of the Allies in December 1941 brought with it the prospect of a more protracted war and probable defeat, the research projects began to be pursued with more urgency. A number of experiments were performed to test the limits of human endurance in simulated war conditions to find appropriate means to prevent death and lasting disabilities. The experiments started in February 1942 with a project to devise effective rescue techniques for pilots ejecting at high altitudes. Within a few months, a number of other projects followed, the most extensive of which focused on the control of epidemics. The researchers found their needed human subjects in concentration camps, crowded with thousands of moribund inmates.

Since the inmates generally were considered an unaffordable liability for a nation at war, the researchers had no qualms about subjecting them to the most brutal non-therapeutic medical experiments imaginable. After all, the suffering of these supposedly unworthy individuals served the cause of preserving the lives of countless more worthy members of a society requiring superhuman strength to prevail in a total war of mutual annihilation. News from the Russian front and Allied saturation bombing of German cities helped to make such arguments convincing.

German Medical Experiments During World War II

THE MEDICAL EXPERIMENTS CAN be grouped as follows:

A. Rescue of fliers and sailors
B. Treatment of war injuries
C. Reconstructive surgery
D. Controlling epidemics
E. Biochemical warfare
F. Eugenics

The first five groups were considered directly war related the last only indirectly. It constituted part of the National Socialists' program to reinvigorate their national body by eliminating from it perceived poisonous elements by so-called eugenic means, a program that provided much of the rationale for the war itself. Elimination mostly meant extermination, but also included such measures as sterilization and chemical behavior control. Some of the experiments by geneticists and anthropologists like Otmar von Verschuer and his assistant Josef Mengele, who used inmates for the study of human heredity, belong to this category.

Rescue of Fliers and Sailors

GERMANY'S BATTLE FOR AIR superiority over Britain and control of the high seas in 1940–41 had met unexpectedly strong resistance from a technically superior airborne fighting force, resulting in high losses on both sides. Flyers bailing out from their damaged planes into the ice-cold seas surrounding the British Isles slowly froze to death if not rescued. With the entry of the United States into the conflict, employing their high-flying Boeing B-17s and Thunderbolts, even greater German losses seemed imminent. The German industry responded by developing a still higher flying and faster plane with a novel jet engine, the Messerschmitt ME-163. To provide fliers with proper safety equipment, some Luftwaffe physicians received an assignment from their high command to study the effects of high-altitude ejection and subsequent descent with and without oxygen equipment.[24]

High altitudes were simulated in low-pressure chambers at an experimental station built inside the camp at Dachau. Nearly 200 inmates were used as subjects between March and August 1942. These purportedly condemned prisoners were promised a pardon for their participation. Seventy to eighty of the nearly 200 inmates died in the experiment. The apparent cause of death was brain embolism, incurred as a result of low atmospheric pressure shortly after simulated ejection at record heights of up to 68,000 feet. To determine the exact cause of death, some subjects were dissected while submerged in water to locate embolic air bubbles in their circulation while the attached cardiogram still registered heartbeats.[25]

   In May 1942, the scope of the project was extended to include experiments
designed to find the most effective rescue methods for fliers stranded in water
at low temperatures. It was generally known that body temperatures still
dropped for hours after rescue. Standard techniques of slow external rewarming and orally administered heart stimulants still resulted in high mortality rates.
Searching for more effective techniques, the Luftwaffe physicians performed
a series of hypothermia experiments on nearly 300 concentration camp inmates,
this time including not only condemned prisoners but political prisoners and
prisoners of war as well. Hypothermia was rapidly induced through submersion in ice-cold water, with and without a protective flier's suit, and sometimes
even without narcotics. Once hypothermia was achieved, various warming
techniques were administered, including quick submersion in hot baths, mas-
sages and hot wrappings. One experiment required tight embraces of the
frozen stiff, but still living, subject by one or more females with encouraged,
and sometimes completed, intercourse. Eighty to ninety subjects either died
in the water as a result of cardiac failure or during attempted rewarming.
Some of the experiments were performed on inmates cooled down in open winter air. The experiments ultimately proved that rapid rewarming was the most
effective rescue technique. It called for immediate placement of the subject into
very hot rather than lukewarm water, as had been thought previously.
   By 1943, the focus of aerial confrontation had shifted from the cold seas
surrounding the British Isles to the warmer Mediterranean. Germany by then
had lost dominance of the Northern air space, but over the waters surrounding Crete and Malta, British and German fighter planes still engaged in a grim
fight for air superiority, with especially high casualties among the reckless
German flyers. Those who found themselves floating in the Mediterranean did
not have to fear cold temperatures as much as lack of potable water for the surviving body. The Luftwaffe therefore ordered research to find a portable kit
with equipment to desalinate seawater. By the end of 1943, two such kits had
been developed by two different laboratories.
   The first contained an apparatus that indeed removed sufficient quantities
of salt from seawater to make it potable. But its operation required a considerable amount of scarce silver. The second device did not remove salt from seawater. It only added sugar solutions to make it palatable, but it was inexpensive
to produce.
   When the nephrologist Hans Eppinger, the most authoritative voice in the
matter, suggested that it might even increase the body's natural capacity to
extract salt from sea water, it was decided to test the method on Dachau
inmates. The test was performed on forty-four Gypsies during summer of
1944.[26] One group drank the sweetened seawater, one drank natural seawater,
and one drank no water at all. Since no one had ever survived more than twelve
days without water, all forty-four subjects had to undergo the experiment for

exactly twelve days. No one died during the experiment, though one subject may have succumbed later to complications. The anticipated result that the added sweetener had no effect on the condition and length of human survivability in the end was inconsequential. By the end of 1944, German forces had lost control over all seas and were merely prolonging the inevitable day of total defeat and the unconditional surrender called for by the rapidly advancing Allies.

Treatment of War Injuries

OF THE MILLIONS OF war casualties everywhere, many lost limbs or even their lives because their wounds were treated improperly or too late, especially in the case of front line soldiers. Prevalent treatment methods were critically flawed and access to medical care shown wholly inadequate, particularly after the German invasion of the U.S.S.R. Thousands of newly wounded, exhausted soldiers showed up daily with severe infections only to find scarce supplies and overwhelmed medical staffs. Quick surgical removal of infected areas, not sparing whole limbs, became the standard procedure for the more fortunate.

Topically applied medication proved relatively ineffective, sending great numbers of soldiers unnecessarily to early graves. One particular antibiotic drug named sulfonamide, however, in many cases seemed to at least temporarily slow the spread of infection. To measure and attempt to improve its effectiveness, physicians performed experiments in inmates of the women's concentration camp at Ravensbrueck.

Here, sixty Polish women, imprisoned for suspected sabotage, were forced to undergo torturous experiments from July 1942 to September 1943. Physicians inflicted simulated war wounds by implanting wood shavings, ground glass, and oil, together with bacteria such as tetanus and streptococci in their legs. The subsequently infected areas were then treated with sulfonamide and other antibiotics. To test their effectiveness, one group of women served as controls, receiving no treatment at all. At least three women died as a result, and all suffered permanent leg injuries. Considerable anxiety attended the researchers' experiments, as they had been informed that British efforts to find potent antibiotics were much more successful. Sulfonamide remained ineffective and the Germans found no better drug. However, British researchers, with considerable help from their American colleagues, developed the highly effective penicillin without ever torturing a single individual. This new medication was made available to Allied soldiers during the last part of the war.[27]

Most war wounds resulted from penetrating injuries caused by bullets and shells, or massive objects crushing bones and organs. Many others stemmed from burns, suffered increasingly by the German population in 1942 as the

Allies stepped up their saturation bombings of German cities with incendiary explosives. Phosphorous bombs in particular struck everyone with fear, because they turned people into living torches. The use of poison gas was outlawed by the Geneva Convention and the Hague Agreements because of its devastating result on human lives during World War I, but those rules provided little security in a war fought with flagrant disregard for all human life. The bombardment of cities and, for that matter, the torture and killing of war prisoners in medical experiments, were outlawed as well.

Trying not to be caught unprepared, the National Socialist leadership braced the country for possible gas attacks and ordered the preparation of adequate protective measures, including medical remedies for gas burns. Gas masks were produced and distributed to every resident, but they would protect only the airways, not the skin. More intensive research needed to be done to find remedies for gas designed to burn the skin as well. Again, this research included excruciating and deadly experiments performed on inmates. Experiments with mustard gas had been performed as early as December 1939.

If there had ever been any concern for the lives of the subjects, it certainly had disappeared when the war reached its more brutalizing level a few years later.[28] Starting in November 1942, inmates of the Natzweiler camp were subjected to a number of highly toxic gases to study the possible prophylactic and therapeutic effect of certain vitamins and ointments.[29] Of perhaps several hundred subjects, as many as one-fourth may have died in the experiments.[30] A typical report of an experiment to study the effectiveness of a new drug, hexamethylenetetramine, on phosgene burns, reads thus:

> Of 4 test subjects, the first was protected orally, the second intravenously, the third received an intravenous injection of Hexamethylenetetramine after the poisoning, in order once more to ascertain the effect of therapeutic treatment, the fourth was not treated at all. The four subjects were placed in the chamber in which a phial containing 2.7 grams of phosgene was smashed. The test subjects remained in this concentration for 25 minutes. The phosgene content was measured three times during inhalation. The readings showed an average concentration of 91 mg per cbm. The subject protected intravenously remained healthy, and did not show the least signs of difficulties of symptoms, the orally protected subject contracted a slight pulmonary edema, subsequently bronchopneumonia and pleurisy, from which he recovered. One control subject also survived his pulmonary edema; the second died a few hours later, and the autopsy showed the characteristics of very serious pulmonary edema.[31]

The experiments apparently yielded very little useful information. Additional experiments were conducted on Buchenwald inmates in November 1943 to find a cure for burns caused by phosphorus bombs. Most of the subjects suffered serious injuries. Apparently, no helpful medication was ever found.

THE ROAD TO NUREMBERG

Increased abscesses to tissue and bones posed another serious problem during the war, particularly in the overcrowded concentration camps. Inadequate diet, deplorable sanitary conditions, and lack of medical care created a highly infectious and contagious environment, causing many fatalities. When the standard methods of topically and orally applied drugs, including sulfonamide and various exploratory medications showed little effect, more experimental means were tried. Abscesses were induced in healthy inmates to study their responsiveness to different treatments through all stages of infection. One control group would receive no treatment. In one recorded study, forty Catholic priests were subjected to such experiments at Dachau in August 1942. Ten died as a consequence. According to one witness, the subjects left untreated, on the whole, were harmed less than the subjects who received experimental treatment. At least three subjects died in similar experiments performed on inmates at Auschwitz.[32]

Reconstructive Surgery

AS THE NUMBER OF wounded soldiers and civilians rose dramatically with each day the war progressed, efforts to deal with the devastating consequences soon became frantic. The dogged determination of soldiers and populations on all sides to fight it out to the bitter end lowered many of the civil standards Europeans had held for centuries. In particular, the National Socialists' unwavering zeal to win this "battle for survival" with a spirit of unquestioned sacrifice and remorselessness generated a climate of brutality toward victims not seen before and not believed by many who were not directly affected.

As the number of maimed and crippled people grew, the German physicians frantically searched for more effective methods of healing and rehabilitation. Again, they found their subjects in the camps. As one of the subjects later recalled:

> The following were carried out: (a) bone breaking, (b) bone transplantation, (c) bone grafting. As to (a): On the operation table the bones of the lower part of both legs were broken into several pieces with a hammer, later they were joined with clips . . . or without clips . . . and were put into a plaster cast. This was removed after several days and the legs remained without plaster casts until they healed. As to (b): The transplantations were carried out in the usual way, except that whole pieces of fibula were cut out, once with periostium, another time without periostium . . . As to (c): Bone grafting. These operations were with the school of Prof. Gebhardt. During the preparatory operation two bone splints were put on the tibia of both legs; during the second operation such bone splints were cut out together with the attached bones and were taken to Hohenlychen [for the benefit of patients in that nearby hospital]. As a supplement to the bone splint operations, such operations were carried out also on 2 prisoners who suffered from deformation of bones of the osteomyelitis type.[33]

Such orthopedic operations had been performed before, though never on deliberately mutilated limbs of healthy individuals. Complete transplantation of bones from one person to another, however, was novel. A surgeon removed a complete shoulder blade from a female inmate at Ravensbrueck and transported it to Hohenlychen, where a different surgeon inserted it into a male patient, whose cancerous shoulder blade had been removed earlier. The young man lived cancer-free with the inserted bone for nearly three years, while the "donor," probably a retarded woman who could have lived without her missing bone, was killed shortly after surgery, according to a witness.[34] Apparently no other heteroplastic bone transplantations were performed. The focus remained on homoplastic experiments, such as orthopedic resection and grafting, where related problems of tissue and nerve regeneration could be studied in more detail as well.

Controlling Epidemics

FEAR THAT THE DECIMATION of French troops through typhus during their 1812 campaign into Russia could repeat itself during the German campaign into Russia led to a number of research projects on epidemics. It probably created more victims than all other medical research projects combined. Typhus indeed struck invading German troops in late-1941.[35] Deaths occurred quickly and in great numbers, as infected soldiers died within one or two days. Military physicians immediately designed projects to study how to halt the spread not only of typhus but most other epidemic diseases as well, including influenza, typhoid, jaundice, yellow fever, malaria, tuberculosis, and hepatitis. Experimental stations were set up in Buchenwald, Natzweiler, Dachau, and Sachsenhausen. As usual, the dangers of the experiments were concealed from the inmates. Some even volunteered initially for the promise of greater food rations. Hundreds of subjects were injected with the cultivated viruses or viral blood of infected inmates and later inoculated with different vaccines to study their comparative effectiveness. Control groups received no inoculations.

In the experiments conducted at Buchenwald, the main experimental station, which had its own vaccine-producing laboratory, the fatality rate among the inoculated inmates was as high as 15 percent. It was even more devastating among the control groups, where almost every other person died.[36] One group fared yet worse. Three to five people always remained untreated for the purpose of supplying highly viral-infected blood. Nearly every one of those "passage persons" died.

At Dachau, thirty people died in malaria experiments between 1942 and 1945, conducted on as many as 1,000 inmates. They were exposed to malaria-infected mosquitoes or received injections of infected mosquito gland extracts. Similar experiments were conducted at Sachsenhausen and Natzweiler with epi-

THE ROAD TO NUREMBERG

demic jaundice. Such research continued until the last days of the war. Some months before the war ended, several physicians were still testing an already disproved theory, which asserted persons stricken with tuberculosis develop greater immunity response with increased bacterial infection. Hundreds of Neuengamme inmates were so infected, and many died. The last experimental series on twenty Jewish children was halted abruptly because of advancing Allied soldiers. But before they could be saved, the children were killed in the last minute, perhaps to destroy incriminating evidence.[37]

Some of the more effective vaccines—developed in various laboratories around the nation, some at the Buchenwald laboratory itself—were administered to infected and threatened populations and soldiers. Vaccines were apparently not offered to the inmates of concentration camps, where by the end of the war the specter of death by epidemic disease was overshadowed only by the horrors of mass killings in the gas chambers. Some evidence shows that German authorities deliberately channeled infected inmates through many Eastern populations in order to spread the disease as widely as possible.[38] The same authorities also "quarantined" thousands of tuberculosis-infected Poles in concentration camps and eventually decided to control the epidemic by sending the incurable cases to the gas chambers too. A more literal equation of the extermination of an epidemic virus in a human body and the extermination of an epidemic "virus" in a "communal body" is hardly imaginable.

Biochemical Warfare

GERMAN MILITARY PHYSICIANS NOT only engaged in research to help soldiers and civilians injured by war on their own side, but also tried to develop weapons to injure and kill those on the enemy side. In the first Nuremberg trial against the top National Socialist leaders, the International Military Tribunal affirmed:

> In July 1943, experimental work was begun in preparation for a campaign of bacteriological warfare. Soviet prisoners of war were used in these medical experiments, which more often than not proved fatal. In connection with this campaign for bacteriological warfare, preparations were also made for the spreading of bacteriological emulsions from planes, with the object of producing widespread failures of crops and consequent starvation. These measures were never applied, possibly because of the rapid deterioration of Germany's military position.[39]

A research center, named the Cancer Research Institution, was set up in 1942 near Posen, where the mentioned experiments apparently were conducted. Since, however, no evidence of the experiments could be secured, the U.S. Military Tribunal subsequently concluded: "It might well be that [the defendant Kurt] Blome was preparing to experiment on human beings in connection with bacteriological warfare, but the record failed to disclose the fact that he had actually conducted experiments."[40]

There is, however, no doubt that experiments with bullets containing the lethal poison aconitin nitrate were conducted in September 1944 at Sachsenhausen as part of an execution of five allegedly condemned inmates. Bullets were shot into their thighs, releasing crystalline aconitin, which caused a painful reaction with death following in two hours. The physician at the scene later gave the following report to the court:

> The sight of this execution was one of the most horrible experiences of my life. On the other hand, I could not shorten the symptoms for in the first place, there was no antidote against aconitin available. If it is in the circulation then there is no possibility of removing it. In the second place, it was the express purpose to find out how long the symptoms for poisoning last in order in later cases to be able to use an antidote, which it was hoped would soon be discovered.[41]

Little is known about origin and utilization of these poison bullets. At the latter trial, in an obvious effort to deflect responsibility, the defense claimed that they had been found on Russian prisoners, supposedly alerting German troops to this new weapon in the hands of the Allies. Poison bullets may have been developed already by the U.S. military during World War I, but none were ever found to have been used in combat by either side.[42]

Eugenic Experiments

VICTORY IN WAR, THE National Socialists hoped, would establish the hegemony of a physically and spiritually rejuvenated German nation over all of Europe and other parts of the world. It would allow Germany to build an empire in the conquered lands to the east. Much like the Americas or Australia earlier, those lands would offer new settlement opportunities for an overpopulated Central Europe. And much like the older colonial holdings of Britain and France, they would also serve as a dumping ground for undesirable elements of the home population, in particular the Jews. Considered to be the main carriers of the poison of Bolshevism and liberalism, they were to be forcibly resettled in an undetermined, yet to be conquered territory, most likely an inhospitable part of Russia, and "work for a living." Madagascar and Palestine were also considered. But when military setbacks spoiled those plans, the National Socialist leadership seemed to favor a quick "final solution": extermination.

Some of the stronger members of the Jewish population should be spared, however, to serve as slave laborers, it was argued, at least as long as they would be strong enough to work. Sterilization and castration should prevent further propagation. This suggestion was first made to Heinrich Himmler, the head of the SS, by the head of Hitler's Chancellery, Viktor Brack, shortly after Germany's early victories in the Soviet Union: "The thought alone that 3 million Bolsheviks, at present German prisoners, could be sterilized so that they could be used as laborers but be prevented from reproduction, opens the most far-reaching perspectives."[43] Brack, a defendant at the trial, wrote in June 1942:

> Among 10 Million of Jews in Europe are, I figure, at least 2–3 Million of men and women who are fit enough for work. Considering the extraordinary difficulties the labor problems presents us with, I hold the view that those 2–3 Million should be especially selected and preserved. This can, however, only be done if at the same time they are rendered incapable to propagate."[44]

Because common surgical methods would have more than exhausted available time and medical staff to sterilize and castrate potentially millions of women and men, hasty efforts to find speedier and more cost effective methods received full backing from top National Socialist leaders. Three methods in particular were considered: orally administered drugs, intrauterine injection, and radiation.

Orally administered drugs was the first method explored. A German researcher, Madaus, had induced sterility in rats, rabbits, and dogs with an extract of the South American plant caladium seguinum. One official suggested to Himmler that "the necessary research and human experiments could be undertaken by an appropriately selected medical staff basing their work on the Madaus animal experiments in cooperation with the pharmacological institute of the Faculty of Medicine of Vienna, on the persons of the inmates of the Gypsy camp of Lackenbach in the Lower Danube."[45] But because the findings were not conclusive, and a more extensive cultivation of this tropical plant caused problems in the colder European climate, German authorities focused on the two remaining alternatives instead.

Auschwitz became the site of sterilization experiments with intrauterine injection. Inflammatory solutions, probably containing jodipin, iodine, and silver nitrate, were injected into the woman's uterus, swelling the inside walls, fallopian tube, and ovary, inflicting lasting damage. Himmler received word in June 1943 from the physician in charge of the experiments that "the moment is no longer far off when I can say: by one adequately trained physician in one adequately equipped place with perhaps 10 assistants (the number of assistants in conformity with the desired acceleration) most likely several hundred—if not even 1,000 [women] per day," can be stelilized.[46] After experiments had been performed on hundreds of women in Auschwitz and later also in Ravensbrueck, the method was still "in need of refinement," a term that apparently referred to excessive vaginal bleeding and prolonged and incapacitating abdominal pains. The "refinements" obviously were not completed in time to consider the method's implementation.

Hence, radiation came to be the favored method. Experiments in Auschwitz had shown that subjecting testicles for two minutes to a dose of

500–600 r and ovaries for three minutes to 300–350 r would permanently destroy their ability to produce ova and sperms. Substantial burns to the radiated areas were not considered a serious problem. The subsequent removal of the subjects' ovaries and testicles to determine the extent of the damage led to some infections, which not everyone survived. Despite all this, Brack reported to Himmler: "The experiments in this field are concluded. The following results can be considered established and adequately based on scientific research. If any persons are to be sterilized permanently, this result can only be attained by applying X-rays in a dosage high enough to produce castration with all its consequences."[47]

National Socialist leaders favored the radiation method not for any perceived scientific merits, but because "castration by x-rays . . . is not only relatively cheap, but can also be performed on many thousands in the shortest time," and also because "the irradiation can take place quite imperceptibly."[48] Concealing the true nature of the operation promised the desired results, as the leaders had already learned when concealing gas chambers as showers. Sterilization and castration rooms could be concealed as office counters, as the report to Himmler shows.

> One practical way of proceeding would be, for instance, to let the persons to be treated approach a counter, where they could be asked to answer some questions or to fill in forms, which would take them 2 or 3 minutes. The official sitting behind the counter could operate the installation in such a way as to turn a switch which would activate the two valves simultaneously (since the irradiation has to operate from both sides.) With a two-valve installation about 150–200 persons could be sterilized per day, and therefore, with 20 such installations as many as 3,000–4,000 persons per day. In my estimation a larger daily number could not, in any case, be sent away for this purpose.[49]

As the war in the East grew in ferocity, and as the existing separation of prisoners by gender made procreation an unlikely event anyway, the sterilization and castration program apparently dropped off the National Socialist leaders' priority list and was never implemented. But many of the hundreds of sterilized and castrated subjects of experimentation, along with many of the thousands of handicapped and otherwise undesired people sterilized already before the war by traditional surgery, lived to tell their story.

Along with socialists, liberals, Jews, Gypsies, so-called asocials and habitual criminals, homosexuals were to be eliminated too. Because homosexuality transcends all groups and certainly was not uncommon in the ranks of the regime's many organizations idolizing masculinity, such as the Storm Troopers, it confronted the promoters of radical purges with a dilemma. Rather than apprehend a fairly sizable part of the population, including high-ranking officials, the regime classified homosexuality as a glandular disorder, for which a cure was hoped. Laws prohibiting homosexual activity were enforced selectively. Those arrested and convicted on the charges or taken into "protective custody", i.e., concentration camps, tended to belong to lower-income groups and parts of the population whose loyalty to the regime was questionable at best. But their number was considerable, and they formed sizable groups in various concentration camps.

Some homosexuals became subjects in endocrinological experiments to increase and regulate the flow of testosterone in their system. Testosterone stimulates male genital development and directs formation of secondary male characteristics. In July 1944, at least five homosexual Buchenwald inmates were used to test the theory that externally provided testosterone showed maximum therapeutic effect when administered in crystalline form pressed into tablets and implanted under the skin. The crystals would break down and enter the blood stream at a steady determinable rate, approximating the natural rate. Testosterone injections directly into the blood stream, by contrast, had a minimal effect. After implantation of the tablets, the subjects remained five days at the Buchenwald hospital and were discharged for further observations, for which no records seem to exist.[50]

The Jewish Skeleton Collection

NEVER DOUBTING GERMANY'S FINAL victory, the German anatomist August Hirt envisioned a purified Nordic race controlling the destiny of other races from the superior, controlling position. Certain so-called destructive races, the "poisonous germs" inside the other races, most notably Jews, eventually would disappear from this hierarchy. But the legacy of their troubled existence should be preserved as a warning in anthropological museums. At the trial, some of the defendants were charged in assisting Hirt in the killing of more than hundred Jews to obtain skeletons for that purpose. The skeletons of "Jewish-Bolshevik Commissars" were to be preserved to demonstrate the physical peculiarities of a deadly but extinct parasite after the end of the war.

Hirt tried to elicit the support of Himmler for his project with the following note of February 1942:

> There exist extensive collections of skulls of almost all races and peoples [Voelker]. Of the Jewish race, however, only so very few specimens of skulls stand at the disposal of science that a study of them does not permit precise conclusions. The war in the East now presents us with the opportunity to remedy this shortage. By procuring the skulls of the Jewish Bolshevik Commissars, who personify a repulsive yet characteristic sub-humanity, we have the opportunity of obtaining tangible, scientific evidence.[51]

Himmler complied, and in late 1943, eighty-six Jews were "shipped" from Auschwitz to Hirt in Strasbourg, where they then were killed. Advancing

Allied soldiers found corpses preserved in alcohol at Hirt's Anatomical Institute at the end of the war.

Medical Results of the Experiments

AT THE TRIAL, THE defendants argued that their experiments and other measures had been legitimate means in aiding the German war effort. But there is no evidence that suggests that they made a difference. Victor von Weizsaecker observed at the conclusion of the war that they neither improved the fighting ability of German troops in the field nor protected the health of the people at home.[52] The reason was not just that the German authorities were unable to implement the experiments' findings fast enough during the troublesome war years, but that there were no findings to be implemented. His view was typical for all those who publicly evaluated the experiments after the war while dissociating themselves from the crimes committed. Aside from hardened Nazis, it was quickly assumed by anyone learning of the experiments, of which little if anything was known before the trial, that no physician with any professional standing would have associated himself or herself with systematically mutilating and killing people for any reason, total warfare or not, and that the defendants represented a small minority of sinister careerists. But the experiments quickly threw a giant shadow over the entire German medical system, especially outside Germany. The leading British medical journal *The Lancet* commented at the time of the trial that "German medicine, which once rivaled that of any European country, has fallen into sad disrepute. The decline dates from 1933. . . . Germany, in common with other Continental countries which she occupied, has been isolated from the course of progress in other lands . . . the universities have been bombed and their life disrupted."[53]

The British Government in 1946 authorized the creation of a committee for the evaluation of the medical crimes, the British Advisory Committee for Medical War Crimes. It was headed by Lord Moran, the private physician of Winston Churchill. He quickly became a central figure in Britain's controversy over the introduction of a national health care system proposed by the new Labor government. Conservative opponents argued that any government control over health care matters could only be ruinous to the nation, as the German example had just demonstrated. Lord Moran's concluding report was short and seen as an endorsement of the conservative position. It contains the following summary:

> The experiments on malaria at Dachau were unsatisfactory from all points of view. . . .
> The experiments designed to discover whether Hexamethylenetetramine did or did not
> protect patients when used after or before exposure to phosgene shows that there was

some protection, if the substance was used prophylactically; but none if it was used after exposure to phosgene. The experiment was neither well designed nor carried out. . . .

The experiments of orthopedic interest have to do with the treatment of wounds by sulphonamides, and those relating to regeneration of bone after resection and grafting, regeneration of soft tissue after resection, and the transplantation of whole bones all failed because of the inadequately trained experimenters, the ill-planning of the experiments and the inadequacy of the controls and recording. The experiments with artificial abscesses and with poisoned bullets were extremely crude and appeared valueless. . . .

The experiments dealing with the effects of cold, including freezing, and the attempts to use sea water for drinking purposes, and the experiments on nutrition, endocrinology and the effect of high altitudes on individuals might have led to useful information had they been properly planned and carried out by trained staff. Some of the findings where in accord with known facts, none added to scientific knowledge of the subject, so that their real contribution was nil.

The bacteriological researches were extensive. . . . Most of the experiments were haphazard in execution and all seemed to lack proper planning or integration while the workers [usually inmates] were singularly ill chosen.[54]

A former inmate and medical aid at Buchenwald, Eugen Kogon, who later testified at the trial, wrote of the bacteriological experiments in which he assisted that, "the scientific value of these tests was either nil or else of but insignificant proportions."[55] The two medical experts for the prosecution, Leo Alexander and Andrew Ivy of the United States, concurred. Hence, the chief counsel for the prosecution, Telford Taylor, remarked in his opening speech at the trial that "these experiments revealed nothing which civilized medicine can use."[56]

This did not mean that the records were not searched further for possible useful information, or that none was found. Upon examining available protocols of some freezing experiments, Alexander recommended as early as July 1945, while American troops were still fighting in the Pacific, that "the method of rapid and intensive rewarming in a hot water bath of 45 degree C (40–50) of people in shock from exposure to cold, especially in water, should be immediately adopted as the treatment of choice by the Air-Sea Rescue Services of the United States Armed Forces," which apparently were going by textbook medicine and used the less efficient method of slow rewarming.[57]

None of the physicians who had performed the Dachau freezing experiments were alive or available at the time of the trial, but some who had performed the high-altitude and seawater experiments were. At least three were employed after the war to advise the U.S. military on its own very similar experiments, even using the German air pressure chambers. Whatever useful knowhow the German researchers may have provided, it did not save them from ultimate indictment by the U.S. military in September 1946. Still, one of the physicians who were later acquitted continued his work on the potability of seawater for many years at Randolph Field in Texas. Also, after the trial, the Army

Chemical Corps hired the former head of the German biological warfare program, conveniently acquitted as well, to continue his research for the United States.[58]

Evidence suggests that since then, much more knowledge produced by the experiments may have been used, probably unadmittedly, by various physicians, researchers, and private and public organizations in various countries, including the United States. A Hastings Center Report of December 1984 states that "at least 45 research articles published since WW II have drawn upon data from Nazi experiments. Most of these articles are in the field of hypothermia research."[59] But some have been in aviation medicine, immunology, and other fields. And many more such articles no doubt have been published since then. Researchers in the United States and elsewhere, especially in the field of genetics, still rely on data that appeared in scientific works steeped deeply in the racist principles of National Socialist ideology.[60] The U.S. Environmental Protection Agency's unacknowledged use of data from the German phosgene experiments, in which many concentration camp inmates died, became public only after protests by some employees in 1988.[61]

The traumatic toll in human suffering caused by Nazi experimenters thus far may have prevented critics from attempting to account for the discrepancy between the general dismissal of these experiments by members of the medical profession and others and the co-option of whatever useful knowledge they may have produced. A considerable feeling of uneasiness must be the price paid by those who knowingly may benefit by this co-option yet feel helpless in facing the dilemma.

One of the few scholars who addressed this problem with some authority is the German geneticist Benno Mueller-Hill in his work *Murderous Science*, published in German in 1984. He states that humanistic concerns prevent anyone from ascribing any scientific value to the experiments at all, but adds that "they could not have been judged 'bad science' if they had been carried out on mice."[62] Indeed, the German physicians and responsible administrators had relegated their fellow human beings to the status of laboratory mice and had produced at least some usable results probably unobtainable by methods based on humanistic principles.

Robert Berger, a cardio-thoracic surgeon at Harvard Medical School, disagrees. Analyzing hypothermia experiments on Dachau concentration camp inmates with fatal outcomes, he found the data flawed, in some instances probably fabricated, and its findings unreliable.[63] They are unreliable mainly because the experimenters lacked conscience. Hence any debate about possible scientific merits of the experiments for him is pointless. Indeed, the very idea that people who had devised and conducted experiments in which the death of the subject was one of their "variables" should have an opportunity to defend their actions seems preposterous. But such an opportunity was given them after the war.

CHAPTER 2

The Trial—
A Legal Analysis

The Precedent: The Major Trial
Before the International Military Tribunal

LONG BEFORE THE END of the war, the three principal Allies had agreed to place top German and Japanese leaders on trial, though separately, before an international court for acts of aggression against other countries and inhumane treatment of their soldiers and civilians. On November 1, 1943, Stalin, Churchill, and Roosevelt released the Moscow Declaration, which in part reads:

> The United Kingdom, the United States and the Soviet Union have received from many quarters evidence of atrocities, massacres and cold-blooded mass executions, which are being perpetrated by the Hitlerite forces in the many countries they overrun and from which they are now being steadily expelled. The brutalities of Hitlerite domination are no new thing, and all the peoples or territories in their grip have suffered from the worst form of government by terror. What is new is that many of these territories are now being redeemed by the advancing armies of the liberating Powers and that in their desperation, the recoiling Hitlerite Huns are redoubling their ruthless cruelties. . . .
>
> . . . those German officers and men and members of the Nazi party who have been responsible for, or have taken a consenting part in, the above atrocities, massacres, and executions, will be sent back to the countries in which their abominable deeds were done in order that they may be judged and punished according to the laws of these liberated countries and of the free governments which will be created therein.[1]

The Declaration concluded with the following statement: "The above declaration is without prejudice to the case of the major criminals, whose offenses have no particular geographical localization and who will be punished by the joint decision of the governments of the Allies." This would allow the Allies to deal with Hitler and the other German leaders separately.

Earlier that year, after Allied landings in North Africa and the defeat of German troops in the battle of Stalingrad, Churchill and Roosevelt had declared the war in Europe could be concluded by nothing less than Germany's unconditional surrender. This concept was accepted by Stalin at the first meeting of the Big Three in Teheran several days after the Moscow Declaration. That declaration provided Hitler and his party leaders with the evidence they needed to show the German people that this was indeed total war, with no possibility of negotiated surrender. Hence for the National Socialists, the war turned into a suicidal mission of survival.

Only once, in July 1944, was the war effort almost halted when dissenting military and civic leaders made an abortive attempt to assassinate Hitler and cease hostilities. Hitler survived; the dissenters, after a mock trial, were executed. The carnage of troops, primarily at the Eastern front, and of civilians, primarily in German cities, along with the mass extermination of death camp inmates, continued unabated for many more months. Shortly after Soviet and Western Allied troops met at the Elbe River and west of Berlin, the unconditional surrender of Germany took place on May 7, 1945, to the Western Allies in Rheims and a day later to the Soviet Allies in Berlin. The major Allied countries, now including France, quickly agreed on a format for the planned trials. Their representatives met in London and established an International Military Tribunal with all necessary powers. The London Agreement, signed into law on August 8, 1945, contained a Charter, stipulating the Tribunal's jurisdiction, laws, and procedures.

Jurisdiction was established "for the trial and punishment of the major criminals" who, "acting in the interests of the European Axis countries [Germany and its allies], whether as individuals or as members of organizations, committed any of the following crimes."[2] The list included crimes violating 1) laws to keep peace, 2) laws to preserve the life and health of captured soldiers and foreign nationals, and 3) laws to abstain from inflicting harm on civilians, either as individuals or members of distinct political, racial or religious groups; referred to in short as crimes against peace, war crimes, and crimes against humanity.

Between November 20, 1945, and August 21, 1946, twenty-two top National Socialist leaders were tried by the International Military Tribunal in a case that served as a legal precedent for twelve cases before the subsequently created American Military Tribunal against lower-ranking officials, the first of which proceeded against twenty-three physicians and administrators in the

Medical Trial. A brief introduction to the Main Trail should be helpful in trying to analyze the subsequent trials.

Count One of the indictment in the Major Trial charged the defendants
with breaking the London Agreement's law against planning to violate any of
the other laws of the Agreement. According to the indictment, the defendants
"participated as leaders, organizers, instigators, or accomplices in the formulation or execution of a common plan or conspiracy to commit, or which
involved the commission of, Crimes against Peace, War Crimes, and Crimes
against Humanity."[3]

Eight defendants were convicted on that count, though only for conspiracy to break the peace between nations as charged under Count Two, despite
their objection that no international law condemned the intent to break peace
or the intent to break laws that govern warfare, and that the London
Agreement's conspiracy law constituted new law, hence could not be applied
ex post facto. The defendants filed the same objection with respect to all
other laws contained in the London Agreement, i.e., that they were retroactive laws calling into question the whole legal basis of the tribunal.

In anticipation of this challenge, the framers of the London Agreement had
placed a procedural injunction on the challenge, something the defendants tried
to circumvent with various procedural maneuvers of their own, but without success. The members of the court were aware, however, that at least with respect
to the conspiracy law, the defense's objection was not without merit. Conspiracy
laws were largely absent from continental Europe's legal tradition, because evidence for violations is difficult to obtain. Conspiracy to commit a crime without doing so, such as a planned overthrow of a political system, may perhaps
be verifiable by nothing but personal testimony. Such laws can easily be abused
to prosecute political enemies, or simply unpopular opinions, as was indeed
done by the National Socialists themselves. But conspiracy laws had a place in
Anglo-Saxon legal traditions, including that of the United States. When the
London Agreement was drawn up, the British representative, not without some
reservations and against French and Russian recommendations, endorsed the
American proposal to include a conspiracy clause in the law condemning
aggressive warfare.[4]

Count Two charged the defendants with breaking the peace as conspired
to according to Count One. In the language of the indictment, the defendants
were held responsible for "participating in the planning, preparation, initiation,
and waging of wars of aggression which were also wars in violation of international treaties, agreements and assurances."[5]

Given the overwhelming evidence presented by the prosecution, including the attack on Poland, the invasion of the U.S.S.R., and so on, the tribunal
had few problems finding twelve of the sixteen defendants so charged guilty.
But this verdict also presented legal problems that came to haunt the subse-

quent trials. The law distinguished between conspiring and planning to commit crimes; indeed, four defendants were found guilty of planning without conspiring to commit crimes. But no one was found guilty of conspiring to commit crimes without also planning them. That may be attributable not to the subtleness of the law as much as to the fact that few National Socialists could have assumed any of the leadership positions as held by the defendants without vigorous endorsement of the goals of National Socialism.

In theory, any verbal or written endorsement of the openly proclaimed goal of National Socialists to annex sovereign territory of other nations by aggressive means, as urged in Hitler's *Mein Kampf*, for instance, constituted an act of conspiracy. But so did Lenin's call to overthrow the capitalist order of Western countries subscribed to at the time by Stalin and certainly the Soviet judges on the bench, a fact that should have caused some embarrassment among the Western judges sitting on the same bench.

More problematic, perhaps, was the Allies' apparent intent not to condemn all aggressive wars, which could have made them liable for their own aggressive wars, colonial wars, for instance, but only to condemn "wars in violation of international treaties, agreements and assurances," which colonies generally had not been privileged to receive. The tribunal insisted that it merely enforced existing law as written in the charter of the London Agreement. A further difficulty stemmed from the fact that the actual treaties, agreements, and assurances between Germany and other nations violated by the defendants contained no provisions specifying criminal responsibility and consequences for possible offenders. Here the tribunal decided that such matters form part of a common, nonverbal understanding between the respective parties, a point the defense never accepted.

Count Three charged the defendants with such war crimes as murder and mistreatment of prisoners of war and civilians of occupied territories, wanton destruction of life and property, and other atrocities "not justified by military necessity." For the most part, these crimes had been enumerated in existing international law, chiefly the Hague Rules of Land Warfare of 1907 and the Geneva Convention of 1929, which constituted the core of the London Agreement's law against war crimes. The defendants' rhetorical "not guilty" plea on all of the charges leveled against them was least convincing with respect to the crimes cited under Count Three. Here the law was very clear and not retroactive. And the amount of evidence presented by the prosecution was overwhelming. It exposed the law's inadequacy to do full justice to the case.

The Hague Rules and the Geneva Convention were conceived in a chivalrous spirit of conditional warfare. They contained such rules as allowing fighting troops to secure their wounded and protected the life and property of civilians in occupied territory. The Geneva Convention in its amended version of 1929, the year that started the Great Depression, contains no provision for dealing with the kind of total warfare that shocked the world just a few years later, despite such earlier warnings as the genocide of the Armenians in World War I and the treatment of civilians to the Russian Civil War that followed. Bradley Smith, perhaps the foremost analyst of the Nuremberg trials, writes that

> . . . the total war and mass ideological movements have greatly extended the scope, form, and havoc of war in the twentieth century. Many of the victims of World War II could make no claim for protection on the basis of codified rules such as those of Geneva or The Hague, for those agreements had not been prepared for a world of gas chambers and atomic weapons. Those who had slaughtered civilians to terrorize a government or break the popular will of the opposition were not clearly chargeable under Count Three. The Nazi persecutors and exterminators did not violate most of the traditional rules of warfare—a conclusion that was simply impossible for the battered people of Europe to accept in 1945.[6]

Indeed, anyone who saw pictures of the liberated concentration camps must have shrunk at the thought that those who had planned and operated them could not be held responsible because no law would fit their crime. The most the perpetrators could be charged with under existing statutory law was mistreatment and murder of prisoners of war and civilians of occupied countries, but not citizens of their own country or the extermination of whole national, religious, racial, political, and other populations. And not even every perpetrator could be so charged. As leaders of a sovereign nation, those who held ultimate responsibility for these crimes were immune to prosecution from foreign jurisdiction.

The framers of the London Agreement had anticipated such arguments and had taken care that they could not serve as an escape hatch for the defendants. Statutory law, the framers determined, rests on natural law, articulated in the humanitarian principles to which all civilized nations, including Germany, have traditionally subscribed. According to these principles, mass extermination constitutes a crime against humanity from which no one can claim exemption. And since natural law has been endorsed by civilized nations at least as far back as the Enlightenment, it does not constitute new law. In this view, the inviolability of natural law found statutory expression in the London Agreement, which defines crimes against humanity as, "murder, extermination, enslavement, deportation, and other inhumane acts committed against any other civilian population, before or during the war; or persecutions on political, racial or religious grounds in execution of or in connection with any crime within the jurisdiction of the tribunal, whether or not in violation of the domestic law of the country where perpetrated."[7]

Indictment under this law constituted Count Four. The framers of the London Agreement did not translate universal natural law into universal statutory law, but confined statutory law to cover acts committed "before and during the war" when executed "in connection with any crime within the jurisdiction of the Tribunal." In other words, the law could be applied only to specific acts committed by citizens of Germany and allied countries before and during the war. That prevented the defendants from arguing that the countries that sat in judgment over them may have violated the law themselves, as the forced deportation and incarceration of Japanese-Americans or the mass bombing of civilian populations might have shown. The prosecution found sufficient legal means to indict eighteen of the twenty-two defendants for crimes against humanity under Count Four. Eighteen were also indicted for war crimes under Count Three. Sixteen defendants were found guilty on one count or the other, fourteen of them on both.

Most critics of the trial have focused on the following two points. The more serious of the two faults the tribunal with the suspension of the time-honored legal principle *nullum crimen sine lege*—there can be no crime without a law. This action placed the signatories of the London Agreement in bad company. The National Socialists too had suspended the principle in 1935 in order to promote their racial policies.[8] But rather than choose between subverting the law and letting the defendants off free, none other than the U.S. Supreme Court Justice Nathan April suggested their summary execution as an expedient act of politics instead.[9]

The second critical point relates to the close similarity of the wording of the London Agreement, the law by which the defendants were tried, to that of the indictment. To be sure, the indictment is longer, but in their essential parts, law and indictment read the same. This suggests that the tribunal was a staged event to place the stamp of approval on the forgone conclusion that the defendants were guilty, exposing the trial as a ritualistic act of revenge. Finding three of the defendants not guilty by reason of insufficient evidence, in this view, merely constituted a legitimizing part of the ritual.

Of course, the defendants themselves were aware of these weaknesses of the trial and exploited them wherever possible. The tribunal interpreted such exploitations as undue challenges to the integrity of the court and confined the defendants to due process as articulated in the London Agreement, whose Charter stipulated that, "neither the Tribunal, its members nor their alternatives can be challenged by the prosecution or by the Defendants or their Counsel."[10] The ultimate court of appeal was to be history.

The Medical Trial

Preparing the Trial

THE LONDON AGREEMENT GAVE the Allies the power to try and punish "major war criminals" only. To try other war criminals, the Agreement's Charter stipulated that "[i]n case of need and depending on the number of the matters to be tried, other Tribunals may be set up; and the establishment, functions, and procedure of each Tribunal shall be identical, and shall be governed by this Charter."[11] For this purpose, the governing authority for Germany as a whole, the Allied Control Council, on December 20, 1945, enacted Control Council Law No. 10, "for the prosecution of war criminals and other similar offenders, other than those dealt with by the International Military Tribunal."[12] It contained the same laws as listed in the charter, defining crimes against peace, war crimes, and crimes against humanity, plus one new law, membership in organizations declared criminal by the International Military Tribunal at the Major Trial: namely the Secret Police (Gestapo), the SS, and the leadership corps of the National Socialist Party. Control Council Law No. 10 gave the different military authorities of Germany's four occupational zones (Soviet, French, British, American) the power to set up their own military tribunals. The military government of the American Zone established the American Military Tribunal on November 2, 1946. Case No. 1 was the U.S. vs. Karl Brandt, et al., or the Medical Trial.

The Medical Trial developed out of the Major Trial. Investigations into the activities of the head of the Luftwaffe, Hermann Goering, had produced a considerable amount of material implicating the Luftwaffe's physicians in torturous and fatal experiments on human subjects, notably high altitude, freezing, and seawater experiments. The prosecution soon expanded the investigation into all human experiments performed during the Hitler regime and discovered routine abuse of concentration camp inmates in similar experiments by other military branches, except the Navy.

The evidence compiled implicated hundreds of physicians and administrators, many of whom were dead, in hiding, or out of jurisdiction. Because the concentration camps were under the sole supervision of the SS, it seemed that the head of this organization, Heinrich Himmler, and its chief physician, Ernst Grawitz, bore principal responsibility for the atrocities. Both had committed suicide at the end of the war. So had the regime's highest official for public health, Leonardo Conti. Of those who had performed medical experiments in person, the two most notorious physicians, Joseph Mengele and Sigmund Rascher, escaped justice as well. Mengele was in hiding, and Rascher had been executed by the SS during the last days of the war. The chief prosecutor at the eventual trial, Telford Taylor, later admitted:

> The choice of defendants and the choice of subjects in the Nuremberg trials were largely determined by factors not altogether under the control of the people who were organizing the trials. To put it bluntly, a great deal depended upon who was available to be tried. A great many people who might have been tried had either been killed or had died during the war. Right at the end of the war there had been quite a number of sui-

cides of people who would have been very much in demand at Nuremberg. Other people were hiding and could not be found.[13]

Further problems emerged when the initial cooperation among the Allies deteriorated and Western powers could no longer count on an automatic transfer of suspects in Soviet custody. The legal basis for trying suspected war criminals changed after the Major Trial, subjecting subsequent trials to the growing political tension between the three Western powers and the U.S.S.R. Jurisdiction for the subsequent trials was placed in the hands of the Allied military government for Germany, the joint Control Council, which empowered the four countries to hold separate tribunals in their respective zones of occupation against Germans suspected of crimes committed in that zone.[14] But such subjects often resided in different zones, requiring tedious extradition maneuvers between occupation forces. If crimes were committed outside Germany, the authorities of those countries had the first right to try suspects according to the laws prevailing there.

Despite those limits to their efforts, the military authorities of the U.S. zone were determined to continue prosecution of principal suspects in class action suits, which meant, prosecution of the most responsible members of particular groups and organizations that had incriminated themselves during the Hitler regime. Prominent cases were tried before a U.S. military tribunal, others before army courts. British and French occupation forces, less bent on enforcing justice in this way in their own zones of occupation, complied with the American plan and handed over requested suspects. Soviet forces did not.

The Defendants

THE PROSECUTOR'S EVENTUAL LIST of defendants contained the following names, listed by rank and position occupied in the National Socialist system:

> **Karl Brandt**: Gruppenfuehrer in the SS, personal physician to Chancellor Adolf Hitler, Commissioner for Health and Sanitation
> **Siegfried Handloser:** Lieutenant General, Medical Service, Chief of the Medical Services of the Armed Forces
> **Paul Rostock**: Chief of the Office for Medical Science and Research, Surgical Adviser to the Army
> **Oskar Schroeder**: Lieutenant General, Medical Service, Chief of Staff of the Inspectorate of the Medical Service of the Air Force
> **Karl Genzken**: Gruppenfuehrer in the SS, Chief of the Medical Department of the Waffen SS (Combat SS)
> **Karl Gebhardt**: Gruppenfuehrer in the SS, personal physician to the head of the SS, Heinrich Himmler, Chief Clinician of the SS and Police, President of the German Red Cross
> **Kurt Blome**: Deputy Reich Health Leader

Rudolf Brandt: Colonel in the SS, personal administrative officer to Heinrich Himmler, Chief of the Ministerial Office of the Ministry of the Interior

Joachim Mrugowsky: Senior Colonel in the Waffen SS, Chief Hygienist of the SS and Police, Chief of Hygiene Institute of the Waffen SS

Helmut Poppendick: Senior Colonel in the SS, Chief of the Personal Staff of the Reich Physician SS and Police

Wolfram Sievers: Colonel in the SS, Manager of the Cultural Heritage Society, Director of the Institute for Military Scientific Research

Gerhard Rose: Brigadier General of the Air Force, Hygiene Advisor for Tropical Medicine to the Chief of the Medical Service of the Air Force, Chief of the Department for Tropical Medicine at the Robert Koch Institute

Siegfried Ruff: Director of the Department for Aviation Medicine at the German Experimental Institute for Aviation

Hans Wolfgang Romberg: Physician on the Staff of the Department for Aviation Medicine at the German Experimental Institute for Aviation

Victor Brack: Senior Colonel in the SS, Chief Administrative Officer in Hitler's Chancellery

Hermann Becker-Freyseng: Captain, Medical Service, Chief of the Department of Aviation Medicine of the Medical Inspectorate of the Air Force

Georg August Weltz: Lieutenant Colonel, Medical Service, Chief of the Institute for Aviation Medicine (Munich)

Konrad Schaefer: Physician on the Staff of the Institute for Aviation Medicine (Berlin)

Waldemar Hoven: Captain in the SS, Chief Physician of the Buchenwald Concentration Camp

Wilhelm Beiglboeck: Consulting physician to the Air Force

Adolf Pokorny: Physician, specialist in skin and venereal diseases

Herta Oberhauser: Physician at the Ravensbrueck Concentration Camp

Fritz Fischer: Major in the Waffen SS, Assistant Physician to Defendant Karl Gebhardt

Of the twenty-three defendants, Karl Brandt and Siegfried Handloser had held the highest ranks. During the last year of the war, Brandt headed all medical emergency operations as Reich Commissioner, responsible only to Hitler, whom he attended as escort physician. Without his at least tacit approval, it is unlikely that medical experiments could have been performed. He definitely initiated and supervised the execution of the earlier euthanasia program. As Chief of the Medical Services of the Armed Forces, Handloser too must have given at least tacit approval to the general pursuit of human experiments, if not of specific projects. Both defendants carried major responsibility for the experiments by virtue of their office. The lower the ranks of the defendants, the closer their involvement in the execution of the experiments. Most of the court's sessions were devoted to determining the degree of responsibility of each defendant for each of the charges of the indictment, a tedious task, given the Hitler regime's feudal bureaucracy. The task was less difficult where direct participation in the experiments could be demonstrated.

For the experiments pertaining to the rescue of flyers and sailors, performed on inmates at Dachau, principal responsibility rested with the defendants

Schroeder, Ruff, Weltz, Becker-Freyseng, Schaefer, and Beiglboeck. As Chief of Staff of the Inspectorate of the Medical Services of the Air Force, Oskar Schroeder carried supervisory responsibility for these experiments, commissioned by the Air Force High Command. The other defendants participated to various degrees in their planning and execution. Romberg assisted in the execution of the high-altitude experiments, and Beiglboeck had sole responsibility for the execution of the seawater experiments. The former were designed and executed by the SS physician Sigmund Rascher, eventually killed by order of Himmler, and the latter were designed by Hans Eppinger from the University of Vienna, who escaped indictment through suicide. Primary responsibility for planning and executing the freezing experiments rested with Rascher and the also deceased Ernst Holzloehner from the University of Kiel.

The human experiments to determine the most effective treatments for war-related injuries and corrective surgery were planned and conducted primarily by Karl Gebhardt, head of the SS Hospital at Hohenlychen. He had the main responsibility for experiments with incendiary bombs, mustard gas, and sulfanilamide, as well as bone, muscle, and nerve regeneration, performed on inmates of nearby Ravensbrueck concentration camp. Gephardt acted with great autonomy under the protection of Himmler, whose personal physician he was. In theory, Genzken, as Chief of the Medical Department of the Waffen SS, shared supervisory responsibility. The SS also had its own Hygiene Institute in Berlin, headed by the defendant Joachim Mrugowsky, with a Department of Typhus and Virus Research at Buchenwald, headed by the deceased Erwin Ding-Schuler, who conducted the immunology experiments on the camp's inmates with the assistance of Waldemar Hoven. Many of the vaccines tested at Buchenwald were provided by Gerhard Rose, who tried to find ways to improve their effectiveness and develop new ones at the Robert Koch Institute. Eugen Haagen, from the University of Strasbourg, designed and conducted similar experiments on inmates at Natzweiler and Schirmeck.

Germany's apparent effort to prepare for biological warfare could not be substantiated in court, but some evidence linked Mrugowsky to experiments with food poisoning and poison bullets, and Kurt Blome to research on spreading harmful germs among soldiers and civilians.

The prosecution was able to present overwhelming evidence showing that experiments had been conducted to develop means to eliminate undesired segments of the population through various means of mass sterilization and castration. Only shifting circumstances of war prevented the project from becoming operational on a larger scale. Implicated in particular were the defendants Karl Brandt, Victor Brack, Helmut Poppendick, and Adolf Pokorny. Rudolf Brandt, Himmler's personal secretary, and Wolfram Sievers, the manager of the SS's Cultural Heritage Society, were indicted primarily for providing researchers with organizational and material support, in particular the release of concentration camp inmates for the many torturous and often fatal human experiments.

In his opening statement before the Tribunal, Telford Taylor presented the following characterization of the defendants:

> The twenty physicians in the dock range from leaders of German scientific medicine, with excellent international reputations, down to the dregs of the German medical profession. All of them have in common a callous lack of consideration and human regard for, and unprincipled willingness to abuse their power over, the poor, the unfortunate, the defenseless creatures who had been deprived of their rights by a ruthless and criminal government. All of them violated the Hippocratic commandments which they had solemnly sworn to uphold and abide by, including the fundamental principles never to harm—'primum non nocere.'
>
> Outstanding men of science, distinguished for their scientific ability in Germany and abroad, are the defendants Rostock and Rose. Both exemplify, in their training and practice alike, the highest tradition of German medicine. Rostock headed the Department of Surgery at the University of Berlin and served as the dean of its medical school. Rose studied under the famous surgeon Enderlen at Heidelberg and then became a distinguished specialist in the fields of public health and tropical diseases. Handloser and Schroeder are outstanding medical administrators. Both of them made their careers in military medicine and reached the peak of their profession. Five more defendants are much younger men who are nevertheless already known as the possessors of considerable scientific ability, or capacity in medical administration. These include the defendants Karl Brandt, Ruff, Beiglboeck, Schaefer and Becker-Freyseng.
>
> A number of others, such as Romberg and Fischer, are well trained, and several of them attained high professional position. But among the remainder few were known as outstanding scientific men. Among them at the foot of the list is Blome, who has published his autobiography entitled 'Embattled Doctor' in which he sets forth that he eventually decided to become a doctor because a medical career would enable him to become "master over life and death."[15]

The careers of the three defendants without medical degrees consisted of little more than loyal service to their superiors and organizations. Victor Brack wielded considerable power as head of Hitler's Chancellery, as did Rudolf Brandt as administrative secretary to Himmler. Their power consisted primarily in their ability to act on their own interpretation of their superior's will, which included the power of life and death over many victims. But they did not belong to the circle of ultimate decision-makers. The same can be said for Wolfram Sievers, the manager of the SS Cultural Heritage Society.

Taylor's characterization of the defendants later was echoed by the psychiatrist commissioned to examine each defendant's state of mind, Francois Bayle, a representative of the French Scientific Commission on War Crimes. During the trial, he subjected every defendant to interviews and tests to determine his personal character traits, level of intelligence, ability to make judgments, and emotional stability.[16] He soon found that this group of defendants by no means was a cohesive cohort.

At first glance they seemed to have many things in common. They had all lived a life of stuffy, middle-class respectability and for the most part had gone through the predictable steps of high-school graduation, university studies, early career moves, marriage, children, and getting ahead in a world fraught with unusual challenges. With a few exceptions (Handloser, Schroeder, Schaefer, Ruff, Pokorney), they had joined the Nazi Party, either for political motives or, more likely, economic opportunism. Most of them had joined the Party during the time of the global depression that started in 1929. Some of them had also joined the SS. This meant that they had to disavow any religious affiliations or other forms of faith and loyalty and become ideological soldiers in the cause of Hitler. In return they received privileges and professional advantages that otherwise would probably have remained out of their reach. None of the defendants noted by Taylor for their scientific and administrative work belonged to that group of Nazi Party and SS officials, except Karl Brandt, the main defendant.

Karl Brandt was 42 years old. The youngest members sitting in the dock were 35, (Schaefer, Romberg, Oberheuser); the oldest were 61 (Handloser, Genzken). Bayle found the personalities of the different defendants were as diverse as those of any other group of comparable size. On the basis of his tests and interviews, for instance, he concluded that Oskar Schroeder was a man of moral rectitute and that Waldemar Hoven was a debauched cynic with no sense of moral values whatsoever. Handloser and Rostock, who like Schroeder were noted by Taylor for their professional achievements, Bayle found to possess highly developed and stable personalities. Schroeder and Handloser, and particularly Rostock, also showed high levels of intelligence. Schroeder was a perfectionist. But he was also very impressionable and often uncertain of his own judgments. And he demonstrated a definite need for affection. Handloser too showed a tendency to be perfect, but it was coupled with a tendency to be in charge. He was even-tempered and of conservative disposition. A tenacious can-do type with rigid work habits, he had an alert mind and got things done. But, as Bayle put it, he lacked brilliance. Rostock, by contrast was less rigid, more individualistic, though often driven by impulsiveness and anger. The most impressive level of intelligence according to Bayle was displayed by the aviation scientist Siegfried Ruff. A man of remarkable creative powers and imagination, his mind generated ideas whose originality Bayle found close to being brilliant. However, Ruff's personality lacked stability. Suffering from a sense of impatience, he could be outright impetuous. The internationally renowned authority on tropical diseases, Gerhard Rose, did not fare any better. His tests too revealed remarkable intelligence, but also a lack of mental stability. Bayle found Rose to be irritable, petulant and disagreeable. A strong sense of self-satisfaction clashed with a foreboding sense of pessimism.

Bayle's investigation of Karl Brandt showed him to be of penetrating intelligence, but lacking in clear judgment. His very combative personality was held in check by a deep sense of stoicism. His thinking was decidedly non-traditional, or radical, making his embracing of Nazi doctrine perhaps the easiest to understand. Brandt engaged Bayle in conversations about the, as he saw it, politically-tainted intent behind his efforts to produce accurate character profiles of the defendants for the court. Bayle wrote that Brandt conducted those conversations "not without charm." Brandt, who apparently had resigned himself to his fate early on, seemed to assume the role of the person whose place he had come to occupy on the bench, Hermann Goering. Both Goering and Brandt showed signs of bi-polar personalities.

In his opening statement before the tribunal, of all the defendants Telford Taylor had placed Kurt Blome "at the foot of the list." As a medical administrator and cancer researcher he had left nothing noteworthy behind other than a record of faithful service to a bankrupt regime. He apparently had managed to destroy all evidence of atrocities connected with his research of biochemical warfare at an institute he headed in Posen. Bayle described him as an asocial and disorganized antagonist, incapable of making objective judgments, and someone who portrayed himself as a martyr of justice.

Given Bayle's assessment of the defendants in general, however, there were others who more truly deserved to be "at the foot of the list," such as Waldemar Hoven. Dull-minded and unstable, superficial and confused, the chief physician of Buchenwald lacked any sense of morals. Morbidly self-indulgent, he saw other people primarily as a means for his own sensual gratification. But his irritatingly insolent behavior, Bayle concluded, could not mask a suicidal sense of paranoia.

Joachim Mrugowsky, Chief Hygienist of the SS, did not look much better either. Slow of mind, driven by near savage material instincts, he oscillated between brutal and placid behavior patterns, between combative and inertial moods.

Karl Gebhardt, Himmler's personal physician and President of the German Red Cross during the last phase of the war, also ranked low in Bayle's reports. The tests revealed an underdeveloped personality of a man of some, but not exceptional, intelligence. Obsessed with base ambition, opinionated and asocial, Gebhardt nevertheless showed a gift for managing his affairs with a practical sense of irony.

The only woman in the group, Herta Oberhauser, physician at the womens' camp in Ravensbrueck, of all defendants seemed to have had the greatest difficulties adapting to the role as prisoner and defendant. Monotonously obsessive, irritable and inhibited, she showed a highly aggressive personality that lacked, Boyle remarked, feminine characteristics. Although she was a methodical and laborious worker, she lacked basic talent for making sound judgements.

The rest of the defendants to various degrees showed similar and other flaws, which for the most part overshadowed any of their perhaps less deplorable traits. Bayle found their personality, on the whole, to be unstable and impressionable, their intelligence mediocre, their judgements unclear, and their behavior aggressive. Still, he found that the character of the SS General Karl Genzken showed courage and his judgment honesty, but the character of Wolfram Sievers, Head of the SS Cultural Heritage Society, on the other hand was diabolic and his judgment mindless. The character of Rudolf Brandt, Himmler's secretary, was amoral and his judgment absurd. Bayle's evaluations, of course, were made under the most unusual of circumstances, which did not necessarily favor the production of accurate information. But most of his findings were corroborated by the information produced in the courtroom.

The trial was held in Nuremberg. The Allies, especially the U.S., had favored Nuremberg as a site for the International Military Tribunal, and later the American Military Tribunal, because it had been the site of Hitler's Nazi Party rallies. Trials here would symbolize defeat of the Hitler Regime and, perhaps, a new beginning for Germany. Also, Nuremberg had been the site where in 1935 the infamous race laws were announced that had laid the foundation for the Jewish genocide. A suitable building for holding the trials in the bombed out city was found too. A Bavarian appellate court at the outskirts of Nuremberg, the Palace of Justice, had survived the bombing attacks without much structural damage. It contained all necessary facilities, and the necessary repairs could be completed in time, if barely. After a few opening sessions in Berlin, the International Military Tribunal and its entourage moved to Nuremberg in October of 1945, where the Major Trial was held for one year. It would be followed by twelve subsequent trials, held by the American Military Tribunal, of which the Medical Trial would be the first.

Nuremberg was one of Germany's most damaged cities. The once proud town whose roots can be traced to the early days of the Middle Ages had been the site of Hitler's Nazi Party rallies that, together with death camp pictures, have remained the most indelible images of Hitler's reign. In 1946 the city was a mere shadow of its former self and looked like something one would more fittingly expect to see described in Dante's *Inferno*. A sea of ruins and rubble, there were few buildings left intact sufficiently to stage the planned tribunals following the war.

Life after the fire-bombings had resumed with an eerie sense of normality. Many people emerged ghostlike from the rubble to pursue a daily routine of searching for generally elusive items of survival. With millions of men having become casualties of the war, most of the early clean-up work was done by women, called Truemmerfrauen (rubble-women). Rebuilding had to wait. In November of 1946 people started to dig themselves into the rubble even

deeper in expectation of a harsh winter, having experienced one of the cold-
est winters in memory the year before.

When the well-known writer Rebecca West arrived in Nuremberg to report
on the trials, she noted that the Germans had not dug out their dead from the
ruins after air raids, a difficult task especially at the end when the raids were fre-
quent and people to do the digging dwindling. "It was for this reason," she
wrote, "that all German towns stank on hot days in the summer of 1946, and
sometimes there would be seen on the rubble lit lanterns and wreaths, set out
by mourners who were observing an anniversary. Neither did they make the
proper effort to furnish artificial limbs for their war casualties, and an appalling
number of one-armed and one-legged men were to be seen in German
streets."[17]

The news of the Major Trial had been followed with mixed interest, but
the news of the Medical Trial found little response among the German population. The Allied powers, mainly in the Western Zones of occupation, had facil-
itated the reemergence of a free and definitely anti-Nazi press almost
immediately upon assuming authority in Germany. But newspapers, where they
were affordable, were of more use as fire-starters, window-covers, clothes-lin-
ers, shoe-inlays, grocery-bags, cigarette papers, or mandatory trade-ins for the
purchase of many other paper goods. The execution of some of the top war
criminals who had been found guilty at the Major Trial had just taken place.
Much of the uncertainty and curiosity as to what to expect from the Allies had
given way to concerns of rebuilding households and reconstructing society.

The Medical Trial opened its first session on November 21, 1946, in the
same courtroom where the Major Trial had just been concluded, with the following indictment of the defendants:

> The United States of America, by the undersigned Telford Taylor, Chief Counsel for
> War Crimes, duly appointed to represent said Government in the prosecution of war
> criminals, charges that the defendants herein participated in a Common Design of
> Conspiracy to commit and did commit War Crimes and Crimes against Humanity, as
> defined in Control Council Law No. 10, duly enacted by the Allied Control Council
> on December 1945. These crimes include murders, brutalities, cruelties, tortures,
> atrocities, and other inhuman acts, as set forth in Counts One, Two, and Three of this
> Indictment. Certain defendants are further charged with Membership in a Criminal
> Organization, as set forth in Count Four of this Indictment.[18]

As in the Major Trial, Count One of the indictment charged all defendants
with conspiracy to commit war crimes and crimes against humanity. In the
Medical Trial, these crimes were defined as "medical experiments upon concentration camp inmates and other living human subjects, without their consent, in the course of which experiments the defendants committed the
murders, brutalities, cruelties, tortures, and other inhuman acts."[19]

Count Two listed the experiments as war crimes in the following order:

A. High-altitude experiments
B. Freezing experiment
C. Malaria experiments
D. Lost (mustard) gas experiments
E. Sulfanilamide experiments
F. Bone, muscle, and nerve regeneration and bone transplantation experiments
G. Seawater experiments
H. Epidemic jaundice experiments
I. Sterilization experiments
J. Spotted fever (typhus) experiments
K. Experiments with poison
L. Incendiary bomb experiments

The prosecution further charged some of the defendants with three medical atrocities not of an experimental nature:

A. The murder of 112 Jews for a skeleton collection
B. The murder and mistreatment of Poles with allegedly incurable tuberculosis
C. The murder of hundreds of thousands of undesirable persons in nursing homes, hospitals, and asylums disguised as an euthanasia program

Count Three charged the defendants with crimes against humanity, evidenced by medical experiments "upon German civilians and nationals of other countries."[20]

Count Four charged the defendants Karl Brandt, Genzken, Gebhardt, Rudolf Brandt, Mrugowsky, Poppendick, Sievers, Brack, Hoven, and Fischer with membership in a criminal organization, namely the SS. This was pursuant to a declaration of the International Military Tribunal that certain organizations of the Hitler regime were criminal, making membership in leading positions and voluntary endorsement of their National Socialist ideology a punishable offense. Aside from the SS, the National Socialist Party, the Secret Police, and its affiliated Security Forces were declared criminal also.

The defendants pleaded not guilty as charged, arguing that they had not violated existing law at the time, and that they had carried out the orders of superiors necessitated by national emergencies. Their arguments were countered by the prosecution's contention that existing law could not be limited to written statutory law but had to include inalienable natural law as well, manifest in the philosophic literature of all civilized nations. They also cited the

Charter of the London Agreement, which had declared any appeal to superior orders an invalid means to reject criminal responsibility.

The Charter had also been written to facilitate the tribunal's task of evaluating evidence for and against the formal charges without allowing for the possibility of challenging the legal basis of the charges themselves. Indeed, the sheer volume of the evidence was so overwhelming that the capacity of the tribunal was more than exhausted by merely sticking to this primary task.

Count One: Crimes Against Peace—Conspiracy

THE PROSECUTION CHARGED THAT "between September 1939 and April 1945 all of the defendants herein, acting pursuant to a common design, unlawfully, willfully, and knowingly did conspire and agree together and with each other and with diverse other persons, to commit War Crimes and Crimes against Humanity as defined in Control Council Law No. 10, Article II."[21] Conspiracy, as distinguished from mere planning, referred to the original conception of the performed experiments. Given their technical nature, it may not be surprising that some, if not most, originated in the minds of research physicians who subscribed to the National Socialist view that popular health is best served by disregarding, and when necessary, sacrificing the health and life of those designated as harmful and parasitic individuals. Rose's typhus experiments and Gebhardt's sulfanilamide experiments may be the best examples. The commonality of these designs, the agreement to execute them "together and with each other and with diverse persons" was more difficult to ascertain. Given the organizational structure within which they occurred and the general secrecy with which they were pursued, not much discussion was needed or agreement sought after superior approval was given. The number of individuals responsibly participating in this process seldom exceeded a handful. The prosecution maintained "each experiment constituted a criminal conspiracy in and of itself. None of the experiments were formulated and executed by one man."[22]

When the defendants contended that they had been generally unaware of other projects or experimenters, the prosecution countered that "the conspirators may not know each other or such others' part in the plan, nor, indeed, all the details of the plan itself. He may know only his own part. That is enough if there is an intentional contribution to the whole."[23] There were occasions where a general sense of conspiracy could have pervaded: the medical conferences organized by the various branches of the Armed Forces. Here physicians presented papers on current research projects, including those on concentration camp inmates. While direct references to this fact were avoided, and thus appeared in no protocol, it must have been apparent from the presentations to anyone familiar with the subject. Personal conversations between presentations probably filled in the rest.

When Ernst Holzloehner and Sigmund Rascher reported at the Aviation Medicine Conference in October 1942 on the rate of temperature drop in humans after immersion in ice-cold water until the occurrence of death, no one could have concluded that the data were measured on a stranded pilot in the North Sea, as the two presenters apparently implied. During an interrogation before the trial, Becker-Freyseng, who had attended the presentation, admitted, "it was rather well known that those men were experimenting on concentration camp inmates."[24] He retracted this generally incriminating admission during the later proceedings and pointed out that, besides himself, ninety other physicians attended the conference. He added that "most of the others are at liberty today and some of them have high positions."[25]

Nobody among the ninety-plus physicians inquired how, let alone protested, the conditions under which the data presented were obtained. Holzloehner gave the same presentation two months later at a medical conference of the Consulting Physicians of the Armed Forces, organized by Handloser, with the same result. The situation at other conferences was similar. The record shows that only once did any of the assembled physicians openly protest the way concentration camp inmates were subjected to torturous and fatal experiments.

Gerhard Rose left no doubt about his disgust at the Third Conference of Consulting Physicians of the Armed Forces in May 1943. But his remarks changed nothing. On the contrary, Rose himself would later use concentration camp inmates for his own immunological experiments, and the number of inmates who suffered injuries and death as a result of such experiments increased during the last two years of the war.

During the closing phase of the trial the defense counsels filed a common motion to dismiss Count One of the indictment because it violated international law and custom, including the London Agreement and the Decisions of the International Military Tribunal, which proceeded in accordance with it.[26] The defense argued, "[i]t is apparent from arguments and presentation of evidence that the Prosecution holds the viewpoint that the defendants are guilty of the crime of conspiracy, which is independent of the individual, possibly criminal acts." But this, the claim goes, is illegal in the present case, and all subsequent cases before the American Military Tribunal, for the following two reasons. First, international, not American, i.e., national, law applies, represented by the four victorious powers in common, in conjunction with the law of the land, i.e., German law. Second, the prosecution's view contradicts the internationally recognized legal principle of nullum crimen sine lege, which also constitutes part of German law.

With respect to the first point, the defense argued that conspiracy was not recognized as a crime in France and Russia. And of the four powers, France and Russia were most entitled to set legal standards for the trials, since they had been occupied by German forces during the war. It also reminded the court that charges of conspiracy traditionally were an instrument of governments and rulers, including dictators like Hitler, to silence unwanted critics. With respect to the second point, the defense argued that even the International Military Tribunal had earlier rejected conspiracy as a punishable offense when it did not result in the commission of war crimes and crimes against humanity, and that a disregard of this rule would constitute an illegal application of retroactive law.

The defense acknowledged that the International Military Tribunal had ruled that conspiracy to wage aggressive war was, however, a punishable crime independent of the commission of war, arguably a rule that created new and retroactive law too. But the defendants in the Medical Trial were not charged with this particular crime.

The prosecution protested the defense's motion to drop conspiracy charges with the argument that "it never occurred to the framers of the London Charter that, by including a reference to conspiracy with respect to crimes against peace, they would thereby raise the implication that conspiracy was excluded in the field of war crimes and crimes against humanity."[27] Hence, the prosecution concluded that "the decision of the International Military Tribunal in this respect is wrong," because "it would be useless, anomalous, and harmful if the doctrine of conspiracy is held to be applicable in the case of crimes against peace but not in the case of war crimes and crimes against humanity." With respect to the defense's protest of the American Military Tribunal's application of American law in the medical and other trials in lieu of international and German law, the prosecution showed the defense's double standard in its argumentation, since it did not protest the Tribunal's typically American, and for the defense beneficial, concepts of the right of defendants to testify on their own behalf or the court's obligation to acquit anybody whose guilt cannot be established beyond any reasonable doubt.

On July 14, 1947, five weeks before the pronouncement of its verdicts, the tribunal granted the defense motion to discuss the conspiracy charges in a ruling containing the following statement:

> It is the ruling of this Tribunal that neither the Charter of the International Military Tribunal nor Control Council Law No. 10 had defined conspiracy to commit a war crime or crime against humanity as a separate substantive crime; therefore, this Tribunal has no jurisdiction to try any defendant upon a charge of conspiracy considered as a separate substantive offense.
>
> Count I of the indictment, in addition to the separate charge of conspiracy, also alleges unlawful participation in the formulation and execution of plans to commit war crimes and crimes against humanity which actually involved the commission of such crimes. We, therefore, cannot properly strike the whole of Count I from the indictment, but, insofar as Count I charges the commission of the alleged crime of conspiracy as a separate substantive offense, distinct from any war crime or crime against humanity, the Tribunal will disregard that charge.[28]

Count Two: War Crimes

COUNT TWO OF THE indictment charged the defendants with war crimes as defined in Control Council Law No. 10, which listed atrocities already mentioned in The Hague Regulation of 1907 and the Geneva Convention of 1929. The charged crimes comprised the specific experiments described in the previous section, performed "without the subjects' consent, upon civilians and members of the armed forces of nations then at war with the German Reich and who were in the custody of the German Reich in exercise of belligerent control," in the course of which the defendants committed "murders, brutalities, cruelties, tortures, atrocities, and other inhumane acts."[29]

The prosecution presented an impressive amount of material showing that the defendants, to various degrees, had been "principles in, accessories to, ordered, abetted, took consenting part in, and were connected with" the charged crimes. Official and private letters, memorandums, experimental protocols, scientific reports, photos, affidavits, and, most importantly, eyewitness accounts left little doubt that no defendant could claim convincingly not to have been, at the very least, "connected with" some of the atrocities with which they were charged, and that a number of defendants had indeed been principals.

Of the two major tasks facing the tribunal, determining the extent of the defendants' commission of the charged crimes and establishing the degree of their culpability for them, the latter proved to be the more challenging. For the most part, the defendants did not deny their active role in the various medical atrocities, on foreign nationals as well as Germans, if only to the extent demonstrable with available evidence. But they did deny most or all culpability for them.

Romberg and Beiglboeck fully acknowledged their respective roles as active experimenters in the Luftwaffe's high-altitude and seawater experiments, respectively, making them liable for the deaths of at least four experimental subjects. But those in superior and consulting positions—Ruff, Weltz, Becker-Freyseng and Schroeder—admitted to little more than vague knowledge of them, in some cases received supposedly after the fact.

Gebhardt, Fischer, and Oberhauser acknowledged their active role in experiments with simulated war injuries and reconstructive surgery on camp inmates, mostly women. Gebhardt even took a certain measure of professional pride in claiming the principal part in their design and execution. His superior Genzken, however, professed general ignorance of these experiments.

Rose admitted his leading role in epidemic research, much of it performed on camp inmates as well, his earlier objections to this admitted inhumanity notwithstanding. But he placed much of the responsibility on his dead superior Gildemeister.

Mrugowsky played down his leading role in similar research and placed all of the responsibility on his own dead superiors, Grawitz and Himmler.

Karl Brandt accepted responsibility only for the euthanasia program during the time it was officially decreed by Hitler, i.e., the first two years of the war. Since the victims were German, he argued, he was not guilty as charged. He too claimed general ignorance of subsequent medical experiments and insisted that he assumed formal responsibility for such matters only with his appointment as Reich Commissioner eight months before the end of the war. At the time he was thoroughly occupied with protecting the health of millions of civilians suffering from Allied saturation bombings of German cities.

With the possible exception of Gebhardt, none of the defendants accepted major responsibility for any of the deeds with which they were charged. When evidence linked them to particular atrocities, they invoked superior orders and their soldierly duty to obey. In particular, the three defendants who were not physicians—Rudolf Brandt, Sievers, and Brack—insisted throughout the trial that they had worked in a secretarial capacity for the ultimate decision-makers, Himmler and Hitler.

Not only did the defendants, for the most part, present themselves as mere followers of higher orders, but they also maintained that they had acted, to the best of their knowledge, within the limits of existing law. The highest expression of existing law for them was identical with the word of the leader of the nation, Adolf Hitler. Hitler's claim to be a creator of new law, and the interpreter of old law, had received some legal sanction from the Enabling Act of 1933, a constitutional emergency measure giving the government's executive branch the extraordinary power to legislate without parliamentary approval in some designated areas. His predecessors in the Weimar Republic had invoked the measure as well, but nobody had claimed it to be anything but a temporary means to deal with crippling economic problems and social unrest. With the help of such legal advisers as Carl Schmitt and Ernst Forsthoff, Hitler used the act as a means to reintroduce more traditional, partially orally based, legal theory, which upheld a ruler's right to promulgate law single-handedly, a medieval concept that still had found some justification in Rousseau's argument that rulers had not only a right but a duty to enforce a nation's General Will.

Hitler's subsequent claim that his word prevailed over statutory law created considerable judicial uncertainty, mostly in the legal profession and the civil service. Except among ideologically committed, usually younger, officers in the military, his word alone was not generally accepted as law until it had passed through various bureaucratic procedures and had become a matter of public record. But many of the orders to which he gave the full weight of the law were sanctioned in the name of national security. To assure their unquestioned execution, Hitler and his trusted National Socialist leaders had created the SS, an ideological fighting force whose members swore unquestioned loyalty to him-self, and whose head, Himmler, eventually became chief of the German police and Secretary of Internal Affairs.

A personal, if less rigorous, loyalty oath to obey Hitler was required also of all civil servants, and an extensive indoctrination of the public by the Minister of Propaganda, Joseph Goebbels, was intended to ensure acceptance of any of Hitler's measures, no matter how much it conflicted with written law. Thus was it possible for Hitler, at least after the outbreak of the war, to order the secret killings of asylum inmates under a so-called euthanasia program. The execution of the program still caused nightmarish legal, not to mention moral, dilemmas for all those who carried responsibility for the inmates' welfare and assisted in the program while opposing the program's circumvention of famil-iar basic laws and standard procedures.[30] Hitler eventually had to stop the pro-gram because of an outcry from some of the deceived family members and the moral outrage expressed openly by some church officials.

To prevent such public interference with their own designs, the National Socialist officials in charge of medical research assigned projects of human experimentation to the military, mostly the SS. Military physicians designed, supervised, and performed all experiments on human subjects. Only the Luftwaffe apparently contracted with civilian consultants, two of whom were the defendants Ruff and Romberg. All experiments were performed in concen-tration camps, which were under the sole command of Himmler and his doggedly loyal SS, sworn to utter secrecy. Here the experimenters found thou-sands of confined individuals, many destined to die, whose sufferings seeming-ly were of little consequence to the world outside. According to the National Socialists' corporate conceptions of society, the inmates were enemies of the state from which society had to be protected, but who could still make a real contribution as experimental subjects. And it all seemed legal as long as Hitler gave his endorsement. And even if he did not give it formally, it was assumed to exist in his less formally expressed intentions or simply in the doctrines of National Socialism, which Hitler voiced on several occasions and which his rul-ing entourage received as legal, often sacred, commands.

Distinctions between Hitler's stated orders, known policies, and general intentions could easily be blurred to fit a researcher's ambition, manifested, for instance in the reply of Gebhardt to the questions of the prosecutor Alexander Hardy about his sulfanilamide experiments:

> Q. [Hardy]I understand you to testify that Hitler had approved of medical experimen-tation on concentration camp inmates, and that his position was reached by you no later than 1942, and that you specifically learned about it when the sulfanilamide experiments were under discussion. Isn't that true?
> A. [Gebhardt] Quite . . .

Q. Let's get this straight. I understand that you talked to Grawitz about the sulfanil-amide experiments early in July, or shortly prior thereto, and that both Grawitz and Himmler gave you to understand that Hitler had approved in principle the use of concentration camp inmates for purposes of medical experimentation. Isn't that right?
A. Yes, that is correct.[31]

This statement was not corroborated, however, by the two highest-ranking defendants, Karl Brandt and Handloser, who claimed to have been unaware of any such approval by Hitler. For them, this was a logical position to take, however, since they also claimed to have been equally unaware that any human experiments ever took place.

Asked whether the two defendants' statements would not contradict his own, Gebhardt replied:

I think that one can explain this [apparent contradiction] by means of individual example or experiments as far as I know they arose. First of all, you are making one principal mistake to overestimate or underestimate information from Hitler or Himmler, according to how it fits into the particular stage of trial. The situation was certainly not that—and, mind you, I was not there—that Hitler might have said, "Now, then, whatever can be cleared up now in the medical field will now be cleared up in a big way through experiments," so that there would have been an order to all official departments that whoever had anything to do with this matter should be consulted. This certainly was not the situation, because then there would have been experiments in many other fields. . . .

Do you think that history will ever ascertain how cautiously and how generally Hitler's wishes and instructions were expressed?

On the other hand, I am sure that it was enough—and mind you, this is all assumption on my part—it was necessary for him only to say to Himmler "Good Heavens, you have a wonderful way there. Why shouldn't they experience the same fate as people at the front?" That was enough for Himmler to take up the matter . . . but it is quite sure that Brandt and Handloser up above were never touched with a general order.[32]

Those defendants who were not directly involved in the conduction of human experiments tended to show ignorance of any possible Hitler order, whose knowledge could only be incriminating, while those who had been so involved claimed that there must have been one, since they hoped it to be vindicating. But there was little disagreement among them about their perceived obligation to obey specific military orders to conduct experiments. With a few exceptions, the defendants had been members of the Armed Forces and argued that they were soldiers first and physicians second. Especially in wartime, they had to execute specific military orders like any other soldier everywhere else, even if it meant possible violation of nonmilitary legal codes, customary medical practice, or personal convictions.

Fischer was most insistent on this point when asked why he had assisted Gebhardt in his torturous experiments on inmates:

These actions took place not in 1947 but in 1942, during the war, at the very height of the war. At that time in my conclusions I was not a free civilian physician, but I was— that is the way I felt—that I was, as I say, a medical specialist who acted only as a soldier with the duty of obedience. When I received these orders which were antagonistic to my inner feelings, I found myself confronted with a gigantic authority. This authority was the state, represented by Hitler and, on the other hand, and supplemental to that, a medical authority that had an international reputation. This authority, namely Dr. Gebhardt, whose life work I knew, was a person who inspired me with confidence. If he decided to carry out these experiments as necessary experiments, then perforce I must believe that they were necessary, and I was also told by him that in the life of a human being, and in the life of a nation, situations arise in which the individual is under obligation to stifle his inner objections in the interest of the community.

I cannot believe, even today, that his were motives other than those under which soldiers act on the front when under orders they committed acts they would never have committed, and which were against their innermost personal feelings. I believe that the situation is analogous. I believe that my situation was the same at the time, the same situation in which the individual soldier fires a torpedo against a ship and another soldier is under orders to drop bombs on an unprotected city. Here again I cannot believe that they were individuals who are acting in accordance with their individual instincts. Rather I know that they too had to overcome their innermost objections and felt themselves to be justified in what they were doing through the fact that they were acting under military orders.[33]

Accordingly, Hitler, as chief of the military command, carried ultimate responsibility for all orders, which relieved all soldiers of personal responsibility.

Karl Brandt added that this responsibility was shared by the state and its institutions. He was unequivocal about this in a reply to Judge Harold Sebring dealing with the low-temperature experiments:

Q. [Sebring] Witness, for the sake of clarification, let us assume that it would have been highly important for the Wehrmacht to ascertain, as a matter of fact, how long a human being could withstand exposure to cold before succumbing to the effects of it. Do you understand that? Let's assume secondly that human subjects were selected for such freezing experiments without consent. Let's assume thirdly that such involuntary human subjects were subjected to the experiments and died as a direct or indirect result thereof. Now, would you be good enough to inform the Tribunal what your view of such an experiment is—from either the legal or the ethical point of view?
A. [Brandt] I must repeat once more, in order to make sure that I understand you correctly. When assigning the experiment the following thing was assumed: highest military necessity, involuntary nature of the experiment, and the danger of the experiment with eventual fatality. In this case I am of the opinion that, when considering the circumstances of the situation of war, this state institution which has laid down the importance in the interest of the state at the same time takes the responsibility away from the physician if such an experiment ends fatally and such responsibility has to be taken by the state.[34]

The prosecution rejected the claim that Hitler could dictate law and, personally or through state institutions, assume responsibility for its enforcement. Instead it argued that the defendants had to uphold statutory law, and a law regulating medical experimentation with humans existed since 1931. In response to the deaths of at least 75 children who died of tuberculosis meningitis after being inoculated with a new vaccine containing tubercle bacilli, the German Minister of the Interior issued Reich Guidelines that prohibited the use of minors for innovative therapies and medical experimentation and required informed consent of adult subjects.[35] The proper legal status of the Guidelines has always been debatable. In the minds of the defendants, they were superseded by guidelines and laws issued during the Hitler regime. Most defendants, in fact, claimed ignorance of the 1931 Guidelines.

When questioned on the subject at the trial, Kurt Blome, the earlier Vice President of the powerful Reich Chamber of Physicians, replied as follows:

> Q. [Counsel Sauter] Dr. Blome, to be sure, you yourself did not carry on any experiments and were not actively participating in the carrying out of experiments. However, during the Hitler period you were deputy leader of the Reich Chamber of Physicians. Consequently, you are able to give partly reliable data on the options that were held at that time; now tell me, during your time of office, did any laws either in Germany or outside of Germany become known to you—laws passed regarding experiments on human beings?
>
> A. [Blome] No such questions were ever asked of the Reich Chamber of Physicians either in peace or in war. Laws for this in Germany are not known to me, aside from Himmler's remarks to me in regard to the carrying out of experiments of military importance during the war. Nor do I know anything positive about laws passed on these matters in foreign countries. In conversations with colleagues, I occasionally heard that America had passed some such law, mainly in the Southern states, a law providing that experiments on human beings could be carried out on condemned criminals for scientific purposes, but I have no positive assurances that this is so.
>
> In my opinion, on the question of carrying out experiments on human beings for research purposes and particularly since the beginning of this century, such experiments became very numerous, which can be seen from international medical literature. That is to say, this is more or less a matter of the law of custom, if I can so express myself, which in the course of decades has become part of the usual research practice.
>
> Q. Did the Reich Chamber of Physicians, of which you were the deputy president, either before or during the war, lay down any policy for German physicians, from which the doctors could see what it was permitted for them to undertake experiments on human beings and what was not permitted; were such policies, or indications of such given to the medical profession?
>
> A. No, I have already said that no such questions were asked of the Reich Chamber of Physicians.[36]

Blome's argument, mostly implicit and similarly advanced by all defendants, was that custom rather than law regulated physician-patient relations and medical research on humans everywhere. The custom of using prisoners for medical experiments had its origin in the United States, notably in Joseph Goldberger's pellagra experiments on inmates of a Mississippi penitentiary in

1915. The defense argued that Germany had not crucially deviated from the custom during the Hitler years, given the brutalizing conditions of the war. This prompted the prosecution to present a rebuttal with the testimony of an expert, Andrew Ivy. A physiologist from the University of Chicago and chairman of the State of Illinois's medical ethics committee, he presented himself more as a medical and ethical rather than a legal authority on the matter, and for that reason will be discussed more in the following chapter.

Ivy did not dispute Blome's observation that, on the whole, medical practice and research is guided more by custom than by law, but he argued that the parameters of this custom have long been established by timeless Hippocratic principles of comforting the ill. He further argued this principle had been grossly abandoned by many German physicians during the war years. Physicians in the United States and elsewhere had not abandoned those principles, even when they did use prisoners as subjects, because no one ever underwent a medical experiment without informed consent, and no one was ever subjected to such torturous and fatal experiments as performed in German concentration camps. Ivy did not find it objectionable to reimburse prisoners, or others, for their willingness to become medical subjects with tangible rewards, as had been practiced in the United States, though he rejected the observed practice of rewarding such services with reduced or commuted sentences.[37]

But even if the court were to rule in favor of the defendants' claims that their experiments had been legal and customary—excluding the most blatant atrocities of such physicians as Rascher and Mengele, who were not in the dock, and Hoven, who was—they were committed, for the most part, on foreign civilians and prisoners of war, few of whom, if any, had volunteered or been informed of the full dangers of the experiments. Even if all the selections had been made by the SS and not themseves, the experimenters could not claim ignorance of that fact. Hence, under international law, if not the London Agreement, their experiments still constituted ill treatment and murder, for which they could be held individually responsible.

Here the defendants claimed, to the best of their knowledge, all human subjects had been volunteers, and their final selection was not made by the experimenting physicians but by members of the SS on explicit orders from Himmler. As head of the SS, no experiments could have been made, and no camp inmates could have been used, without Himmler's explicit approval, and sometimes active support. But he apparently did not initiate these experiments, as much as he may have pressed for them later on. They were initiated by the experimentors themselves.

The story of Luftwaffe Captain Sigmund Rascher is a case in point. Through his wife, he had personal contact to Himmler, which he exploited to the utmost to advance his career. On May 15, 1941, Rascher wrote the following letter to his SS superior:

Dear Mr. Reich Leader:
My humble thanks to your warm congratulations and the flowers on the occasion of the birth of my second son! It is a lusty boy again this time, though he arrived three weeks prematurely. Perhaps you will permit me to send you a snapshot of the two children some time.
. . . Cannot two or three professional criminals be made available for these experiments? The experiments will be conducted at the "Air Force Ground-Level Testing Station for High-Altitude Research" in Munich. The experiments, during which, of course, the test persons may die, will proceed with my collaboration. They are definitely of importance in high-altitude flight research and cannot be conducted with monkeys, as has been tried, since monkeys react altogether differently. I have talked about this matter in strict confidence with the deputy air surgeon who will conduct these experiments, and he shares my view that the problems in question can be clarified only be way of experiments on human beings. (Feebleminded persons might also be used as testing material.)[38]

Himmler granted the request, and Rascher performed his first high-altitude experiments on inmates at Dachau with the assistance of Romberg and the consultation of Ruff and Weltz. After at least three obviously programmed deaths had occurred, Romberg, Ruff, and Weltz severed their ties with Rascher, who continued such terminal experiments on many more inmates by himself. He reported his findings to Himmler, including the observation that death occurred at high altitudes as a result of embolism caused by low air pressure, and that cardiac activity continued long after all other vital signs had ceased.

This particular observation caught the attention of Himmler, who responded with the following note:

Dear Dr. Rascher:
I still would like to answer your letter which you had included in your reports to me. I found the latest discoveries of your research especially interesting. Now I would like to ask you for the following:
1. The experiments shall be repeated on additional men sentenced to die.
. . . .
3. In particular, the experiments should provide information whether it is possible that the heart, with its ability to keep functioning for such a long time, is able to call these men back to life.
Should such an experiment succeed, the condemned subject's sentence naturally is commuted to life in concentration camp.
Friendly regards and Heil Hitler.
Your H. Himmler[39]

Something disturbed Rascher in this letter, and he sent Himmler a note requesting clarification:

Until now I have had only Poles and Russians at my disposal for these experiments, including some condemned to death. I am in the dark so far whether paragraph three cited above applies to them as well and whether their sentences are to be commuted to life in the concentration camp if they survive several of the most hazardous tests.[40]

The answer, signed by the defendant Rudolf Brandt, informed Rascher "that the formerly given directive by the Reich Leader SS to pardon subjects does not apply to Poles and Russians."[41]

With one possible exception, the Tribunal could not establish that any inmate had in fact been so pardoned or, for that matter, that any of the inmates had indeed been condemned convicts. Rascher's Russians and Poles were mostly prisoners of war under the protection of international law.

Eugen Kogon, an inmate and medical assistant at Buchenwald, who appeared as a major witness at the trial, wrote the following account:

> I myself, for more than two years, from March 1943 to April 1945, served as a so-called Ward Clerk at Buchenwald, and during this period the secret lists of prisoners selected for these experiments passed through many hands. I know of no single case in which one of these human guinea pigs had been previously sentenced to death by a court of law. I am reliably informed that the situation was not different in the other camps. . . . in actual practice the human subjects were for years picked by camp headquarters by methods now familiar. They were generally convicts and homosexuals, with a sprinkling of political prisoners of all nationalities.[42]

With respect to Rascher's high-altitude experiments, Kogon wrote:

> A mobile unit was set up at Dachau in the camp street, between Block 5 and the adjacent barracks. The area was isolated from the other hospital buildings so that outside observation was impossible. The unit consisted of a high enclosed box on wheels, with built-in instruments for the measurement of pressure, temperature, and altitude. The equipment made it possible to simulate conditions during an ascent to high altitudes and during rapid descent. Heart action of the subjects was measured by an electrocardiograph. Autopsies were conducted immediately upon death ("the blood does not yet boil at an altitude of 70,000 feet" reads the final report of the "experts," dated July 28, 1942). On one occasion, during on autopsy, Rascher found the heart of the victim still beating. He thereupon instituted a whole series of killings, solely for the purpose of establishing the length of time during which the human heart remained active after death.
>
> Naturally the "Sky Ride Wagon," as it came to be known in the camp, inspired panic among the prisoners. The first victim had been requisitioned from the Labor Utilization Office as a special detail to be granted supplementary rations. Some innocents had actually volunteered. But within a few days sinister rumors were heard. There were no more volunteers. Thereafter the victims were simply taken from the barracks on one pretext or another. Newcomers were especially popular as subjects. Frequently "The Captain," as he was known in the camp, went stalking for suitable victims himself.[43]

Obviously, no unified system for selecting human subjects was followed. Once Himmler or one of his designates, such as the head of the criminal police, Arthur Nebe, had approved a request to use inmates for specific medical experiments, selections were made by camp headquarters at the advice of the physicians or, as in the case of Rascher, by the physicians themselves.

Rascher's brutality in finding victims apparently was matched only by Joseph Mengele's at Auschwitz. Mengele stalked the camp in constant search for suitable specimens for various hereditary projects. The only defendant at the trial who had demonstrated a similarly sadistic penchant to play master over life and death was Waldemar Hoven, the camp physician at Buchenwald and occasional assistant to Erwin Ding-Schuler. He played a crucial role in putting together rosters of individuals marked for experiments and used his power to play favorites among inmates, engaging their assistance in making selections from among their enemies. Also with their assistance, and by his own admission, he killed at least 50 to 60 such enemies himself.[44]

Aside from Hoven, Herta Oberhauser, the only woman in the dock, was also the only other camp physician among the defendants. She too had played primarily an assisting role in the experiments by providing postoperative care for Gebhardt's female subjects at the Ravensbrueck camp for women. She admitted to at least four killings of postoperative moribund individuals but seemed to have played no part in the selection of the subjects.[45]

None of the other defendants had been stationed permanently inside a camp. When they entered camps, it was primarily to inspect, supervise, and conduct human research. At the trial they insisted they did not take part in the selection of their subjects themselves, they did not know or care about how camp headquarters selected them, and they had accepted the assurances of the SS that everything had the sanction of law. But at the very least they must have provided medical criteria for the selections, and they certainly had the power of disapproval when they were not met. The SS, in other words, provided a convenient service. They apparently did not interfere when physicians did want to pick their own subjects, however.

Himmler, in turn, seemed primarily interested in reserving his own power of approving the use of inmates for medical experiments in general. During the last phase of the war, when the requests for subjects considerably increased, he delegated and specified this power more formally. When in February 1944, Ding-Schuler requested convicts for his typhus experiments in Buchenwald, for instance, Himmler gave the following order:

> I agree that professional criminals be taken for experiments with the typhus vaccine. But only these professional criminals should be chosen who have served more than 10 years in prison; that is not with 10 prior convictions but a total penalty of 10 years. SS-Gruppenfuehrer Nebe is to supervise the disposal of these inmates. I don't wish the physician to pick out inmates without any counter control.[46]

A few months later, on May 15, 1944, Himmler documented what had been established practice by then, according to Kogon, at the urging of physicians like Ding-Schuler, who may have already anticipated postwar legal consequences:

I hereby order that medical experiments to be carried out in concentration camps must have my personal approval. This order is to go into effect immediately.

All offices within the SS and Police which deem necessary the carrying out of a medical experiment in a concentration camp will have to submit to the Reich Physician SS and Police application stating the proper reasons. In this application information on the problems involved, the extent of the experiments to be carried out, the number of prisoners needed as well as the presumable duration of the experiment will have to be clearly shown.

The Reich Physician SS and Police will submit the application to me along with the critical opinion of the Chief Surgeon (Oberster Kliniker) concerning the technical aspects, and the opinion of the Gruppenfuehrers Nebe and Glucks.[47]

The Chief Surgeon was the defendant Gebhardt. When asked by the prosecutor whether the Polish women in his experiments had volunteered or whether the experiments were imposed without consent in lieu of a death sentence, which they supposedly had received, he replied:

I can only assure you, and if you ask me ten times, it was not my intention whether you considered that negligence on my part, or not, I don't care; I would be lying if I told you anything else. I was glad that Himmler took this legal side, as to the status of the doctors, and I was told someone at the top took charge of this matter. I had no reason at that time to doubt the German state authorities in any way, or to distrust Himmler. How it worked out in detail was not a point of discussion in any way for me.[48]

The evidence presented by the prosecution left little doubt that the experimenting physicians had themselves participated in the selection of their subjects. But the evidence against those sitting in the dock was largely circumstantial. And those for whom there was sufficient evidence were not sitting in the dock.

Hence the defendants flatly denied any responsibility for any selection, typified by the following statements of Weltz, who had been a consultant for the high-altitude experiments performed by Rascher. When asked, "how carefully did you outline to the concentration camp commandant what type of subject you wanted?" Weltz replied: "Schnitzler, the adjutant of the Reichsleitung, informed the camp commander in our presence that his orders from Hitler were, one, that Himmler had given permission for the experiments; two, that all of us were to participate in them; three, that they were to be volunteers and that they were to be habitual criminals."[49]

The defense could have rested its case right there, after having demonstrated the supposed innocence of the accused by reason of the claimed legality of the acts committed and the lack of personal responsibility for any illegal acts committed. But it went one step further. It contested the prosecution's definition of foreigner. Since war crimes were crimes committed against foreign nationals only, the definition was crucial, at least in some cases. Gebhardt, Fischer, and Oberhauser, for instance, had almost exclusively performed, or

assisted in, experiments on Polish women. But they claimed that at the time
the women had been residents of German territory subject to German law. As
evidence they presented the Soviet-German Boundary and Friendship Treaty
of 1939, which had divided Poland between, and had placed the citizens
under the respective jurisdiction of, Germany and the U.S.S.R. For the
American Military Tribunal this was a moot point, because in a precedent setting rule, the International Military Tribunal, with the help of a Soviet judge,
had already decided that the Treaty was inadmissible evidence.

The defendants charged with atrocities against inmates whose nationality
could not be established with certainty—Becker-Freyseng, Schaefer, and
Beiglboeck in the case of the seawater experiments, and Weltz, Ruff, and
Romberg in the case of the high-altitude experiments—generally claimed to
have been told by the SS, or to have been under the justified assumption, that
they were German residents. Non-German names, unfamiliarity with the
German language or foreign accents supposedly generated no doubts but
rather reflected political changes and high demographic mobility during the war
years.

Karl Brandt even claimed that efforts were made to save foreign asylum
inmates from the euthanasia program he had directed and for which he accepted responsibility. But his arguments did not convince the Tribunal, which concluded in its final judgment:

> We have no doubt that Karl Brandt—as he himself testified—is a sincere believer in the
> administration of euthanasia to persons hopelessly ill, whose lives are burdensome to
> themselves and an expense to the state or to their families. The abstract proposition of
> whether or not euthanasia is justified in certain cases of the class referred to is no con-
> cern of this Tribunal. Whether or not a state may validly enact legislation which impos-
> es euthanasia upon certain classes of citizens is likewise a question which does not enter
> into the issues. Assuming that it may do so, the Family of Nations is not obligated to
> give recognition to such legislation when it manifestly gives legality to plain murder and
> torture of defenseless and powerless human beings of other nations.
>
> The evidence is conclusive that persons were included in the program who were
> non-German nationals. The dereliction of the defendant Brandt contributed to their
> extermination. That is enough to require this Tribunal to find he is criminally respon-
> sible in the program.[50]

The Tribunal's position respecting the subjection of foreigners to medical
experiments was the same, typically expressed in its judgment of Gebhardt:

> Whatever may be the right of the state with reference to its own citizens, it is certain
> that such legislation may not be extended so as to permit the practice upon nationals
> of other countries who are held in the most abject servitude and subjected to experi-
> ments without their consent and under the most brutal and senseless conditions.[51]

Gebhardt's claim that his experiments were performed on condemned prisoners of war in lieu of an execution, the tribunal rebuffed as follows:

It is claimed by Dr. Gebhardt that all of the non-German experimental subjects were selected from inmates of concentration camps, former members of the Polish resistance movement, who had previously been condemned to death and were in any event marked for legal execution. This is not recognized as a valid defense to the charge of the indictment.

The Polish women who were used in the experiments had not given their consent to become experimental subjects. That fact was known to Gebhardt. The evidence conclusively shows that they had been confined at Ravensbrueck without so much as a semblance of a trial. That fact could have been known to Gebhardt had he made the slightest inquiry to them concerning their status. Moreover, assuming for the moment that they had been condemned to death for acts considered hostile to the German forces in the occupied territory of Poland, these persons still were entitled to the protection of laws of civilized nations. While under certain specific conditions the rules of land warfare may recognize the validity of an execution of spies, war rebels, or other resistance workers, it does not under any circumstances countenance the infliction of death or other punishment by maiming or torture.[52]

The Tribunal also disputed the argument that many inmates had volunteered and the defendants had no specific responsibility to check on the subjects' status if the selection had in fact been made by someone else, especially since the torturous nature of the experiments made anything but forced subjection inconceivable. Given the abject conditions of concentration camp inmates, the entire question of volunteering for this matter seemed rather spurious to the tribunal. Given the fact that more often than not the physicians themselves had been the initiators of the experiments, the Tribunal also rejected the argument that they merely executed orders from higher up. This had become particularly clear in the case of Gebhardt, where the judgment reads as follows:

We cannot see the applicability of the doctrine of superior orders as a defense to the charges contained in the indictment. Such doctrine has never been held applicable to a case where the one to whom the order is given has free latitude of decision whether to accept the order or reject it. Such was the situation with reference to Gebhardt. The record makes it manifestly plain that he was not ordered to perform the experiments, but that he sought the opportunity to do so.[53]

Finally, with respect to the defendants' claim that the acts for which they were indicted had been legal under German law, the Tribunal apparently felt no ruling was needed, but a mere affirmation of its jurisdiction under Control Council Law No. 10 would suffice. Under this law, not only acts committed against foreign citizens were indictable, but acts against German citizens as well. Since this provision was a novelty in international law, its framers accorded it a separate status. Specific, and in many respects novel, acts of aggression against others, especially members of national, racial, and religious groups, were classified as crimes against humanity, no matter who committed them or where they were committed. Hence, Control Council Law No. 10 overrode existing

German law. The prosecution charged all defendants with the commission of such acts of aggression under Count Three, which will be discussed below.

The tribunal found fifteen of the defendants guilty of war crimes as charged: K. Brandt, Handloser, Genzken, Gebhardt, R. Brandt, Mrugowsky, Sievers, Rose, Brack, Becker-Freyseng, Hoven, Beiglboeck, Oberhauser, and Fischer. In eight cases, the tribunal felt that evidence did not prove the defendants' guilt beyond reasonable doubt, but indicated this was no absolution from responsibility.

Count Three: Crimes Against Humanity

THE FRAMERS OF THE London Agreement declared certain acts of aggression to be punishable crimes against humanity. According to the text, transcribed into Control Council Law No. 10, they consist of "atrocities and offenses, including but not limited to murder, extermination, enslavement, deportation, imprisonment, torture, rape, or other inhuman acts committed against any civilian population, or persecution on political, racial or religious grounds whether or not in violation of the domestic laws of the country where perpetrated."

Crimes against humanity differ from war crimes in two crucial respects: in what is charged and who is charged. Whereas war crimes refer to such atrocities as ill-treatment and murder of prisoners of war and civilians from occupied territory, crimes against humanity refer to such atrocities committed against "any civilian population," especially against individuals merely because they belong to discrete political, racial or religious groups.

Since these atrocities were crimes "whether or not in violation of the domestic laws of the country where perpetrated," Control Council Law No. 10 took precedence over national law—past, present, and future. Henceforth, violators could be tried by a foreign court for acts committed against citizens of their own country. The Major Trial before the International Military Tribunal therefore became a precedent-setting case in international law, though not without much skepticism on the part of critics who doubted the feasibility of applying the law and the will of the international community to enforce it when appropriate.

All defendants were charged with war crimes as well as crimes against humanity. The double charge prevented the defendants from escaping conviction on war crime charges by claiming ignorance about their medical subjects' nationality, as they indeed had tried to do. When the victims were German or their nationality was uncertain, the atrocities committed against them were still crimes, namely crimes against humanity, for they were members of a persecuted political, racial or religious group. In this way, the tribunal could guarantee that hardly a crime committed by the defendants would go unpunished and that their victims, dead or alive, would find some measure of belated justice.

The rationale for outlawing every kind of atrocity, regardless of the nationality of the victims, reflected the determination to punish the perpetrators and to reveal the especially gruesome nature of these atrocities and the genocidal motives behind them.

The vivid testimony regarding the victims' suffering in concentration camps graphically demonstrated the gruesome nature of the defendants' acts. The task of exposing their genocidal motives proved to be more difficult. The prosecution had to show the defendants selected, or approved the selection of, subjects on the basis of political ideology, racial identity, or religious conviction. But given the evidence presented to the tribunal, particularly the testimony of Eugen Kogon, discussed under Count Two, no officially prescribed or generally observed method of selection existed. In most cases, much depended on the whims and prejudices of individual camp guards.

According to Kogon, in Buchenwald, as in all the other camps, the lot fell heavily on homosexuals, along with common criminals and so-called asocials. Those categories had not been recognized by the framers of the London Agreement as members of persecuted groups, despite the fact that they too had been marked for elimination from the general population by the National Socialists. Hence, the prosecution could only charge the defendants with political, racial, and religious persecution, and it presented its evidence accordingly.

The most obvious case of racial persecution was manifest in the collection of Jewish skeletons, in which Sievers had played a crucial part. This case served more as a testimony to the National Socialists' plan to exterminate the entire Jewish population than the defendants' bias in selecting human subjects. Since most of the defendants did not deny their embrace of National Socialist doctrines, their support of the project could be assumed, whether they knew of it or not. That racial groups, as defined by the Nuremberg Race Laws, had been targeted, if not always used, for medical research was evident in the case of Beiglboeck's seawater experiment. In a letter to Himmler regarding these experiments, Ernst Grawitz, the highest-ranking SS physician, suggested Jews or Gypsies.

Himmler decided on Gypsies.[54] The SS even managed to find some volunteers among the approximately one thousand Gypsies at Buchenwald for a so-called work assignment, of which forty-four were sent to Beiglboeck's experimental station in Dachau. The subjects were Czech, Polish, Russian, and German.[55] When briefed by Beigleboeck on the real purpose of their presence, apparently without explaining the full dangers of the experiment, they still agreed to serve as medical subjects, but only because they imagined a worse fate if they refused.[56]

Beiglboeck tried to exonerate himself of the charge of crimes against humanity by insisting that the Gypsies had been placed in concentration camps, and subsequently selected for the experiment, not because of their racial or ethnic background but because of their asocial behavior. So-called asocials were not listed as members of a persecuted group in Control Council Law No. 10. Since their nationality supposedly was uncertain too, he argued their selection for and subjection to painful experimentation did not constitute crimes under Count Three or Count Two.

Beiglboeck further argued that incarceration of asocials was not uncommon in other countries, that it fell under the purview of sovereign states, and that it was legitimate under such circumstances as war. His counsel presented the argument as follows:

> My client is charged with having committed crimes against humanity. Control Council Law No. 10 unfortunately does not contain a definition of crimes against humanity . . ., but it has to be persecution against people for political or racial reasons. Therefore, I want to say that we are not dealing with racial persecution, but those are people who for other reasons have been in the concentration camps.[57]

Asked by his counsel "what you, as a physician, mean or would understand by the term 'asocial'," Beiglboeck replied:

> In our books on psychiatry where we discuss such matters, the chapter on the question of "asocial" and "anti-social" elements is one of those most difficult to deal with. Speaking from a medical point of view, the term "asocial" would cover a person who in most cases has an inborn, sometimes hereditary defect of his ethical instincts; that is, a type who not by reasoning but on the basis of instinct cannot abide by prevailing rules and laws of society.
>
> Furthermore, these people, of course, do not like to work, also one of the requirements of human society, and from these two roots for the individual there derives a vicious cycle. The more criminal he becomes, in the widest meaning of the word, the more he comes in conflict with human society, so society, of course, tries to counteract that. He considers this to be an injustice because he thinks that the demands of society are unjust and inapplicable. Therefore, he considers himself persecuted although innocent to commit further violations against laws and regulations, and that brings about the term of the "asocial" and "anti-social" as a sociologic term rather than a medical one. The physician is only interested in that certain inner defect, the lack of a natural, healthy sense of ethics and the fact that in many cases this is hereditary; and as birds of a feather flock together and as just the fact of vagrancy—that is the resentment against settling down, to the same extent as resentment against every type of compulsion—belongs into that picture, it happens frequently that two asocials get married. Even more frequently they didn't get married but they have children together and that brings it about that asocial families, entire asocial families, come into existence; and on these families studies have been made, especially in the United States, where as far as I know these studies have become very famous; and in these families one can find the entire scale of examples which we considered covered by the term "asocial." These families distinguish themselves in some cases only by hating to work. Other members of family are habitual thieves. A third category again may be vagrants. The fourth type may be real criminals all the way to the habitual criminal. Among the female members of these families prostitution is extremely widespread.
>
> All that comes apparently from some psychological aberration which seems to be

the clue to the reason why these inclinations show to a different extent in various families. Generally, resentnment of every kind of authority is apparent. There are many
among them who may have other defects, have a greater or high degree of intelligence.

    As far as I know—and I only know it from occasional reading of medical studies—
in Germany especially the question of heredity of such instincts was greatly emphasized,
purely from the medical point of view, but how the legal form was found that, of course,
I could not say.[58]

At the request of the Tribunal, Beiglboeck's counsel obliged and provided the defense's legal definition of an asocial person: "We designated as asocial the person who consciously commits acts against human society and by
these acts is asocial, an enemy of society, that is the concept we have. In
English it can be expressed by the term, a-social [sic] is an enemy of society."[59]

Beiglboeck's argument that the race of his medical subjects, and by implication of all medical subjects, was coincidental to the supposed real reason for
their incarceration and eventual selection for experiments, namely their asocial
behavior, could not be backed up with any kind of evidence and contradicted
political theory and practice under the Hitler regime. National Socialists identified races by genetically fixed correlations of physical and mental characteristics and prejudged all individuals accordingly.

The supposed laziness of Gypsies, for instance, believed to be evident in
physical appearance, did not save their more industrious members from collective mistreatment. Jewishness was treated as a social disease that would not even
save such German patriots as Fritz Haber or geniuses like Albert Einstein.
Living under German rule and not being German was by definition an act of
nonconformity, and hence asocial.

Through various more or less subtle appeals to the Tribunal, Beiglboeck
and his codefendants tried to tell the judges that things were not all that different in the United States. And it is difficult to imagine that the judges had
any illusion that in their country the treatment of African-Americans, Native
Americans, and Asians in the past, and even the present, was much less humil-
iating than the Germans' treatment of Jews and Gypsies. But the unprecedented inhumanity witnessed in the German death camps left most people immune
to the defendants' suggestion that the balance sheets of horror were
comparable.

In its eventual judgment of Beiglboeck, the Tribunal ruled that "it is
apparent from the evidence the experiments were essentially criminal in their
nature, and non-German nationals were used without their consent as experimental subjects. To the extent the crimes committed by defendant Beiglboeck
were not war crimes they were crimes against humanity," i.e., aimed to harm
a specifically designated group.[60]

Beiglboeck's experiments were war crimes to the extent they were committed against non-German nationals and crimes against humanity to the

extent they were committed against Gypsies. Since under Western legal tradition it is not customary to convict someone for the same deed under more than
one law, it remained a matter of interpretation whether Beiglboeck's inhuman
treatment of his non-German victims was punishable under Count Two,
because they were foreign nationals (war crimes) or Count Three, because they
were Gypsies (crimes against humanity). The deliberately ambiguous text of
the Tribunal's judgment implied Beiglboeck morally, if not legally, had committed both crimes.

The same was true for all other defendants. All twenty-three were indicted for war crimes as well as crimes against humanity. Of the fifteen who were
convicted, no one was found guilty on just one of the two charges. Thus link-
ing the two counts, the Tribunal did not have to decide concretely which acts
constituted violations according to Count Two and which according to Count
Three.

Gebhardt's argument that the Polish women on whom he operated were
residents of annexed German territory and so subject to German law is another case in point. Even if the tribunal had upheld his claim that his atrocities did
not constitute war crimes, it merely would have exposed them as crimes against
humanity, in this case, "inhumane acts committed against any civilian population . . . on . . . racial . . . grounds."

Of the defendants who had not inflicted inhuman treatment and murder
on the victims themselves, but had planned, ordered, or administratively assisted in their mistreatment, the prosecution generally could produce more evidence to prove commission of war crimes than crimes against humanity, as in
the case of Handloser and Schroeder. But in a few cases, evidence to prove the
commission of crimes against humanity was overwhelming.

Victor Brack, for instance, the chief administrative officer in Hitler's
Chancellery, was one of the principal organizers of the regime's extermination
programs. In June 1942, he suggested to Himmler many of the millions of Jews
marked for the gas chambers could be used as slave laborers, but not before
being castrated or sterilized. At the trial Brack tried to convince the Tribunal
this suggestion was a mere stalling device to save as many Jews as possible from
certain death in expectation of German victory in the East and a subsequently expected change of policy from extermination to resettlement.[61]

This was a futile attempt to escape the hangman's noose. Extant correspon-
dence showed that he had pursued his task with too much zeal and too little
effort to stall anything. He had eagerly promoted research in different areas
of mass sterilization methods and eventually recommended the use of concealed
x-ray techniques (described in the previous chapter) as the cheapest and
quickest.

In its closing statement, the prosecution focused on three points that figured most prominently in all of the defendants' statements: lack of knowledge,

denial of personal authority, and soldierly duty of obedience. All defendants claimed general ignorance of the atrocities committed, including those for which they had been indicted personally, except those where denial of knowledge would have meant clear perjury in view of available evidence. The statement "I have heard of that for the first time here in Nuremberg" was often heard when the defendants sat in the witness box.

Even when they had to admit knowledge, they generally claimed to have done little more than pass on or execute legal orders of superiors who had died in the meantime, chiefly Hitler, Himmler, Grawitz, Conti, and Bouhler. The illegal aspects of such orders, such as the selection of inmates for medical experiments, were usually handled by other persons, generally unknown. This led the prosecution to this conclusion:

> One of the common defenses which has been utilized rather extensively in this case is a variation of the old "shell game"—now you see it, now you don't. . . . Blome, according to his story, was only deputy of the "good" Conti while the "bad" Conti went his criminal way without assistance of his chief collaborator. Poppendick and Grawitz had the same unique relationship. Genzken and Mrugowsky perform a similar bisection of Ding; while the right hand was in the vaccine production plant at Buchenwald under their command, his left hand performed the criminal typhus experiment at the direction of Grawitz, and never the twain did meet.[62]

The one defendant who may indeed have known more about the medical atrocities than any of the others, namely Himmler's personal secretary, Rudolf Brandt, played the role of the ignorant messenger to the point of visibly irritating the prosecution, which observed, "His testimony before the tribunal can be summed up in the one sentence: 'I remember nothing.' Aside from a description of Himmler as something in the nature of a Jekyll and Hyde, he contented himself with giving answers to leading questions from his attorney which were calculated to reveal him as a disembodied stenographic automaton or a mechanically proficient half-wit."[63]

In the end, all defendants claimed to have done little more than their expected duty as soldiers and civil servants. And if indeed some orders were questionable in either a legal or a moral sense, supposedly there was little they could have done but to obey at a time when Germany was fighting for its sheer survival.

No defendant was more insistent on this point than Fischer, who acknowledged to some degree that the excruciating surgical experiments he and Gebhardt had performed on Polish women had caused irreparable damage and unspeakable suffering to the victims. The prosecution rebuffed his claim:

> He knew at the time he performed these experiments that he was committing a crime. He knew the pain, disfigurement, disability, and risk of death to which his experimental victims would be subjected. He could have refused to participate in the experiments

without any fear of consequences. This he admits in saying, "It is not fear of a death sentence or anything like that, but the alternative was either be obedient or disobedient during war, and thereby set an example, an example of disobedience." Such an admission removes any basis for mitigation. A soldier is always faced with the alternative of obeying or disobeying an order. If he knows the order is criminal, it is surely a hollow excuse to say it must be obeyed for the sake of obedience alone.[64]

There was, the prosecution showed, a third choice: resignation. The defendants could have resigned from questionable projects. Given the evidence, however, most of them not only carried them out approvingly, in many cases they initiated and designed them.[65] Their rationale, no doubt, was not merely to help Germany survive in its professed struggle against enslaving Bolshevism, but to help establish a German-dominated, fascist Europe, especially aimed at pressing Eastern nations into servitude.

While such prospects had attracted many Germans into the ranks of National Socialist organizations long before the war, no professional group had been as enthusiastically supportive of them as the physicians. Any physician officially affiliated with the Hitler regime had probably done more than reluctantly obey orders and was unlikely ever to have thought of resigning from anything.[66] Of the twenty-three defendants, ten had joined the ranks of the SS, the military elite that provided the ideological backbone of the regime. Their claim merely to have followed orders, often reluctantly, found no credible ears on the judges' bench.

The Tribunal found fifteen of the defendants guilty of crimes against humanity as charged in the indictment. These were the same defendants who had also been found guilty of committing war crimes. In eight cases the Tribunal found that the evidence presented did not prove guilt beyond reasonable doubt.

Count Four: Membership in Criminal Organizations

COUNT FOUR OF THE indictment charged:

> The defendants Karl Brandt, Genzken, Gebhardt, Rudolf Brandt, Mrugowsky, Poppendick, Sievers, Brack, Hoven and Fischer are guilty of membership in an organization declared to be criminal by the International Military Tribunal in Case No. 1 in that each of said defendants was a member of Die Schutzstaffeln der Nationalsozialistischen Deutschen Arbeiter-Partei, commonly known as the "SS" after 1 September 1939. Such membership is in violation of Paragraph I (d) Article II of the Control Council Law No. 10.[67]

In their attempt to hold individuals who committed atrocities during the Hitler regime responsible for their actions and simultaneously dismantle much of the political infrastructure that made them possible, the Allies planned to outlaw all institutions and organizations that provided the regime's ideological backbone, aggressive leadership, and repressive police force. To that end, the signatories of the London Agreement through its Charter had empowered the International Military Tribunal to declare certain organizations to have been criminal. Volunteer members of these organizations could be held liable for atrocities committed by any of its members. The organizations were: the leadership corps of the National Socialist Party, the Secret Police (Gestapo) and the SS (Schutzstaffeln). The Tribunal also considered declaring the SA (Sturmabteilung), the cabinet, and the general staff to have been criminal but ruled against it on the grounds of insufficient evidence.

Ten of the defendants were accused of having been members of the SS. Established in 1925 as a black-uniformed protective guard of the National Socialist Party, the SS became an elite corps of extremely obedient political soldiers under the direction of Heinrich Himmler, trained to go on suicidal combat missions and eliminate all so-called enemies of the state with brutal repression. In the end, this included outright extermination of large segments of Europe's civilian population.

The SS grew rapidly and eventually created its own medical branch, complete with hospitals, medical schools, and research facilities. The SS physician Ernst Grawitz was placed in charge of the medical arm. The ten defendants who had joined the SS had done so between 1929 (Brack) and 1936 (Genzken), when Himmler tried to boost the elitist image of the SS by wooing especially the sons of educated and wealthy families to join the ranks and provide the kind of leadership that could restructure a purportedly decaying European society on the basis of personal authority and loyalty.

Given the charge under Count Four, the only evidence needed for a conviction was proof of membership, and that was a matter of public record. Since none of the defendants ever contested that record, Count Four never became a subject of debate during the nine-month-long proceedings. Such debates had filled days of hearings before the International Military Tribunal, where the defense had argued, in vain, that organizations could not be declared illegal retroactively, and that membership itself could not automatically constitute a criminal act for members who may not have endorsed the principles or participated in the activities that prompted the court to find the organization illegal. The defendants contested the legality of this law, but this was a moot point for the American Military Tribunal, and all ten were duly convicted.

Except for Poppendick, the defendants were also convicted of war crimes and crimes against humanity. Membership in the SS merely seemed to confirm the heinous motives behind the latter crimes. Though Poppendick was implicated in all of these crimes, there was not enough evidence to convict him. As chief physician of the Race and Settlement Office since 1941 and physician for special assignments in Grawitz's office between 1939 and 1943, he handled

THE TRIAL—A LEGAL ANALYSIS

correspondences and attended meetings dealing with most, and possibly all, human experiments. But since he had not directly participated in their performance, the Tribunal found that this was insufficient ground for conviction.

For example, it stated, with respect to the Ravensbrueck experiments:

> We are of the opinion that Poppendick had knowledge of the criminal nature of the experiments conducted by Gebhardt and Fischer at Ravensbrueck, but the defendant's criminal connection with any such experiments has not been proven by the evidence.[68]

Similarly with regard to the hormone experiments conducted on homosexuals at Buchenwald:

> Certainly the evidence raises a strong suspicion that he was involved in the experiments. He at least had notice of them and of their consequences. He knew also that they were being carried on by the SS, of which he was and remained a member.
>
> This Tribunal cannot, however, convict upon mere suspicion; evidence beyond a reasonable doubt is necessary. The evidence is insufficient to sustain guilt under Counts Two and Three of the Indictment.[69]

In the end, the tribunal convicted Poppendick on Count Four alone:

> The Defendant Poppendick is charged with membership in an organization declared criminal by the Judgment of the International Military Tribunal, namely the SS. Poppendick joined the SS in July 1932. He remained in the SS voluntarily throughout the war with actual knowledge of the fact that that organization was being used for the commission of acts now declared criminal by Control Council Law No. 10. He must therefore be found guilty under Count Four of the Indictment.[70]

Poppendick was the only defendant in the Medical Trial found guilty because of membership in an organization declared to be criminal and on none of the other charges. And he was the first person to be found guilty exclusively for such membership. None of the defendants at the preceding Major Trial could have been charged with such criminal membership, because the organizations themselves were still under indictment.

Indicted were the Reich Cabinet, the General Staff and High Command, the Storm Troops (SA), the Leadership Corps of the National Socialist Party, the Secret Police (Gestapo), including the Security Service (SD), and the Schutzstaffeln (SS). Only the last three were declared to have been criminal, since they in particular were the more instrumental tools in the atrocities committed under the Hitler regime.

As much as the International Military Tribunal tried to avoid it, its ruling did raise the specter of collective guilt, which had been applied most disturbingly by the National Socialists themselves. To them, membership in the Communist Party, for example, or the racial designation of "Jewish" in accord with the 1935 "Law for the Protection of German Blood and German Honor" called for automatic punishment. To avoid any such association, the International Military Tribunal had declared:

1. Membership alone in an organization declared criminal is not enough to come within the scope of the declarations of organizational criminality.
2. Persons who had no knowledge of the criminal purposes or acts of the organization, and those who were drafted by the State for membership, unless they were personally implicated in the commission of acts declared criminal by Article 6 of the Charter as members of the organization, should be excluded.[71]

Nonetheless, since every member at the very least must have been aware of the very purposes that led to this organization's criminal status, more than a million people were subject to indictment. In practice, no one was prepared, economically or otherwise, to take on such a task. Therefore, membership in criminal organizations became primarily an aggravating factor in the indictment of the more blatant cases of war crimes and crimes against humanity.

Subsequent trials were held before a number of different Allied Zonal as well as German courts, and a number of denazification laws prevented many, but by no means all, former members of such organizations from holding public office or certain civil service positions during the postwar years.

In some respects, Count Four took the place of Count One's charge of conspiracy, which had been dropped from the indictment. In both cases the prosecution tried to show the defendants advanced National Socialist goals by conspiring to wage aggressive wars with the intent to commit war crimes and crimes against humanity. Under Count One, all defendants had participated in this and should be held accountable. Under Count Four, only the ten SS members could be held accountable. The International Military Tribunal had ruled:

A criminal organization is analogous to a criminal conspiracy in that the essence of both is cooperation for criminal purposes. There must be a group bound together and organized for a common purpose. The group must be formed or used in connection with the commission of crimes denounced by the Charter.[72]

No one observing the Nuremberg Trials could have doubted the Tribunal's intended double function: to administer justice and teach a lesson. The lesson was that the doctrines of National Socialism constitute little more than ideological tools of oppression for power-hungry dictators and their adherents. The tribunal, no doubt, hoped that by exposing the National Socialists' heinous deeds with the totalitarian nature of the doctrines behind them, the world would never allow a Hitler regime to rise again. Nobody had promoted these doctrines more fervently than the members of the SS, including the ten medical defendants who had joined the organization. Most defendants had also been members of the National Socialist Party. By comparison, party membership required less of an ideological commitment and demanded no explicit undertaking to obey the dictates of the organization above existing law. By exposing SS membership and all it stood for, the tribunal exposed the worst aspects of the Hitler regime, and the eventual sentencing of the defendants reflected this clearly.

Verdicts and Sentences

ON AUGUST 20, 1947, the Tribunal read its verdicts to the defendants. Of the fifteen who were found guilty of war crimes and crimes against humanity, seven were sentenced to death by hanging. All seven had been members of the SS: Karl Brandt, Gebhardt, Mrugowsky, Brack, Sievers, Rudolf Brandt, and Hoven. Seven were sentenced to prison for life: Handloser, Schroeder, Genzken, Rose, Fischer, Becker-Freyseng and Oberhauser. Only Genzken and Fischer had been SS members. Beigleboeck, not an SS member, received a fifteen-year prison term. Poppendick was sentenced to ten years in prison for SS membership alone. Of the seven defendants who were acquitted, no one had been a member of the SS: Blome, Rostock, Ruff, Weltz, Romberg, Schaefer, and Pokorny.

The sixteen defendants who had been convicted petitioned the Military Governor of the American Zone, Lucius Clay, for a reversal or commutation of their sentences, citing everything from attestation of highest moral character by respected antifascist personalities to violations of procedural rules by the Tribunal to their detriment.

Karl Brandt presented the story of his death sentence, received from a German court martial during the last days of the war, as proof of his eventual rejection of National Socialism. Evidence suggested, however, that this episode was a result of an intense disagreement Brandt had with Theodor Morell, Hitler's other physician, over the proper control of Hitler's worsening nervous disorders as the inevitable end of the war drew near.

Hoven's appeal included the argument that his murder of at least sixty, and possibly more, supposedly dangerous concentration camp inmates arrested much of the infighting between rival camp groups and saved the lives of thousands of other prisoners, especially ones who were being politically persecuted.

Perhaps the most bizarre, if not surprising, appeal came from Sievers. As the proceedings revealed, he had been a member of the internal resistance against Hitler, his unfailing service for the regime's bloody pursuits notwithstanding. During the early days of the regime, he had joined the clandestine circle of opponents around Friederich Hielscher. Hielscher, who for his activities spent over a year in a Gestapo prison, testified in court that Sievers's zealous efforts to serve the regime was a mere front to cover up his more subversive work. But Sievers could not show that he actually participated much in the underground work beyond collecting and transmitting privileged information to his group. His participation in various medical atrocities, on the other hand, was well-documented. In passing judgment on his activities, the tribunal concluded, "it certainly is not the law that a resistance fighter can commit no crime, and least of all, against the very people he is supposed to be protecting."[73]

Clay questioned the whole sincerity of Siever's claim, observing:

> If the defendant had actually been opposed to Nazi practices and desired the overthrow of the Nazi regime, he could not have so enthusiastically participated in the criminal experiments and aided the plans for the murder of Jews to complete a skeleton collection.[74]

Clay turned down all petitions, and the seven defendants condemned to death were executed by hanging in Bavaria's Landsberg Prison on June 2, 1948.

The Trial in Review: How Fair, How Just, How Competent?

HARDLY ANYONE FOLLOWING THE events at the Nuremberg Trials could fail to conclude that the defendants had received a measure of fairness and justice much greater than the circumstances warranted. The exceptions were for the most part Germans who had remained sympathetic to reactionary doctrines, if not the specific goals of National Socialism. To them the trials represented little more than imposed victor's justice, a result of defeat in war, a rationalized act of revenge. They concurred with Karl Brandt when he told the tribunal "the sentence has been established beforehand."[75] Their inference was that a victor could not judge a loathed enemy with the degree of objectivity necessary for a fair trial.

Some of the best German minds argued impassionedly to the contrary. Karl Jaspers, for instance, maintained:

> The basic fact that victory in war, not law alone, is the governing point of departure is undeniable. In great affairs as well as in small affairs, what is ironically said concerning military offenses is true: one is punished not because of the law but because he allows himself to be caught. However, this basic fact does not mean that after his victory man would not be able by virtue of his liberty to apply his might for the realization of right.[76]

The fact that three defendants were acquitted in the Major Trial, seven in the Medical Trial, and many more in subsequent trials confirmed Jaspers' trust in the fairness of the applied judicial process. It disproved Brandt's view that the victors primarily sought revenge and all verdicts were predetermined.

The tribunal reiterated its commitment to the presumption of the defendants' innocence in its eventual judgment with the following words: "Under the Anglo-Saxon system of jurisprudence every defendant in a criminal case is presumed to be innocent of an offense charged until the prosecution, by competent, credible proof, has shown his guilt to the exclusion of every reasonable doubt."[77] In seven cases the prosecution was unable to do so. Despite much incriminating evidence, the tribunal held that the defendants' guilt was not evident beyond every reasonable doubt and did not convict.

Blome, accused of killing many Russian prisoners in biological warfare experiments, apparently managed to destroy all evidence at the end of the war, and no surviving victims were found. At the trial, he left no doubt about his allegiance to National Socialism. His position as Deputy Reich Health Leader belied his claim of ignorance of any medical atrocities committed during the Hitler years. Still, the tribunal felt that it had little choice but to acquit him of all charges raised under Counts Two and Three. He had been a high-ranking official in the SA, but the SA had not been declared a criminal organization, despite its notorious role in the persecution of Jews and others during the early days of the regime. Since Blome had never joined the SS, he could not be charged under Count Four.

Poppendick, who also had to be acquitted of all charges under Counts Two and Three despite much incriminating evidence, could at least be convicted and sentenced for SS membership. And while the Tribunal of the U.S. Military felt it could not convict Blome for experiments he may have conducted on Russian prisoners during the war, the Army Medical Corps of the U.S. Military was confident that his knowledge gained from these experiments was valuable enough to hire him three years after the trial ended. The acquittals of Rostock, Weltz, Ruff, Romberg, and Pokorny must have looked similarly controversial, despite the fact that they served as unequivocal testimony to the Tribunal's commitment to uphold the standards of fair trial.

Only the acquittal of Schaefer may not have seemed quite as disturbing. He never joined any National Socialist organization, was drafted into the Air Force, never advanced beyond the rank of sergeant, was assigned to a laboratory of a company with military contracts to find a method to make sea water potable, never used camp inmates in his research, and strongly advised against conducting Poppendick's sea water experiments on scientific and ethical grounds. The prosecution would have been well advised to fill his place in the defense dock with someone from the pool of candidates who had done more to earn it.

The acquittals bore testimony to the trial's judicial fairness and seemed to confirm the justness of the verdicts passed on those who were not acquitted. This outcome could not have been anticipated in the beginning. The prosecution certainly tried to convict every one of the defendants. Critics who would like to render the judgment a political move to appease those who, like

Karl Brandt, viewed the Nuremberg trials merely as a tool of the victorious
Allies to exact revenge must find the diligence with which the judges observed
procedural rules disturbing.

The defendants had ample opportunity to state their case, present evidence,
and summon witnesses. They made more use of this opportunity than the prosecution did, as the tribunal observed in its final judgment:

> During the 133 trial days used for presentation of evidence, 32 witnesses gave oral evi-
> dence for the Prosecution and 53 witnesses, including the 23 defendants, gave oral evi-
> dence for the Defense. In addition, the Prosecution put in evidence as exhibits a total
> of 570 affidavits, reports and documents; the Defense put in a total number of 901—
> making a grand total of 1471 documents received in evidence. Copies of all exhibits
> tendered by the Prosecution in their case in chief were furnished in the German lan-
> guage to the defendants prior to the time of the reception of the exhibits in evidence.
> Each defendant was represented at the arraignment and trial by counsel of his own selec-
> tion. Whenever possible, all applications by defense counsel for the procuring of the
> personal attendance of persons who made affidavits in behalf of the Prosecution were
> granted and the persons brought to Nuernberg for interrogation or cross-examination
> by defense counsel. Throughout the trial great latitude in presenting evidence was
> allowed Defense counsel, even to the point at times of receiving in evidence certain mat-
> ters of but scant probative value.[78]

Most defense witnesses may be placed in two groups: those who had
worked with or knew of the defendants in some official capacity and were now
trying to substantiate their claim of limited responsibility for the atrocities discussed before the Tribunal, and those who knew the defendants less officially
and primarily testified to their moral character. Character witnesses made the
expected variety of statements, i.e., that the defendant was an honest, princi-
pled, and duty-bound person, hardly capable of the cruelty alleged by the
Tribunal.

For many witnesses of the first group, their appearance before the Tribunal
was as much an opportunity to minimize their own role in the regime as it was
an attempt to aid the defendants. In fact, some witnesses at the time were defendants themselves in trials before different courts, and had little to lose and much
to gain by obscuring rather than clarifying the events about which they were
questioned. A former asylum director, Hermann Pfannmueller, who testified
on behalf of Brack, took the occasion to refute an often-quoted statement
ascribed to him, according to which inmates were "useless eaters" who would
be better off dead. One physician, Eugen Haagen, testifying on behalf of
Schroeder and Becker-Freyseng, had performed deadly typhus experiments on
concentration camp inmates at Natzweiler; he tried to convince the tribunal
of their beneficial results for medicine.

The witnesses for the prosecution were mostly survivors of medical experiments. Their ability to face their tormentors with as much controlled compo-

sure as they did certainly constitutes one of the more startling feats of the trial. Only once did a witness, a subject of Beiglboeck's seawater experiments, lose control in the courtroom and lash out against the man who had used him as a human guinea pig. The disfigured legs presented by a Polish woman, who bore physical witness to the medical tortures suffered at the hands of Gebhardt and Fischer, certainly could only suggest the extent of much deeper emotional scars. Eugen Kogon, a Buchenwald inmate who for years had served as Erwin Ding-Schuler's principal assistant, managed to present perhaps the most meticulous account of the atrocities committed there as well as some other camps. His comprehensive and often detailed knowledge of many medical experiments and the people who had performed them allowed him to refer to a number of individuals who should have been sharing the defense bench. His comments again raised questions about the political, legal, and organizational limits of the Tribunal and other courts in apprehending the hundreds and perhaps thousands who were implicated in the medical atrocities but remained at large. Many observers of the Nuremberg trials must have been painfully aware that such limits did exist, and that time was working against those who tried to dispense justice evenhandedly.

Military occupation of Germany in the beginning was not planned to last more than a few years, making it obvious to everyone that the various military courts during that time would be able to indict only a fraction of those implicated in violations under Control Council Law No. 10. Many had gone into hiding, some as far away as South America, and could be assumed ready to return soon after the occupation ended. Therefore, the Allied Control Council empowered German courts to try violators of Control Council Law No. 10 too, but only German citizens suspected of crimes against other German citizens or stateless persons.[79] In fact, Control Council Law No. 10 became part of the German legal system and led to the indictment and conviction of many more perpetrators in later years. Subsequent waivers of respective statutes of limitation allowed these courts to indict suspected criminals indefinitely. As guaranteed by Roosevelt, Churchill, and Stalin in the Moscow Declaration, crimes committed by citizens of other countries and against citizens of other countries were tried by courts holding jurisdiction over the crime location in accordance with local prevailing law. As a result, many more perpetrators were tried, often after lengthy extradition battles with countries where they had taken up residence. This resulted from a broad interpretation of the intent, if not the letter of Control Council Law No. 10, as the case against Adolf Eichmann in Jerusalem attested.

The Nuremberg trials were held to teach a lesson as well as to administer justice. The lesson involved showing the world step-by-step how a supposedly civilized and informed society is politically hijacked by totalitarian-minded individuals and groups causing the death and destruction of millions of innocent people. Telford Taylor left no doubt about this missionary intent during his opening speech before the tribunal:

> It is our deep obligation to all peoples of the world to show why and how these things happened. It is incumbent upon us to set forth with conspicuous clarity the ideas and motives which moved these defendants to treat their fellow men as less than beasts. The perverse thoughts and distorted concepts which brought about these savageries are not dead. They cannot be killed by force of arms. They must not become a spreading cancer in the breast of humanity. They must be cut out and exposed, for the reasons so well stated by Mr. Justice Jackson in this court room a year ago: "The wrongs which we seek to condemn and punish have been so calculated, so malignant, and so devastating that civilization cannot tolerate their being ignored because it cannot survive their being repeated."[80]

Taylor and Jackson tried to expose not only legal wrongs but also, and perhaps to a greater degree, moral wrongs, contained in the ideas and motives seen behind the legal wrongs. Taylor, strongly believing in the righteousness of his own cause, unwittingly showed himself susceptible to these same ideas and motives. References to human beings as "spreading cancer" that "must be cut out" to save humanity belonged to the repertoire of the reactionary minds whose deeds he condemned and wanted to see punished.

To consider Taylor, or anyone else, incapable of acting out his metaphorical suggestion, given the proper circumstances, in contrast to, for instance, Karl Brandt, would deny oneself the full benefit of Taylor's intended lesson, for which he unwittingly provided an example. Like Taylor, the defendants, with the obvious exception of Hoven thought of themselves as devoted citizens serving their country in time of need. Unlike Taylor, they had the misfortune to be confronted with dilemmas of apocalyptic proportions. Taylor's language gave credence to their largely implicit suggestion that, with their situations reversed, the results might well have been the same. The fact that neither Taylor nor anyone else could have been completely unaware of the theoretical possibility of such an outcome placed a great burden on the tribunal's judges to avoid even the semblance of harboring any bias against the defendants or imposing a form of victor's justice.

Some critics argued, however, that such bias was inherent in the wording of the law. As has been mentioned previously, Control Council Law No. 10, one German legal expert argued, violated the legal principle of *nullem crimen sine lege* (no law, no crime), recognized by all "civilized nations"[81] He voiced the familiar argument that the retroactive imposition of the law defining crimes against humanity constituted more an act of revenge than an attempt to introduce justice. The critics who made such arguments were opposed by others who endorsed the official position of the victor nations that the extreme heinousness of the acts committed called for a legitimate exception to the otherwise universally accepted principle of *nullem crimen sine lege*. Some also pointed out these acts must indeed be considered crimes under the principles of "natural law," which had been accepted, if not always codified in detail, by civilized nations for several centuries.[82]

To avoid the perception the Nuremberg trials suffered from an understandable bias against the defendants and the German nation, and were motivated by desires for revenge, many critics, especially in Germany, argued trial personnel should have been selected by the signatories of the Hague Regulations or the recently formed United Nations, and should have included members from neutral nations. Should that have proved impractical, at the very least some German judges should have been allowed to sit on the tribunals alongside judges from the Allied countries. But the Allies had planned otherwise. They expected to be challenged on that point by the defendants, as is reflected in the provision of the London Agreement's Charter that "neither the Tribunal, its members nor its alternates can be challenged by the prosecution or the Defendants or their counsel."[83] To many observers this provision probably confirmed rather than diminished suspicions of bias and was substantiated by Supreme Court Justice Nathan April's remarks that the provision, in fact, contradicted all Anglo-Saxon legal tradition.[84]

April also argued that far from having distinguished themselves for their sense of judicial fairness, the national rather than international character of the Nuremberg tribunals led to some serious procedural shortcomings. This prevented the extension of judicial rights as guaranteed in Anglo-Saxon countries over the areas for which the victorious Allies had assumed jurisdiction. Procuring evidence, for instance, especially the summoning of witnesses, was restricted to the area controlled by one of the four Allies, a fact that, given the scope of the charges, he considered an unacceptable infringement of the proclaimed rights of the defendants.

This became apparent when the Tribunal had to deny a request by the defense to summon the French medical expert George Blanc because he resided in an area under French control, i.e., in an area outside its jurisdiction. When the defense continued to insist on a neutral expert and objected to the summoning of the prosecution's medical expert Andrew Ivy from the United States on grounds of suspected prejudice in a case involving the United States, the tribunal had to admit:

> As to foreign experts, requested by the defense counsel, it was never the policy of the Tribunal to order the production of a witness who resided in a foreign country, because it was impossible to enforce the ordering of any witness who had been pretended and who would voluntarily come here. He could be called by the defendants at any time. That was always open to the defendant. But, due to the matters with which defense counsel is well aware, the Defendants Information Bureau could never undertake to present to summon and procure the attendance of a witness residing in a foreign country as there are too many difficulties and that is a matter of impossibility.[85]

Had the Tribunal been international and indisputably neutral, it also would have had little problem in objecting to the defendants' repeated efforts to discuss medical experiments performed by Americans that supposedly were similar to those they had performed themselves. The Tribunal's repeated objections in the matter could easily be interpreted as a cover-up. A perhaps even greater dilemma stemmed from the fact some of the defendants had continued their experimental work after the war for the U.S. Military. That the tribunal routinely ignored references to this work only raised the feared specter of bias. But full discussions on the subject would have undermined its claimed lack of bias even further. The defense took every opportunity to expose the Tribunal's weakness on this point, as in the following exchange between Ruff and his counsel, Fritz Sauter:

> Q. [Sauter] You were the leader of this institute [German Experimental Institute for Aviation] until spring of 1945. Were you then professionally active thereafter, and if so, when and where?
> A. [Ruff] From the Spring of 1945 until the Autumn of 1945 I was unemployed. From October 1945 to September 1946, I was scientific collaborator of the Aero-Medical Center of the United States Air Forces.
>
> Q. What was your position there, just in general?
> A. My activities were similar to those that I had under the DVL [German Experimental Institute for Aviation].
>
> Q. Were high altitude experiments carried on in this Aero-Medical Center such as you are accused of in this trial?
> A. I experimented in the field of high altitude research and also carried out high altitude experiments in the low pressure chamber as I had done in my institute and of which I am here accused.
>
> Q. Did you use a low pressure chamber such as was used in Dachau.
> A. Yes.[86]

According to the defendant Romberg, who also worked for the Aero-Medical Center, at least six deaths occurred in those experiments. Questioned by the prosecutor Alexander Hardy on the cause of death in high altitude experiments at Dachau, he referred to the American experiments:

> Q. [Hardy] Do you know of deaths caused by a sudden central failure due to stoppage of the blood flow? Is that a known cause of death in medical circles?
> A. [Romberg] I know it now because of the experience of the American Air Forces when they tried to examine the fitness of their flyers. In 6 cases during a prolonged stay - I think that in twelve kilometer altitude—a sudden death occurred.[87]

The defendants no doubt would have also referred to similar experiments performed by Japanese physicians during the war, but they apparently had been unaware or possessed no detailed knowledge of them. If anything, the role U.S.

authorities played after the war in obtaining experimental results for war-related purposes would have seriously jeopardized the Tribunal's position as an unbiased court and Taylor's claim to expose the dangers of violating cherished principles of humanity. The Japanese experiments, performed on camp inmates in Manchuria who were mainly Chinese civilians and prisoners of war, were similar to those performed by German physicians, not only with respect to the kinds of medical subjects explored, but also with respect to the scope and brutality of execution.

To gain as much information as possible about the experiments, of which little was known among the Allies during the war, the Allied Commander in the Pacific, Douglas MacArthur, after the war negotiated with the Japanese to obtain the results of their experiments in return for immunity from prosecution.[88] The deal was made at a time when the U.S. military was preparing to prosecute Germans for similar atrocities. MacArthur, trying to obtain wider political backing for his controversial move, managed to obtain the blessings of the Departments of War and the Navy, as well as the State Department.

A subcommittee of the State-War-Navy Coordinating Committee eventually concluded, "the value to us of Japan's BW [Biological Warfare] data is of such importance to national security as to far outweigh the value accruing from 'war crimes' prosecution."[89] The Nuremberg judges were probably unaware of the American-Japanese deal. But their insistence that the defendants were not as ignorant as they claimed of many atrocities committed during the Hitler regime, and that their appeals to national security were no excuse for committing and covering up crimes, in retrospect lose some credibility.

It is possible U.S. authorities would have tried to strike a similar deal with the German physicians had the experimental results been otherwise unobtainable. But whatever German results were still available at the end of the war— i.e., had not been destroyed as potentially incriminating evidence or irretrievably lost-the victorious powers managed to obtain through careful sifting of captured documents and, after Germany's capitulation, skillful questioning of incriminated personnel. In contrast to the Pacific theater, the Allies in Europe fought until they had occupied almost every square foot held by enemy forces, including every inch of German territory. In their wake, special units searched for and secured any material that could be of some use or serve as evidence in the planned trials, including a plethora of files documenting various activities of the Hitler regime's more clandestine operations. They also identified many of the regime's refugees whose intimate knowledge of customs and places became an indispensable tool in tracking down the more elusive information pertaining to these operations, such as records of the medical experiments.

Leo Alexander of the U.S. Medical Corps, for instance, one of the two medical experts testifying for the prosecution, was an Austrian psychiatrist who had received his medical training in Vienna and Frankfurt. He could move among the German-speaking medical community with native ease and could obtain crucial data where investigators of more discernible foreign appearance might have failed. In June 1945 he visited Weltz at his laboratory near Munich. When he inquired about Weltz's hypothermia experiments, he was given results derived solely from animal testing. Suspecting more, he visited other researchers and laboratories and eventually found evidence in some SS files showing such experiments had also been performed on concentration camp inmates.

Such an approach did not work in occupied Japan, as Japanese-Americans were not entrusted with sensitive assignments. In fact, most were placed in camps as national security risks. Additional factors, such as Japan's surrender before U.S. occupation of the mainland and the relative isolation of the Manchurian camps where the experiments were performed apparently persuaded U.S. authorities to endorse MacArthur's deal, even if it meant covering up crimes in Japan while condemning them in Germany. It is doubtful that the judges at the Medical Trial were aware of the double standard applied in their judgments, but the fact that many officials of their government knew may serve some critics as a welcome tool to exonerate the defendants retrospectively.

The prosecution also failed to live up to expectations. Many observers had hoped for a trial clearly showing how the abandonment of the Hippocratic principles of medicine leads not only to a disregard for individual lives but to a general decline of medical knowledge as well. Prosecutors lacked sufficient medical expertise to confront the defendants on important medical issues and failed to produce enough experts who could. This is all the more surprising since the prosecution by no means underestimated the medical competence of the defendants. In his opening speech, Taylor acknowledged, "they are not ignorant men. Most of them are physicians and some of them are distinguished scientists."[90] At least two of them, Rose and Rostock, were internationally recognized scholars. The defendants left no doubt they considered the qualifications of the prosecutors, as well as the witnesses and judges, to grasp the complexity of their medical research questionable at best.

Responding to some statements by the prosecution and witnesses, for instance, Gebhardt complained that "someone is attacking me, a layman, who is saying he can pass judgment, has no idea of the process of infectious diseases, or what death and dying of thousands means."[91] When questions about seawater experiments by Alexander Hardy revealed his limited grasp of basic human physiology, Beiglboeck mocked, "You have to excuse me, but only a bloody layperson can ask such a question."[92]

The prosecution summoned only two experts to shed its lay image and to enlighten the Tribunal on the more technical aspects of the defendants' medical activities: Leo Alexander and Andrew Ivy. The psychiatrist Alexander concentrated his efforts on analyzing the behavior rather than the research of the

defendants. Only Ivy had advanced knowledge in some of the defendants' spe-
cialties. He was a physician, professor of physiology, and head of the Medical
College of the University of Illinois. He also was an expert on human diges-
tion and had studied specific functions of the alimentary tract. During the war,
he had performed human experiments on prolonged seawater intake and
exposure to high altitudes, and he spoke with considerable authority on the similar experiments of Beiglboeck, Romberg, Ruff and Becker-Freyseng. The tribunal also asked him to give his opinion on the various human experiments
performed by some of the other defendants.

Ivy testified for four days during the closing phase of the trial. With the
exception of Hoven and Pokorny, who had played no significant part in any
of the experiments, all defendants and respective witnesses by then had taken
the stand and their attorneys were preparing closing briefs. But the prosecution opened up discussions on all experiments again and offered Ivy's statements as rebuttals to some defense arguments and evidence presented earlier.
When Ivy argued that the Germans could have obtained their data on high altitude exposure from experiments with animals and declared the seawater experiments a scientific farce, counsel of the implicated defendants objected to his
testimony on cases they considered closed.[93]

When the objection was overruled, they declared themselves ill-prepared
to challenge his medical testimony on short notice and moved that the implicated defendants pose questions to Ivy directly instead. Counsel Fritz Sauter
made the first such motion on behalf of Ruff, which was granted over the objection of the prosecution.[94] Subsequent motions by the attorneys for Rose and
Beiglboeck were granted as well.

Under questioning by the defendants, Ivy's earlier self-assurance about certain medical questions dwindled, as in the following direct exchange with
defendant Ruff, who contested Ivy's earlier statement that German experiments
of slow descent from high altitudes had caused brain damage in the subjects.

> Q. [Ruff] Professor Ivy, do you know of any case in literature where after a brief lack
> of oxygen, ten minutes at the most, any provable damage to the brain was observed?
> A. [Ivy] No. You know as well as I do that that depends upon the extent of oxygen
> lack and its duration. Permanent damage to the human cerebrum will occur if it is com-
> pletely deprived of oxygen from five to seven minutes. That is lethal as far as the human,
> and I might also say the dog's cerebrum is concerned. It is not necessarily lethal inso-
> far as the vital medullar centers are concerned.
>
> Q. Professor Ivy, do you know the work of Buechner and his school on this subject?
> A. No.
>
> Q. Professor Buechner found, and I am certain that similar work was carried out in
> America too, that if one leaves animals for days and hours in such a strong lack of oxy-
> gen that they are just barely kept alive, that even after these days one can find no dam-
> age to the cerebral cortex with these animals.

A. Well, that may depend upon the extent of anoxia to which they have been exposed. He probably determined just the threshold at which no damage occurred, and I have in mind, for example, experiments of Professor Wendell at North Western University where the extent of oxygen saturation of the blood for a period of several minutes was only 20–15, 20 or 30 per cent.

Q. But as far as I remember this work, in a short lack of oxygen, by this I mean a maximum of ten minutes such as occurred in our experiments, in such short experiments no damage to the brain was observed, is that correct?
A. No, I am not familiar with that. There are two factors concerned. One is the degree of oxygen lack, and the time. Those two factors have to be considered, and as you stated in your report, you were working at the upper limits of what you considered to be safety.

Q. Now, Professor Ivy, I am sure you know that the first damage to the brain from anoxia and usually after a long interruption of the oxygen supply is damage to the ganglia, and especially the corpus striatum. These things are known to a far extent from chronic carbon monoxide poisoning and from literature.
A. Yes, that is morphologically speaking. In such experiments, learning ability tests, to my knowledge, have not been applied. There is particular reference to carbon monoxide poisoning.

Q. Professor Ivy, you will no doubt agree with me that in these cases of brain damage in the area of corpus striatum there are so-called Parkinsonianisms.
A. That is correct. I happen to be very familiar with that subject. For example, this week at the meeting of the American Medical Association in Atlantic City, I gave an exhibit on the subject of resuscitation from carbon monoxide poisoning. I happen to be an expert consultant on that subject for the Council on Physical Therapy of the American Medical Association.

Q. Now, Professor Ivy, since you are especially well informed in this field, do you agree with me that the damage which appears after a long period of anoxia, these Parkinsonianisms, that they can be found in neurological tests and in the clinical aspect of the person much better than in an intelligence test?
A. All patients do not manifest the symptoms of Parkinsonianism or paralysis agitans. I should like to also indicate that some of the human beings and animals who have been subjected to carbon monoxide poisoning, human beings, of course, accidentally, will show a clear period after they recover consciousness of from five to ten days in which they are apparently normal. Then they will develop various manifestations of damage to the nervous system or neurological sequelae, which may take the form of tremors in Parkinson's disease, may take the form of amnesia, loss of consciousness, and may be followed by death. So one might reasonably ask whether or not any of these subjects that were exposed to this anoxia as a result of slow descent showed any symptoms after a period of from five to ten days had passed.

Q. I absolutely agree with you on this point, Professor Ivy, I can tell you as far as I recall, that was not mentioned exactly in the report, that the experimental subjects who went through these sinking experiments were under observation for about six weeks afterwards, and that after six weeks the nervous system and the clinical aspect of these experimental subjects showed nothing whatever, and I believe you will agree with me

if I say that with the probability bordering on certainty, that is probability which is the most we doctors can give, it cannot be expected that people suffered damage at any point in the brain.
[Prosecutor McHaney]: I object to the remarks of Dr. Ruff. He is not now testifying. He is engaged in the examination of Dr. Ivy, and I submit that he should restrict his remarks to direct questions to the witness.[95]

More than once a prosecutor, and sometimes a judge, interfered and redirected the examination in Ivy's favor. Apparently suspecting problems, the tribunal limited examination time to thirty minutes when Rose started his questioning of Ivy. As the record shows, the suspicion was not unfounded. During his allotted time, Rose aimed at demonstrating that U.S. physicians in general and military physicians in particular, had performed experiments similar to those conducted by German physicians with respect to scientific value, legal grounding, and ethical orientation, if not scope of execution. That the tribunal, which had prevented most such comparisons up to this point, allowed Rose to question Ivy on this issue without interference may perhaps be attributed to a conviction that, if anyone, Ivy would be the most proper person to lay such claims to rest once and for all.

Rose, contesting Ivy's testimony that human subjects of American experiments had always volunteered, started off with a discussion of yellow fever experiments conducted in 1900 by Major Walter Reed of the U.S. Army Medical Corps in Cuba. Reed had been appointed by the Surgeon General to head the Yellow Fever Board, which worked with the assistance of Cuba's U.S. Military Governor, General Leonard Wood. Rose questioned Ivy as follows:

Q. [Rose] How many members of the American armed forces were used in the yellow fever experiments of Reed? How many of them were there?
A. [Ivy] I do not know.

Q. Is it correct that, outside of the two persons who you mentioned, only coolies who had volunteered for payment were used?
A. According to my information, the two doctors whom I mentioned, Carroll and Lazer, and then American soldiers. I did not know that there were any natives used.

Q. Well, you do not know about it?
A. We do not have soldiers in Cuba or in the West Indies.[96]

Aside from a few Americans, most volunteers had been Cuban residents, mostly Spanish immigrants, who were paid between $100 and $200 in gold for their participation.[97] While they certainly were no "coolies," their economic status was likely barely above subsistence level, and the monetary reward must have been very tempting. The recent arrival of the Spaniards as a result of the Spanish-American War made them more reliable subjects than long-term residents, many of whom had acquired immunity to the disease. The money had been made available by General Wood. Since neither Rose nor Ivy were certain about the details, Rose moved on:

Q. [Rose] How large is the mortality rate in yellow fever?
A. [Ivy] How large? You mean . . .

Q. What is the mortality rate?
A. That is in epidemics or in the experiments of Walter Reed?

Q. Yellow fever in general.
A. I think it is about 50 percent, if I recollect the figure correctly. It varies.

Q. Is it not correct that in the case of all races, with the exception of the Negro, the mortality rate is 80 to 90 percent?
A. I remember that it is quite high.

Q. Is it not correct that the number of experimental subjects in the Reed experiments was more then thirty?
A. I do not remember.

Q. Then there is no point in asking further questions about it if you are not informed about it.

The experiments of Reed and other American researchers were crucial to the prosecution's claim that American researchers, unlike the defendants, had not maltreated, tortured or killed human subjects. Hence, Ivy's testimony was very important, and his shirking answers certainly must have surprised not only Rose. Rose continued with questions about plague and beriberi experiments conducted by Richard Strong in the Philippines between 1905 and 1912:

Q. [Rose] Well, I shall go over to another point. Moreover, from Volume VII of the *Philippine Journal of Science*, you submitted pages 200 and 291. That is the paper by Strong regarding beriberi. Did you read that paper yourself?
A. [Ivy] Yes, I read the paper, and then I had photostats made of the two pages indicating that volunteers were used.

Q. In addition, you also discussed the matter with one of the authors of this paper, did you not?
A. That is correct, Dr. Crowell.

Q. Did I understand you correctly, that you said in your testimony on Friday that none of the experimental subjects died?
A. Yes, I said that to the best of my knowledge none of the experimental subjects died.

Q. And since you read the paper yourself, as you just confirmed to me now, may I perhaps, in order to refresh you memory, ask you to turn to page 379 of this paper? I have put a white sheet of paper in this place. Moreover, the tables 4 to 7 of this paper. Perhaps for the benefit of the Tribunal I may read the important lines. On page 379 it says: "The patient gradually sank and died at 2 P.M. on the following day."

The President: Dr. Rose, from what book are you reading? Will you please read into the record the title of the publication?

Defendant Dr. Rose: *The Philippine Journal of Science*, Volume VII, Section 3, page 379. Further down it says: "Necropsy: One half hour after death." The tables 4, 5, 6 and 7, which follow p. 414, are anatomical presentations regarding this.

(Volume submitted to witness)

After having looked at the text, would you not like to correct the statement you made that there were no fatalities?

A. Yes, there is a fatality. I do not know what it was due to, though.

Q. I thought you read the paper.
A. Yes.

Q. Well, now, if you want to read over all those pages which describe the case history of this man, unfortunately too much of the time that is made to me for questioning you will be lost. Therefore, I shall now proceed.

Ivy's earlier statements that no death had occurred were more likely to be erroneous than deceiving. But either way, Rose was able to put a large dent into the credibility of Ivy's testimony. He proceeded thus:

Q. [Rose] Is beriberi a serious disease?
A. [Ivy] It depends on how far it advances.

Q. Well, you have read the paper through and therefore you know that the case histories of the 29 patients are described exactly in this paper, and how serious degree of illness these patients had. Do you agree? Do you agree with me that beriberi is a disease which causes serious damage to the heart and to the nervous system?
A. Yes, if it is permitted to go to a point where serious damage occurs.

Q. Yes, if one lets it proceed to the extent that the patient dies of it, then, after all, it has proceeded pretty far. The paper says that the experimental subjects could speak neither English nor Spanish, and apparently also not the native dialect which was spoken in Manila, but that one had to speak to them through interpreters in their native dialect. They were apparently illiterates. Do you consider that persons of that kind are able to judge the significance of the beriberi experiment?
A. I think so, when beriberi is endemic in the region from which they come.

Q. Well, you know just as well as I do that beriberi does not occur in the mountain regions of the Philippines.
A. No, I am not sure of that.

Q. But in any case you agree with me that beriberi is such an important problem that the experiments by Strong, from an ethical and scientific point of view, were justified to their entire extent?
A. I have heard no criticism of those experiments.

Q. And you yourself do not criticize them either? You know the paper after all, do you not?
A. Yes, I read the paper the latter part of December, so all of the subject matter is not familiar to me now.

Q. But in any case, at the time you were reading it, you did not have any misgivings about it, did you?

A. No, I was primarily interested in finding out whether the subjects were volunteers and whether they were offered a reward. That was the part of the paper which I had photostatted.

It is indeed unlikely the condemned prisoners understood the full nature of the experiment, but for volunteering, they were "allowed an abundance of cigarettes of any kind they wished, and also cigars if they desired them."[98] And aside from the one subject pointed out by Rose, apparently everyone survived.

Rose then questioned Ivy on the reliability of information given the public about malaria experiments conducted on hundreds of U.S. prisoners during the summer of 1945, suggesting that medical knowledge about the experiments leads to the conclusion that fatalities must have occurred.[99] When Prosecutor McHaney objected to this kind of speculation, Rose turned his questions to human experiments with typhus, which, if anything, must have increased the feeling of many who were present in the courtroom that this part of the trial needed more preparation.

Q. [Rose] You submitted a document to the Tribunal, which was given the Exhibit no. 518, regarding the Veintimillas typhus investigations. You said that the experimental subjects were volunteers. May I ask you how you know that? I know the paper very well, and in the paper itself it is not stated.

A. [Ivy] I am not sure that I said they were volunteers. It states that for this purpose we selected 48 persons from 30 to 40 years of age and on whom no previous typhus infection was suspected, according to anamnesic or historical analysis.

Q. But do you have any other sources of information than the paper itself? Did you speak with Veintimillas himself?

A. I feel quite sure that I did not testify that volunteers were used in this article.

Q. Then I must have misunderstood you. At least over the microphone that is what I heard, and I made a note of it.

A. That may have been implied, the way they were being submitted, and the questions come in, but I know that volunteers were not specifically stated in this particular article, and in the same way they were not specifically stated in the plague experiments of Col. Strong. And when I found the word "volunteer" was not specifically included in the experiment of Col. Strong I called up Dr. Crowell and discussed the matter with him. I could not do that in the case of this article. And I wanted to point out that on page 343 it is stated: "It was obvious that typhus fever in men could be produced by such inoculum, and as we considered it unnecessary to expose human beings to the risk of a certain infection, we therefore relied on guinea pigs for control cases.

Q. I am familiar with that. Are you an expert in the field of testing typhus vaccines?

A. No, I am not an expert in the field of typhus.

Q. But perhaps you know just because of this fact which you just pointed out, namely, on the basis of the fact that no human controls are available, the entire experiments

conducted by Veintimillas and of the typhus experts is not considered of any proba-
tive value?
A. No, I do not know that.

Q. But you do know, don't you, that the reaction of an animal to an infection does not
prove anything in regard to what the same infectious material would cause in human
beings?
A. I do not know that to be true.

Q. But you submitted this paper, this article by Veintimillas, and in this paper the experiment by Franciscassa is mentioned. He conducted a similar experiment and he used
human controls, that is, infected and non-immunized persons. Are you familiar with
that experiment?
A. I am not familiar with that experiment.

Q. But it is mentioned in this paper. Did you overlook it?
A. I did not look up the references cited in this paper.

Q. But this fact, that he used controls who had not been vaccinated, is mentioned in
this paper by Veintimillas, over and above that, do you know that Blanc and Baltassard
conducted a number of vaccine tests of that type, in which the persons who were vaccinated were infected with virulent bacilli, as well as other control objects? Do you know
these experiments?
A. I do not.

Q. Do you know the experiments by Otere, who infected unvaccinated persons with
typhus?
A. No.

Q. Do you know the experiments by Yerein and Laval, who infected two coolies successfully with typhus?
A. No.

Q. Do you know the similar experiments by Sargent and his collaborators?
A. No.

Q. Do you know the similar experiments by Reitano, Mitchell and Richardson, Sparrow
and Lumbroso?
A. No.

Q. Perhaps at least you know the experiments of the Americans, McCalla and Brereton,
who infected two persons with Rocky Mountain spotted fever, and in particular do you
know why as their experimental subject they took a patient who had both legs
amputated?
A. No.

Q. Even though you are concerning yourself with the question of human experiments?
A. Yes.

Further questioning led Ivy again to reiterate his two main points: first, that
despite his demonstrated unfamiliarity with many of the medical and legal issues

raised by Rose and others, non-therapeutic and potentially harmful experiments on human subjects, including prisoners, is permissible as long as participation is informed and voluntary, and that, secondly, in cases where informed and voluntary consent of subjects in experiments performed by U.S. physicians was in doubt, it had to be assumed, even when defendants' could produce evidence to the contrary. More challenges on this point from Beiglboeck and several counsels could not change Ivy's mind on that subject.

Given the importance of the trial, it certainly seems unfortunate that the tribunal had to rely on the expertise of a single medical researcher in determining permissible medical, legal and ethical limits of human experimentation in general and the extent of their transgression by the defendants in particular. Ivy's direct examination by some of the defendants marked perhaps the weakest point in the efforts of the prosecution to show the defendants' guilt and could have been avoided, had it been anticipated. But it apparently came as a surprise to everyone. Ivy had to undergo nearly four days of intensive questioning by prosecution and defense alike and no doubt would have done much better under more favorable circumstances.

However, Ivy probably saw his testimony as a victory in his apparently self-appointed mission to make sure that the Tribunal in its expected ruling to condemn the German experiments on concentration camp inmates would not, perhaps unwittingly, hand down a ruling that by implication would also condemn American experiments on prison inmates.

Earlier during the trial, on January 27, 1947, the prosecution had summoned a psychiatrist and professor of medical history at the University of Erlangen, Walter Leibrandt, to testify to the general admissibility of human experimentation. Leibrandt provided the court with an insider's view of the changes the German medical profession underwent as a result of the National Socialists' seizure of power in 1933. Because his wife was Jewish, he was stripped of his official positions, but managed to survive as a private practitioner, notwithstanding some last-minute efforts by the Secret Police to apprehend the couple for violation of the regime's racial laws. Except for innovative therapy, he condemned any kind of experiment on human beings, even when the subjects agreed to volunteer and the benefits to others were obvious. When asked by the defense whether that meant that he also condemned the malaria experiments conducted during the war on prisoners at Stateville Prison in Illinois, he answered yes.

Ivy, a resident of Illinois and familiar with the Stateville experiments, was in the courtroom during Leibrandt's testimony. He saw an impending dilemma and found a solution. He would rebut Leibrandt's testimony later in the trial by demonstrating that the American experiments, unlike the German ones, were legally and ethically permissible and overseen by public committees.[100] He quickly went to Chicago, enlisted the aid of Governor Dwight Greene for the formation of a public committee, subsequently called the Greene Committee, which he chaired to oversee medical experiments on Illinois state prisoners, and then went back to Nuremberg to report on the committee's activities.

During his testimony on June 12–14, 1947, he suggested the Greene Committee had carefully studied and approved the Stateville experiments and all prison subjects had volunteered after giving informed consent, as required by American Medical Association's Guidelines.

When questioned by the defense, he admitted the prisoners had received reduced sentences for their participation, but argued he had not approved of it and insisted the real motivation of the prisoners was not receiving a reduced sentence but to make a positive contribution to society. He skillfully concealed the fact that the American Medical Association Guidelines had been adopted a few weeks after the beginning of the trial, i.e., after the Stateville experiments, and that the Greene Committee had never met. When asked by the defense whether "the formation of the committee had anything to do with the fact that this trial is going on," he replied, under oath, "there is no connection between the action of this committee and this trial."[101]

In its ruling, the court leaned to the side of Ivy rather than Leibrandt. Ivy, together with Leo Alexander, had supplied the court with a memorandum outlining universally applicable standards for experimentation on human beings, therapeutic and non-therapeutic. They became the basis for the ten principles ultimately endorsed by the court, which came to be known as the Nuremberg Code. The code protects human subjects from abuse by guaranteeing certain safeguards, most notably, perhaps, requirement of informed consent throughout the experiment. In many respects, the code was a summary version of the Reich Guidelines of 1931.[102]

The Nuremberg Code

1. The voluntary consent of the human subject is absolutely essential. This means that the person involved should have legal capacity to give consent; should be so situated as to be able to exercise free power of choice, without the intervention of any element of force, fraud, deceit, duress, overreaching, or other ulterior forms of constraint or coercion; and should have sufficient knowledge and comprehension of the elements of the subject matter involved as to enable him to make an understanding and enlightened decision. This latter element requires that before the acceptance of an affirmative decision by the experimental subject there should be made known to him the nature, duration,

and purpose of the experiment; the method and means by which it is to be concluded; all inconveniences and hazards reasonably to be expected; and the effects upon his health or person which may possibly come from his participation in the experiment. The duty and responsibility for ascertaining the quality of the consent rests upon each individual who initiates, directs or engages in the experiment. It is a personal duty and responsibility, which may not be delegated to another with impunity.

2. The experiment should be such as to yield fruitful results for the good of society, unprocurable by other methods or means of study, and not random and unnecessary in nature.

3. The experiment should be so designed and based on the result of animal experimentation and a knowledge of the natural history of the disease or other problem under study that the anticipated results will justify the performance of the experiment.

4. The experiment should be so conducted as to avoid all unnecessary physical and mental suffering and injury.

5. No experiment should be conducted where there is an *a priori* reason to believe that death or disabling injury will occur; except, perhaps, in those experiments where the experimental physicians also serve as subjects.

6. The degree of risk to be taken should never exceed that determined by the humanitarian importance of the problem to be solved by the experiment.

7. Proper preparation should be made and adequate facilities provided to protect the experimental subject against even remote possibilities of injury, disability, or death.

8. The experiment should be conducted only by scientifically qualified persons. The highest degree of skill and care should be required through all stages of the experiment of those who conduct or engage in the experiment.

9. During the course of the experiment the human subject should be at liberty to bring the experiment to an end if he has reached the physical or mental state where continuation of the experiment seems to him to be impossible.

10. During the course of the experiment the scientist in charge must be prepared to terminate the experiment at any stage, if he has probable cause to believe, in the exercise of the good faith, superior skill, and careful judgment required of him, that the continuation of the experiment is likely to result in injury, disability, or death to the experimental subject.

As significant as the Nuremberg Code may look in retrospect, it was hardly mentioned in the press at the time. The press reports focused on the defendants, the charges, the proceedings, and the ultimate verdict. And even that news seldom made the front page. With the conclusion of the Major Trial, much of the earlier suspense regarding guilt and punishment of the Nazi elite as viewed by the Allies was gone.

Most observers, no doubt, saw the subsequent trials as repeats of the Major Trial, albeit on a smaller scale. The Major Trial had produced twelve death sentences, seven prison terms, and three acquittals. The Medical Trial, the first of the twelve subsequent trials, had produced seven death sentences, nine prison terms, and seven acquittals. Legal and moral arguments on all sides had been registered, and what could be expected was more of the same.

The largest local paper, the *Nuernberger Nachrichten*, had given much front-page coverage to the Major Trial. It only did this once for the Medical Trial, when reporting on the opening session.[103] The verdict nine months later was covered on page three, and the occasional and usually terse updates on the proceedings were even further back in the paper.[104] Other German papers reported these events similarly.

The liberal *Berliner Zeitung* and the communist *Neues Deutschland* both had very short articles of the verdict on page two.[105] Some of the earlier articles had listed the brutal crimes of the defendants in gory detail, but they did not supply much commentary beyond expected condemnation. There was virtually no discussion on the impact the trial had on the ethics of medical experiments on human subjects in the future.

Alexander Mitscherlich's and Fred Mielke's documentation of the trial for the German Commission of Physicians in May of 1947, published as *Das Diktat der Menschenverachtung*, was meant to show the full scope of the failings of too many physicians under the Hitler regime and to initiate discussion on the lessons learned from the trial.[106] The book received limited attention in some papers but was virtually ignored by the German medical profession.

The situation was not very different in the United States. The *New York Times* covered the opening of the Medical Trial on page nine, though the announcement of the verdicts was a front-page story.[107] The Nuremberg Code was not mentioned. Few other papers covered the event. The historian David Rothman later wrote, "the prevailing view was that [the defendants at Nuremberg] were Nazis first and last; by definition nothing they did, and no code drawn up in response to them, was relevant to the United States."[108] For most observers of the trial, the Nuremberg Code probably was more a necessary by-product of meting out justice rather than a guide for medical research. And justice had been done, even if it was victor's justice in the eyes of those who still maintained fascist views.

The Trial—An Ethical Analysis

Theoretical Background for an Overdue Debate

TRYING TO EVALUATE THE Medical Trial, ethicist Robert Burt recently asked his readers to recapture the sense of the trial thus:

> We might recapture this sense by imagining that we ourselves had been judges at Nuremberg and that, before writing the ten standards in our formal judgment, we had presided over the 133 days of testimony about the concentration camp experiments. During those 133 days, we would have heard about camp inmates placed in pressure chambers where the simulated altitude was increased until their lungs and other body organs exploded; we would have heard about inmates plunged into ice water clothed in heavy military uniforms, or stripped naked and thrown outdoors in winter temperatures, where they remained (clothed or naked) until they had frozen to death; we would have heard about inmates purposefully burnt or cut by ground glass and left untreated until they died from the infection of their wounds; we would have heard about inmates whose healthy arms or legs were severed simply to test various surgical techniques for amputations.
>
> After hearing all of this, during more than four months of testimony, imagine now that we adjourned to our conference room and talked among ourselves to arrive at a verdict. How plausible is it, in these discussions, that any of us would say: "The basic problem with these experiments is that the subjects did not agree to participate."[1]

All the judges could do by endorsing the principles guiding human experimentation, Burt writes, is to establish a first line of defense against recurrence of such barbarities. And this is usually the point where ethical analyses of the trial end.

Anyone with any knowledge of the medical atrocities described in the previous chapters may be inclined to wonder what the subject of any ethical analysis might in fact be. Surely, the unfathomable brutality of the acts committed seem beyond any imaginable moral justification. Showing how they were committed, against whom they were committed, and the extent to which they violated prevailing law already overwhelms the patience of the most tolerant observer, let alone that of the still surviving victims and all who sympathize with their plight. Most critics agree that no analysis of the crimes can be neutral and that every analysis must expose evil.

The mere suggestion that the perpetrators could have acted in accordance with ethical principles at all seems preposterous and dangerously close to rendering the atrocities justifiable. But that is precisely what the defendants did. Not only did they argue their deeds were legal and necessary for the survival of their society, but also that they were motivated ethically. The records are replete with testimonies by the defendants asserting good intentions behind savage deeds. Yet more than half a century later, no serious comprehensive examination of the defendants' arguments exists.

Arthur Caplan explains this absence thus:

> One reason for the relative silence of bioethicists concerning the rationales and justifications given by German scientists and physicians during the Nazi era is that it is troubling for those concerned with bioethical issues to contemplate the possibility that those who supported the Nazi regime, who helped supply key elements of the epistemological and ideological foundations of Nazism, and who implemented or quietly endorsed the genocidal policies of the Third Reich did so from firm moral convictions. It is hard to accept the idea that those who committed terrible crimes against helpless persons were, when placed on trial for these actions, willing to present serious moral arguments in their defense. It is easier and less disturbing to simply dismiss the crimes of biomedicine under Nazism as the vicious acts of a small group of lunatics, deviants, and second-rate minds. It is easier, but it is also false.[2]

Even when the arguments of the perpetrators are noted, it is easy to dismiss them as sinister fabrications advanced to escape dreaded consequences or as retroactive rationalizations offered to soothe their own conscience, i.e., something deserving harsh condemnation rather than serious examination. Yet those arguments may also be seen as offering an opportunity to recognize how arguments with manifestly inhuman content can be advanced convincingly for the purported benefit of advancing the cause of humanity and by people who cannot all be dismissed as deranged. Understanding whatever measure of logic and coherence, or absurdity, such arguments contain, may be a useful tool in trying to limit the appeal they may hold for others.

Such an endeavor cannot be undertaken without risk. Arguments like those advanced, for instance, by Gerhard Rose and Karl Brandt may contain a measure of coherence that according to some critics may lend them a disturbing level of credibility. Critics may also charge the professedly serious examination of the defendants' arguments may itself be nothing but a cover for establishing such credibility in the first place.

Robert Jay Lifton opened himself to precisely that kind of criticism when he wrote *The Nazi Doctors*, in his own words, "a study to uncover psychological conditions conducive to evil." Using the method of psychoanalysis, he demonstrated with interviews from surviving camp physicians how they became killers in the guise of healers, namely by developing split personalities and living double lives, one upholding traditional standards of decency and the other pursuing calculated destruction of human lives. Both halves were linked in National Socialist ideology, according to which destruction of poisonous individuals is a necessary measure to heal a sick community.

Efforts like Lifton's, which suggest that no one may be immune to inducements to commit heinous crimes given certain circumstances, put in question the more prevailing view that atrocities like those committed by the defendants have their origin more in certain destructive characteristics that are inexpungably present in certain populations, if not entire societies. To individuals who endorse such a view and feel that they are not part of such a population or society themselves, it offers relief from nagging doubts whether they themselves would have been able to remain immune to committing heinous crimes given extreme circumstances.

Such relief was offered by Daniel Goldhagen's *Hitler's Willing Executioners*.[3] Although academically suspect and endorsed more by a less reflective general public, it received much praise from many distinguished scholars, including German scholars, most notably Juergen Habermas.[4] In many of his works Habermas has tried to show that the generation and acquisition of human knowledge and codes of ethics—ultimately of entire world-views—is fundamentally shaped by human interest, and that this interest is group and class specific. Far from endorsing any kind of epistemological or moral relativism, he argues the many world-views created by people throughout the ages clash, often violently, in a dialectical process that progressively reveals standards of truth and goodness that are universal. Given the dialectical method of Habermas' critical Marxist theory, the clash of the Nazi world-view with the world-views of Soviet communism and laissez-faire liberalism logically led to the defeat of the Hitler regime, a fact that contains lessons especially Germans should heed, and for Habermas, Goldhagen's book provides perhaps a much needed opportunity.

In addition to psychoanalysis and Marxian dialectics, linguistic analyses by such cultural critics as Jacques Derrida, Michel Foucault and Hayden White offer further tools for trying to understand Nazi perpetrators. According to White, for instance, individuals communicate with the help of a number of distinct types of discourse. Each discourse is characterized by a specific linguistic trope that codifies information in recognizably similar ways, whether the information refers to poetic, scientific, ideological or other matters.[5]

White recognizes four such tropes, namely metaphor, synecdoche, metonymy and irony. The use of the metaphoric trope as distinguished from, say, the ironic trope shapes discourses about ideological subjects in clearly identifiable ways. Predominantly it will produce statements commonly identified as anarchist, terrorist and fascist, while the ironic trope will predominantly produce statements commonly identified as liberal. With respect to poetic subjects, on the other hand, the former will predominantly produce statements commonly identified as romantic and the latter predominantly statements commonly identified as satirical. Hence, there exist linguistic affinities between fascist and romantic statements and between liberal and satirical statements.

White insists, however, such affinities cannot be drawn automatically, and the strength of profound thinkers often consists in their ability to link different types of discourses into a coherent whole that may defy such affinities. While this linguistic flexibility places some limits on the analytic strength of White's theory, it is still a helpful, perhaps additional, tool in trying to shed light on the thoughts and actions of people who certainly defy more conventional types of explanations.

Showing that many fascists used a metaphoric type of discourse helps explain why their thoughts and actions generally seemed to puzzle those who used other types of discourses. For instance, when Nazis talked about "eliminating poisonous elements from the ailing body," they metaphorically collapsed the distinctions between "poisonous elements" and certain people in society to where the two became identical. Similarly equated were the "ailing body" and the German nation. The nation, or body, subsumes everybody. "Body" and "everybody" are one.

In the words of the defendant Karl Brandt: "At the moment as a personality is dissolved in the concept of a collective body, every demand put to that personality has to be dissolved in the concept of a collective system. Therefore, the demands of society are put above every individual human being as an entire complex, and this individual complex, the human being, is completely used in the interest of that society."[6] And when the interest of society calls for "eliminating poisonous elements," the metaphoric type of discourse prescribes action very literally. This prescriptive power attributed to language corresponds to the fascist urgency to refashion society swiftly and radically.

In an ironic type of discourse, by contrast, terms such as "collective body" refer to multiple realities, e.g., individuals, constituencies, citizen groups, etc., which resist complete integration into a whole that extinguishes the distinct characteristics of the separate realities. Each reality maintains its distinct identity. Which particular reality a specific term signifies is always a matter of contention. Agreement is never final and can always be challenged. Hence, a call for action, as in "eliminate all enemies of state," does not signify a metaphorically unequivocal reality, but many realities, prompting such questions as, "eliminate who?; eliminate how?; eliminate why?" which are characteristic of liberal thinking.

Different types of discourse may also be linked to different concepts regarding good and evil. For those who believe an envisioned communal body has an existence of its own that subsumes the existence of all its individual members, who have no existence outside the larger whole, goodness consists in furthering the welfare of the whole, even if it comes at the detriment of certain individuals within it. For those who believe it is individuals who provide the ultimate existential basis of society, a basis which itself may have no existence apart from those individuals, goodness consists in furthering the welfare of individuals first, even if it comes at the detriment of society as a whole. This juxtaposition of two distinct principles of goodness is, of course, familiar and is mentioned here only to demonstrate an old dilemma faced by everyone who searches for a single principle with which all others can be judged.

Psychoanalysis and Marxism hold out the promise that attainment of such a principle is possible, if only partially. Modern linguistic theories generally do not. Their ultimate promise is not finding such a principle as much as preserving the freedom to choose between a number of plausible, if ultimately irreconcilable, options.

While linguistic theories further ethical pluralism, they also demonstrate the necessity for compromise between radically different concepts of goodness. Such compromise means having to part with the idea of ethical certainty. History is replete with examples showing this is one thing people dread very much. If fact, they often prefer extreme hardship and death to losing that certainty. When such certainly itself is gained at the price of having faced hardship and death, it is all the more painful to give it up.

Hence, it should be no surprise that the Nuremberg trials were as much an attempt by the victorious Allies, mainly the United States, to affirm the existence of such a single and certain principle: namely the existence of inalienable human rights, as it was an attempt to punish the perpetrators and render justice to their victims. Fighting for this principle, American authorities asserted after Auschwitz and despite Hiroshima, had been the real purpose of the war.

The assertion certainly would have been more convincing had the International Military Tribunal not included Soviet judges, whose inclusion signified more an acceptance of ethical pluralism than an effort to affirm the validity of a universally applicable standard of ethical conduct. The Soviets left no doubt about their rejection of the particular meaning the U.S. was attributing to the trials. The Soviets viewed the trials as primarily demonstrating the triumph of communism over fascism. The only agreement the Allies could reach was that the unprecedented scale and heinousness of German genocidal policies constituted a condemnable assault on millions of innocent people and humanity itself. This agreement provided the basis for the unprecedented law of crimes against humanity included in the Charter of the Allied London Agreement.

For the American authorities, the crimes before the International Military Tribunal remained willful violations of transcultural principles of law and ethics, while for the Soviets they constituted the most barbaric but largely inevitable consequence of the industrialized workforce's struggle for global self-determination. But such distinctions did not mar the subsequent trials held by the U.S.'s Military Tribunals in its restricted zone of occupation. Here attempts to show the defendants' particular moral failings above and beyond any legal transgressions became much more pronounced.

The defendants for the most part responded by reaffirming their fascist doctrines and by charging the tribunal with upholding a "might makes right" doctrine, designed to punish and exact revenge rather than administer justice. As a result, the U.S. military trials in particular presented a showdown between the ethical principles upheld by the courts on behalf of the United States and those upheld by the defendants on behalf of their vanquished regime.

The showdown has many antecedents and its philosophic roots may be traced back to the struggle of Socrates against his enemies the sophists. His affirmation that an absolute principle of goodness indeed does exist and can be proven through logical deduction has often been associated with the beginning of Greece's cultural greatness, but this affirmation came at a price. It tied the individual value of people to the power of their own intellect and their varying abilities to find the new absolute.

Ignorance, mainly a lack of formal education, characterized lack of value, which meant the majority of people had little or no value. The problem eventually was overcome with the rise of Christianity, which affirmed equal value for everyone before a new absolute, a single omnipotent God, who was not found through reason but revealed through faith.

Much of Western Civilization has been characterized by various attempts to synthesize those two opposed traditions: namely Greco-Roman humanism and Judao-Christian religion. During the seventeenth and eighteenth centuries, these attempts slowly yielded to a progressive secularization of society, along with its various promoters and detractors.

A "new spirit of inquiry" fostered a radical kind of skepticism especially toward things spiritual, which prompted Kant to make his well-known statement that he had to limit the power of reason to make room for faith again, faith in the existence of a higher transcendental power. Many subsequent critics found the assumed transcendental power in Hegel's World Idea, a spiritual absolute that Marx transformed into a material absolute, the "dialectical force of history." During the closing phase of the nineteenth century, belief in absolutes came under vigorous attack, chiefly from two sources: Darwin's theory of evolution and Nietzsche's pronouncement of the death of God.

According to Darwin's theory, all facets of cultural existence, including the belief in absolutes, constitute little more than fabricated devices useful only for prevailing in an all-pervasive, blind struggle for existence, with no intrinsic value of their own. Ethical principles, like anything else, assume usefulness, not value, to the degree they serve this goal.

While for Darwin culture was a product of human struggle for survival, for Nietzsche it was the product of human creative powers, the source of all values. Nietzsche tried to liberate the human mind from enslavement to its own creations, such as philosophic principles or religious doctrines. For him, man, not God or some other absolute, was the ultimate creator and judge of all things. Existentialists of various persuasions trace their roots to this idea.

During this past century, fascist minds of all colors have based their various political ideologies on both Darwin's theory of evolution and Nietzsche's brand of humanism. National Socialists in particular insisted life is dominated by a perpetual struggle for survival. They replaced Darwin's mechanically determined, materialistic process of natural selection with Nietzsche's self-conscious will to prevail through spiritual domination. This domination ultimately subordinated all human concerns, including ethical concerns, to the creative imagination of the most gifted. They interpreted Darwin to have meant, incorrectly, that existential struggles take place more between groups than between individuals, and they interpreted Nietzsche, also incorrectly, to have meant the Germanic people had a particular mandate to impose their will on the rest of the Europeans.

Fascists embraced the ethical relativism implied in the theory of Darwin and the elitism in the writings of Nietzsche. Realizing that few people were ready to accept the full import of such arguments, the ideological pacesetters among the National Socialists cultivated the ideal of a Nietzschean superman, a person who had the inner strength to abandon familiar worlds and the ruthlessness to prevail in newly charted territory whatever the cost. Embracing this ideal came to be recognized as a major criterion for acceptance into leadership ranks and membership in such elite organizations as the SS.

Most National Socialists remained dedicated more to an expressly reactionary and decidedly political position and saw their purpose primarily in fighting the envisioned threat of Bolshevism, despite their general endorsement of official and more idealistic sounding doctrines. Their hero was the pedestrian Horst Wessel rather than the intellectual Martin Heidegger. They joined the SA rather than the SS, and they intuitively favored a vulgarized version of

Darwin's theory over the esoteric visions of Nietzsche. Their understanding
of social processes was biological rather than cultural. They generally subscribed
to the view that the German nation with which they identified so strongly had
a historic obligation to preserve its threatened existence, as they envisioned it,
by any means possible, including war against enemies outside their nation,
chiefly rival nations, and within. The list of the latter comprised Bolsheviks, liberals, Jews, Gypsies, asocials, homosexuals, common criminals, and whoever else
would not fit the designated picture of a sober minded, hard working,
community-oriented German. Having learned from history and the Social
Darwinists that in a world marked by perpetual scarcity, passiveness and risk
avoidance lead to extinction, National Socialists promoted preservation through
aggression. Aiding the community aggressively and in a spirit of personal sacrifice constituted the epitome of goodness. Pursuit of individual interests and
self-gratification, especially when they seemed to disregard or harm the larger interests of society, showed depravity and expandability.

After 1933, the year the National Socialists assumed power, these basic
tenets increasingly dominated the daily activities of German society and
obstructed the lives of all who refused to adopt them or were declared genetically unfit to observe them. The resulting plight suffered especially by Jews
serves as the most tragic example. The fascist systems that emerged in Europe
after World War I all adopted some version of this collectivist ethic, without
which they would not have survived for as long as they did. Much effort has
been expended on the question of why in particular so many Germans
embraced it with such unprecedented ruthlessness and brutal disregard for
innocent lives, to the point of self-destruction. The answers arrived at cannot
claim to be conclusive, and much more effort needs to be invested to come to
some kind of consensus.

The defendants at the Medical Trial had all subscribed to this ethic, and
their attempt to justify it before the American Military Tribunal may provide
some helpful clues in this ongoing investigation. The more articulate justifications did not invoke the arguments of Nietzsche or Schopenhauer, as might
have been expected, but the philosophy of Hegel. The orthopedic surgeon Fritz
Fischer, for instance, who during his earlier days had belonged to the coterie
of Stefan George, a well-known poet who had shared Nietzsche's scorn for the
so-called ethics of comfort, resorted to the philosophy of Hegel. According to
Hegel, he argued, the state and the individual live in a perpetually changing
dialectical tension, subject to the fortunes of peace and the demands of war.
Reflecting on such changes during the Hitler regime, Fischer told the Tribunal:

> In peacetime the individual stood in the center and the State was simply the organiza-
> tion for the individual security, and unless one wanted to be an anarchist, one could
> allow in warfare only that law which put the State in the center and adopted a supra-

individual attitude, however, without being able to avoid the conclusion that the individual occupied a secondary position. There were also philosophic bases for this point of view.[7]

Hegel had indeed proclaimed that the state, the political structure of the collective body, was the highest incarnation of an unfathomable World Idea, the highest good, which pursued a rational purpose in this world despite its often seemingly irrational movements. His argument that everything real is rational and everything rational is real could indeed be understood, conveniently no doubt, as a carte blanche to pursue one's own ambitions without limits and without regard for others. However irrational and cruel they might appear on the surface, they would prove to be the most rational means to serve the state, and therewith the World Idea, in the long run. Had Hegel not idolized Napoleon for precisely this reason? He would now, it could be argued, endorse the actions of Hitler and the German nation for the same reason.

Gebhardt indicated that not only Hitler but Lenin and Stalin too had acted in accordance with this dictum, bringing to mind Hegel's argument that the World Idea by necessity is divided against itself and charts its progressive course through history via such tragic confrontations as the battle of Stalingrad and the Normandy invasion.[8]

In this scenario, neither side would be wrong in any universally applicable sense, but both must face legal and ethical condemnation by the other side and accept the consequences in case of political defeat. The prevailing side, by virtue of its victory, more closely approximated the World Spirit's process to unfold itself in accordance with a preexisting but little understood rational purpose.

The losers could present themselves, as the defendants indeed did, as tragic victims who had failed in their active and supposedly noble pursuit of a higher purpose, a status they had denied to their own victims, who had played a more passive role in this conflict. Passivity, as demonstrated, for instance, by many concentration camp inmates, would relegate them to mere sheep that had willingly trotted to Hegel's "slaughterbench of history."

To show their active commitment and so-called noble intentions, the defendants pointed to their wartime records and their often selfless engagement as physicians or administrators. Most of them had served as soldiers in combat, including some during World War I. Some had been wounded, Blome five times. Most experimental physicians testified they had performed dangerous self-experiments.

Rose apparently did so on many occasions, inflicting himself with typhus, malaria, and yellow fever to find adequate vaccines. Weltz, Becker-Freyseng, Ruff, and Romberg performed high-altitude experiments, Beiglboeck and Schaefer thirst experiments, all upon themselves. Ruff, Romberg, and Gebhardt, in fact, asked the Tribunal that the same experiments they had performed on

camp inmates be performed on themselves as evidence that the risk factors for
the subjects had not crucially exceeded acceptable standards.[9] The defendants
in general left little doubt about their self-ascribed role as selfless healers of the
larger community.

Karl Brandt told the Tribunal of his failed efforts as a young physician to
follow Albert Schweitzer to Lambarene in Africa. He went to work in
Germany's principal coal mining district, the Ruhr Valley, instead. Other
defendants, particularly Blome and Gebhardt, demonstrated scorn for physicians interested primarily in financial rewards. And almost everyone mentioned that the confrontation with a general sense of hopelessness among
many patients and countless others during the devastating prewar depression
generated in them strong urges to adopt radical, if painful, medical and political solutions to the crisis, an experience that solidified their embrace of
National Socialism as the only possible cure.

For the prosecution, the invocation of Hegel to render the medical atrocities of the defendants ethically coherent, if not legitimate, constituted not only
a lame attempt to escape deserved consequences for committing inhumane acts,
which remained indefensible by any mental concoction, but exposed the philosophy of Hegel itself as nothing but a blueprint for dictatorship of the worst
kind. This feeling was summarized by Leo Alexander in an article published
shortly after the trial:

> Irrespective of other ideologic trappings, the guiding philosophic principle of recent
> dictatorships, including that of Nazis, has been Hegelian in that what has been con-
> sidered "rational utility" and corresponding doctrine and planning has replaced moral,
> ethical and religious values. Nazi propaganda was highly effective in perverting pub-
> lic opinion and public conscience in a remarkably short time. In the medical profes-
> sion this expressed itself in a rapid decline in standards of professional ethics.[10]

According to Alexander, Hegel had relegated individual human beings to
the totality of the society in which they lived to such a degree they had become
pieces of utility that could easily be dispensed with if they disturbed the personal schemes of those who held total power. As a result, Hegel's philosophy
had become the ideological mainstay not only of National Socialists but of all
totalitarian-minded people in this century, most notably the communists. For
anyone upholding Kant's view that the supreme value of individuals consists
in the fact that they are ends in themselves and not means for something or
somebody else and Locke's view that they are naturally endowed with certain
liberties and equality, of which no one can deprive them with impunity, any
totalitarian philosophy constitutes an antithesis to human values per se, Hegel's
insistence to the contrary notwithstanding. In this tradition of liberal philosophy as represented by Kant and Locke, personal liberties and equality are
inalienable attributes of every individual and constitute generally recognizable,

universal truths characteristic of democratic systems, leaving no room for collective or relative truths.

The Nuremberg trials were staged in part to impress this message on as
wide an audience as possible, not by public proclamation but through a public confrontation of views. When Counselor Otto Nelte, for instance, questioned Andrew Ivy about what a citizen of a totalitarian state should do upon
recognizing the state's objectionable designs in war, Ivy responded without
much hesitation:

Q. [Nelte] Do you consider the actions of the conscientious objector to be as ethically pure as the actions of the soldier?
A. [Ivy] I do.

Q. Then you are saying that men who follow the orders of the state, namely the soldiers, and men who refuse to follow those orders, namely the conscientious objectors,
are ethically on the same level?
A. I do, although I do not agree with them.

Q. Would not the absolute affirmation of the person's right to refuse to serve in the
war lead to the ultimate dissolution of the state and hence to the state's ability to defend
itself?
A. Well, some believe that war is futile and they think they can defend that position.
Others believe that defensive war is necessary and that aggressive war is an evil.

Q. Have you ever seen a case in history where a state admits that it itself is carrying on
an aggressive war? Do not all states insist that they are carrying on a justified and legal
war?
A. That does not make that claim true.

Q. But the citizen of a state must decide whether what he is doing is good or evil. Would
a citizen of the United States believe his own state or believe the views that he hears
over the radio from Germany or France?
A. We have difference of opinion in the United States and we tolerate that difference
of opinion.

Q. I am asking whether the citizen, as a simple citizen, is more or less obliged or coerced
to hear what the state tells him. If, for example, he is called to arms. How is he to decide
whether the reasons for the government's decision are good or bad?
A. In a democracy, the citizens elect their own legislators who determine that totalitarianism and democracy are two different worlds of thought and behavior and it is difficult to reconcile them.

Q. Must not the citizens of totalitarian states obey their governments?
A. I do not believe that they should.

Q. Do you mean to state that the citizen of any totalitarian state should refuse to obey
the orders of his government?
A. I agree.[11]

In other words, since men know by nature what is right and wrong, they have the responsibility to act accordingly, especially when confronted with a totalitarian government. The defendants may have wondered why the U.S. government itself failed to act accordingly in its dealings with the totalitarian regime of the Soviet Union, but they did not make it an explicit point. Rather, they tried to discredit the charges against them primarily by citing medical experiments conducted by American physicians, which supposedly were similar in callousness, if not scope, to those conducted by themselves and by referring to what they considered to be atrocities committed by the U.S. military against civilians in such bombing raids as those experienced by the residents of Dresden and Hiroshima.

As much as the Allies, particularly the United States, tried to show that the heinous acts of the defendants revealed an unprecedented determination by the National Socialists to turn traditional principles of human ethics on their head, the Nuremberg trials remained first and foremost judicial trials. The defendants' claims to have acted in accordance with justified, if not generally recognized, principles of ethics were not discussed in and of themselves as much as they were considered to be either extenuating or aggravating circumstances for acts charged as crimes under laws prepared for these trials.

One of those laws decreed certain acts to be crimes against humanity. It was prompted by the National Socialists' unprecedented extermination of entire political, religious, and racial populations, especially the Jews of Europe. To make this ostensibly ethical atrocity a punishable legal violation, the authors of the law widened the scope of the term humanity to refer not merely to ethical but to judicial matters as well. Otherwise, it would have been impossible to indict the defendants on anything but war crimes charges, as defined by the Geneva Conventions and Hague Regulations.

But existing laws against war crimes did not fit the enormity of the defendants' deeds, which could not have been foreseen when the war crimes laws were endorsed during the earlier part of this century, well before the outbreak of World War II. The signatories of the London Agreement defined crimes against humanity as any inhuman act, such as murder, extermination, enslavement and deportation, against any civilian population and persecutions on political, racial, or religious grounds. This definition was transcribed into Control Council Law No. 10, the basis for the Medical Trial (see chapter II).

Neither the signatories nor the tribunals provided a comprehensive definition of the term humanity, but it generally referred to ethical values as the inviolable sanctity and dignity of all individual human life. Nor did the lawmakers or tribunals expressly state these values were ethical absolutes, but they left no doubt they were recognized and observed by all civilized nations, and that the German nation had violated them not in a justifiable defense of its country but in wanton acts of aggression against innocent and helpless people, often merely because they belonged to despised national, political, racial, or religious groups.

In the Medical Trial, the prosecution presented piles of evidence showing the defendants committed crimes against humanity by singling out members of such groups—Russians, Poles, Gypsies, Jews, and others—for their torturous and fatal medical experiments, and fifteen people were subsequently convicted.

The defendants denied making any selections of subjects themselves. They also pointed to Richard Strong's plague and beriberi experiments and Walter Reed's yellow fever experiments on confined and ill-informed Filipinos and Cubans as examples of earlier harmful and fatal medical research on members of distinct racial and national groups by American physicians.

When the prosecution objected to such comparisons, Fritz Sauter, the counsel for Kurt Blome, who was accused of having performed plague experiments on Russian prisoners, quipped with reference to Strong's plague experiments on Filipinos: "I am interested in determining whether Prof. Blome can be declared a criminal for plague experiments which he did not conduct while some foreigner, who had conducted experiments, is not a criminal but glorified."[12]

When Sauter questioned the prosecution's medical expert Andrew Ivy as to whether the use of confined conscientious objectors for high altitude experiments in the United States during the war was not a politically motivated selection, despite the stated voluntary status of the subjects, Ivy remarked categorically: "We have no political prisoners in America."[13] This statement would be correct only if the Japanese-Americans interned in camps during the war had been placed there for racial rather than political reasons.

For the prosecution at the time, the defendants' arguments, in particular those comparing various human experiments, were meant to be misleading, not only because the German experiments had shown a much greater disregard for individual life than the American experiments had, but also, and more importantly, because they obscured the fact that the German experiments manifested an abuse of subjugated racial and national groups for medical research and were part of a plan first to abuse and then to exterminate such groups in accordance with accepted genocidal policies. Given the inconceivable but nevertheless real magnitude of the genocidal policies as revealed in the major trial, the prosecution could work with the convincing assumption that millions of innocent people could not have been turned into ashes without the active participation of every person holding a position in the Hitler regime like those held by the defendants. And since all the German experiments were performed in concentration camps, many indeed as a prelude to the victims' death in the gas chambers, the defendants' repeated attempts to place their own experiments on the same plane with those of other researchers, especially American researchers, could only evoke a sense of profound alienation among most observers at the time.

More than half a century later, there are many indications that this alienation gives way to a sense of curiosity about any possible scientific merit these experiments may possess or any helpful legal and ethical lessons that may be gleaned from a seemingly safe critical distance. This development must be difficult to bear for any victims still alive, who may not be able to, or ever want to, establish such a critical distance.

The defendants by no means misjudged the prevailing mood inside the courtroom regarding their former activities as dedicated National Socialists in a regime that had created Treblinka and Auschwitz. They tried to counteract this mood the same way they tried to counteract the specific charges of medical atrocities, namely by referring to supposedly comparable atrocities committed by the nation that sat in judgment over them, such as the carpet bombing of Japanese and German towns.

Unlike the medical atrocities, the larger political atrocities were not a subject of formal charges against them. They had been the subject of charges in the Major Trial. Hence, the references took mostly the form of indirect accusations and were largely ignored by the prosecution and judges, who were more interested in the defendants' disregard for specific codes of medical ethics than in comparing balance sheets of horror or taking issue with charges of hypocrisy. Because ethical codes by themselves are not legally binding and are subject to much interpretation even where agreement on basic principles is not in question, the prosecution felt burdened in its efforts to keep the defendants within a limited format of inquiry.

Medical Ethics: Hippocrates and National Socialism

THE PROSECUTION TRIED TO expose the defendants' wanton disregard of generally observed obligations of the physician to be a healer of the sick and a comforter of those in distress. For more than two thousand years, the sick and distressed in Western civilization had viewed the physician as someone who had dedicated his life to promote their individual health and help them in easing personal pain.

Since antiquity, physicians have demonstrated that they honored this trust bestowed upon them by pledging to uphold a set of ethical codes, collectively known as the Hippocratic oath, which is still pledged in various forms by many graduating physicians today. Most of them state that physicians must use all of their skills to treat patients and help them recover from illness and other physical mischief to the best of their ability. They cannot dispense poisonous drugs or abortive remedies. They cannot inflict harm and must keep secret all personal information regarding their patients and professional information pertaining to their work.

The oath also contains a provision regulating the physicians' relations with peers, especially teachers, and relatives. This provision in particular fostered the formation of guilds, which until recently managed to take care of their members' affairs with minimal outside interference, including that of governments. However, in the twentieth century, governments successfully gained some measure of control over medical organizations, usually in the name of protecting the interests of the larger and often indigent populations.

For physicians, this has been less a challenge in countries with a more liberal tradition, such as Britain and the United States, where independent organizations have received more social and legal support. Governmental controls have led to more complicated changes in countries with a more collectivist tradition, such as Russia and to a lesser degree also Germany, where society has demanded that physicians forgo much of their independence for the sake of the greater common good.

The main beneficiary of the liberal interpretation is the individual patient who has sufficient means to gain access to the physician's services, even if it comes at the cost of withholding such services from others. The main beneficiary of the collectivist interpretation are all those who in a liberal system have little or no access to such services, as the government tries to ration them according to need.

The Hippocratic pledge that "I will use my power to help the sick to the best of my ability and judgment" may be interpreted either way.[14] The part of the statement that reads "to the best of my ability and judgment" supports individualist interpretations, and the part that reads "to help the sick" supports collectivist interpretations. But the pledge continues: "I will abstain from harming or wronging any man by it." Either way, the physician pledges to inflict no harm on anyone in his, and nowadays also her, care.

To say the defendants harmed the people entrusted to them, if anything, is a gross understatement, given the extremely excruciating and often fatal medical procedures to which they had subjected them. The prosecution summoned Andrew Ivy and Werner Leibrandt to show the defendants had been bound by the Hippocratic codes and had violated them in the most brutal way imaginable. Leibrandt stated that while a large number of German physicians actively promoted the ideology of National Socialism, which they had long integrated into their practice of medicine, most of the rest simply knuckled under to the demands of the regime with little resistance. They gave up the time-honored principle of aiding the individual and practiced collectivist medicine to promote their careers.

Leibrandt told the Tribunal:

> The doctor, who for thousands of years, even before the Christian era, had the duty
> of treating the individual patient to the best of his ability; this doctor was now made
> a biological state officer by the National Socialist system. This is, he no longer decid-
> ed according to the ethical principles of pre-Christianity and the pre-Christian world
> in the interests of the individual patient, but he was the agent of a class of leaders who
> did not concern themselves with the individual, but considered the individual only as
> an expression of the maintenance of fictitious biological developments of racial ideas
> and thus tore the heart out of the medical profession. The doctor who has no prima-
> ry interest in the patient, who only gives out orders on behalf of a fictitious collective
> economy, according to the law of the Hippocratic oath, is not a doctor.[15]

The defendants did not dispute the charge they had adopted collectivist
medical doctrines but argued they were not at all contradictory to the principles of Hippocratic medicine. Oskar Schroeder, for instance, pointed to the
many Hippocratic writings dealing exclusively with the etiology and cure of ill-
nesses afflicting whole populations without ever mentioning the particular status of individuals at all, such as *Airs, Waters, Places* and others. The physician
who practices medicine in such a demonstrated communal framework supposedly does not care less for the individual but merely protects him or her more
adequately by treating the population as a whole.[16]

According to Karl Gebhardt, he even possesses higher ethical standards
than the physician who tends only to the individual patient does. "All of us will
envy a physician like that," he states with reference to the latter, "but one cannot tell me that this is ethically the best physician for the ethical and clinical
welfare."[17]

Leibrandt left no doubt about the fact that the adoption of a radical collectivist medicine did not mean that, as the defendants contended, individuals received better medical care at the expense of personal attention, but that
National Socialist medicine had relegated individuals to a level where their sole
value resided in their contributions to the collective as determined by the
regime's leaders. Those who failed to make expected contributions or who were
considered a liability came to be seen as easily expendable. This view was partly an extension of, and received much justification from, a much-popularized
Social Darwinism, as has been explained earlier. Accordingly, during times of
national emergencies, individuals who were considered to be a liability should
be forced to either make contributions to the community or be removed from
it. Contributions, according to the defendants, could consist of serving as medical subjects and removal could entail euthanasia. And this, they argued, was
all in the spirit of Hippocrates.

Leibrandt argued such an extreme and inhumane interpretation was the
result of a transition in thinking many German physicians underwent before
and during the Nazi regime. To demonstrate how German physicians made the

transition, Leibrandt pointed to a book entitled *Structure of Public Health: The Third Reich,* by Arthur Guett, the former head of Health Affairs in Hitler's Ministry of the Interior. In his book, Guett argued "the ill-conceived love of thy neighbor has to disappear, especially in relation to inferior or asocial creatures."[18] The defendant Joachim Mrugowsky had made a similar argument in a work of his dealing with medical ethics, *Das aerztliche Ethos.*[19] In response to a question by the prosecution, Leibrandt called both works "a joke of world history."

> Q. [Prosecutor Hardy] Then would you say, Professor, that Guett's description of an inferior social creature is contrary to the ethics of the oath of Hippocrates, is that right?
> A. [Leibrandt] It is a joke of world history that in a book about national socialist professional ethics dated 1943, the oath of Hippocrates was cited word by word, and that there they referred to the contents of this oath, and they considered themselves obligated by that oath. It is further a joke of world history that among the defendants there is one person who wrote a book about medical ethics in which he quotes the identical principles of one of the most famous physicians of the last century, Christian Wilhelm Hufeland, and this is the defendant Mrugowsky. I have to state in this reference that the essential points of the oath of Hippocrates are that the physician is forbidden under oath to commit arbitrary injustice on his patients or to do him any harm. The conception of injustice contained in the Hippocratic oath, which is signified by the Greek term "Aedicia" is one of the most important concepts—note—not of the Christian, but also of the pre-Christian world. The health of the state in the sense of Plato is justice, and injustice which is mentioned in that Hippocratic oath, and the physician is obligated never to harm the individual, never to inflict any arbitrary harm to the individual, that is, to do him injustice. I cannot understand how this Hippocratic oath fits in the national socialist literature of 1943 and at the time when everything happened as the evidence here has shown.
>
> Q. Professor, have not the ethics of the oath of Hippocrates been considered to be the legal and moral code of the conduct of physicians throughout the world for twenty-two centuries?
> A. Yes.[20]

Leibrandt, no doubt, was aware his view was subject to challenge from historians who have maintained the modern understanding of the ethics of the Hippocratic oath contrasted sharply with the standards of medicine as practiced at the time of Hippocrates and many centuries afterwards.

In ancient Greece, physicians frequently assisted patients in committing suicide to end unbearable suffering through a "good death" and performed infanticide as a form of genetic population control. During late antiquity, some physicians performed vivisections and medical experiments on prisoners. Physicians treated patients selectively and refused treatment to people labeled enemies. Provisions of secrecy were ill kept. The Hippocratic oath was not commonly observed, but it was held out as an ideal for the entire profession by the followers of the Hippocratic school, which constituted a minority among physicians throughout antiquity. The school carried on the basic tenets of the Pythagoreans, who preached universal brotherhood of all men.[21]

Not until the rise of Christianity did the Hippocratic codes become the accepted norm for all physicians in Western civilization. In many ways, the Christian principles of universal love and equality of all human souls reiterated the Pythagorean commitment to universal brotherhood. The oath subsequently was revised in some obvious respects. The Greek deities to whom the oath was sworn were replaced by the Christian God. A prescription to give special care to the poor and needy was included, and the profession was declared open to all.[22] This new oath, and the various subsequent versions of it, once considered a mere ideal for the few, became a practical guideline for all, and remains so today.

Since the mid-nineteenth century, however, its injunction against inflicting willful harm was frequently violated when the introduction of the germ theory of disease tempted a growing number of researchers to perform nontherapeutic experiments on hospitalized indigent patients and prisoners. These attempts to develop accurate diagnoses of, and effective cures for, spreading epidemics, foreshadowed the atrocities of the defendants. For this type of research, the defendant Weltz pointed out, the Hippocratic oath contained no guidelines, because:

> When the Hippocratic oath was first formulated there was no such thing as experimental medicine. Experimental medicine is a new development within the last century. It has been highly successful. A medicine not based on the success of experimental medicine is inconceivable today.[23]

Weltz argued the oath was hopelessly outdated and in great need of revision. "It is an honorable document," he stated, "which, however, does not altogether fit present times. If it is to be applied today, its wording has to be changed very extensively."[24] Becker-Freyseng argued the text of the Hippocratic oath had such wide conceptual scope and so many interpretations that "anything and nothing could be proved by it today," and no unequivocally binding set of codes could ever be derived from it.[25]

The prosecution had anticipated such arguments from the defendants and had summoned Leibrandt and Ivy to disprove them. Hence, it had Leibrandt affirm the oath indeed has been considered "the legal and moral code of the conduct of a physician throughout the world for twenty-two centuries," and despite changing interpretations, its basic concepts remained unchanged. In particular, the physician's obligation never to inflict harm "is one of the most important concepts—note—not of the Christian, but also of the pre-Christian world."

This was a clear rebuttal of National Socialist views as expressed by Guett and others that pre-Christian medical practices were considerably different from later Christian practices and the envisioned National Socialist Europe should orient itself on the former rather than the latter. Many German physicians, like Mrugowsky, had indeed argued the Hippocratic writings as a whole, if not the oath in particular, represented much more the aristocratic tradition of antiquity than the egalitarian tradition it ultimately came to represent as a result of Christian influences, an argument the defendants now reiterated at the Tribunal.

When Ivy was asked by the prosecution on the current relevance of the oath, he agreed with Leibrandt.

> Q. [Prosecutor Hardy] Is the oath of Hippocrates the Golden Rule in the United States and to your knowledge throughout the world?
> A. [Ivy] According to my knowledge it represents the Golden Rule of the medical profession. It states how one doctor would like to be treated by another doctor in case he were ill. And in that way how a doctor should treat his patient or experimental subjects. He should treat them as though he were serving as a subject.

> Q. Several of the defendants have pointed out in this case that the oath of Hippocrates is obsolete today. Do you follow that opinion?
> A. I do not. The moral imperative of the oath of Hippocrates I believe is necessary for the survival of the scientific and technical philosophy of medicine.[26]

Later in the proceedings, some of the defendants challenged this unequivocal endorsement of Hippocratic ethics. Mrugowsky's counsel, Fritz Fleming, showed that even today the text of the oath varies from country to country in crucial respects and that some of its earlier provisions are omitted or ignored in most texts. Ivy, for instance, had to agree that the contractual agreements between teachers and students were not and could not be observed today as stated in the oath. After citing a translation of the original text, Fleming engaged Ivy in a discussion on the Hippocratic meaning of helping and not harming patients by additionally citing the text of one of the Hippocratic letters.

> A. [Ivy] The oath continues: "The prescription to make life easy for the patient I shall regard, and I shall avoid doing what can harm or injure the patient?"
> Yes, that indicates a reverence for life, and that you should do nothing in the way of therapy which you know will harm the patient.

> Q. [Fleming] It is precisely this part of the Hippocratic oath that is missing in the French version. From this it can be seen that the various conceptions of the doctor's medical ethics and what his obligations are differ vastly from time to time and that the Hippocratic oath contains nothing but general principles which as you can see from this letter of Hippocrates, which I am going to read to you, were not regarded even by Hippocrates himself in the way that they are regarded and held to be necessary today. In this letter to Hippocrates it says: "I am not justified in taking advantage of the richness of the Persians not in treating barbarians who are enemies of the Greek people or freeing such barbarians from disease."

That is the fifth letter from Hippocrates and you have already said that such an attitude cannot be brought into, or is consonant with, the basic principles of medical ethics,
is that so?
A. Yes, that is not coincident with my principles of the medical ethics, as in reverence
for life, whether that life be friend or foe, when it comes to treating their disease and
sickness.
. . . I might add that I doubt whether Hippocrates wrote that letter.[27]

Ivy's last point favored the argument of the defense more than the prosecution's, because it is doubtful whether Hippocrates wrote the oath either, or
any of the roughly sixty treatises bearing his name.[28] They evidently were written by a large number of physicians and primarily contain instructions regarding diagnoses and treatments of diseases and injuries, but they also deal with
matters of ethics and the aims of medicine as a whole. Their varied origins over
time are evidenced by their considerable discrepancies, including the instructions on proper codes of medical ethics.

Most were written around 400 B.C., during the most active part of
Hippocrates' life, but several were written earlier and some more than a hundred years later. It is most likely, that scholars working at Alexandria combined
them into a collection and ascribed them to the renowned Hippocratic school
on the Isle of Cos. The historian G.E.R. Lloyd has observed "in the absence
of convincing arguments for authenticity, those who have discussed the problem have all too often fallen back on the supposition that Hippocrates must be
the author of the treatises that they happen to value the most highly."[29]

The prosecutors themselves were not concerned so much with questions
of authenticity and historic accuracy, but it occupied the minds of the defend-
ing physicians and the medical experts testifying against them. The prosecution simply tried to show the Hippocratic codes summarized in the oath had
survived as major guidelines for physicians throughout the ages and had governed the practice of all physicians in modern times, whatever their origins may
have been. But it had difficulty dismissing the defendants' arguments that no
consensus existed or was even possible on that particular point, certainly not
across national boundaries. As they did with respect to the legality of the
atrocities with which they were charged, the defendants argued the professional and ethical standards physicians have to observe in their practice of medicine are those of the collective of which they are members.

In their own case, they happened to be those of the German nation.
These standards were affected, they argued, by geopolitical events that threatened the nation's very survival. These events and the ethical standards in
effect at the time justified the extraordinary measures of which they were now
accused. It would be unjust to judge their actions after-the-fact by different
standards that did not prevail when these measures had to be taken.

This was clearly expressed by the counsels for Kurt Blome and Siegfried Romberg when Ivy judged the ethics of the defendants' deeds by standards the American Medical Association had formally endorsed just before the beginning of the trial:

> Here the question is always asked what the opinion of the medical profession in America is. For us in this trial, in the evaluation of German defendants, that is not decisive, but in my opinion the question must be decisive what, for example, in 1942, when the altitude experiments were undertaken at Dachau, the attitude of the medical profession in Germany was. From my point of view as a defense counsel I do not object if the prosecution should ask Professor Ivy what the attitude or opinion of the medical profession in Germany was in 1942. If he can answer that question, all right, let him answer it, but we are not interested in finding out what the ethical attitude of the medical profession in the United States was, because a German physician who in Germany undertook experiments on Germans cannot, in my opinion, be judged exclusively according to an American medical opinion, which moreover is from the year 1945 and was coded in the year 1945 and 1946, was coded for future use: it can have no retroactive force either.[30]

In 1942, the defendants maintained, Germany, along with other European nations, was engulfed in total warfare. The war never touched American soil or threatened U.S. survival. There was little room for Hippocratic compassion and charity, because circumstances demanded the physician act in accordance with duty and obedience. It was their duty to obediently carry out assignments that placed the health and life of certain people in jeopardy to save the health and life of the nation.

In the words of Fritz Fischer:

> During this time in which my people were fighting for their very life . . . the state had the right to take measures that lay beyond the competence of the individual. In that time when 1,500 persons were falling daily on the front and in which several hundred died daily in the homeland as a result of the war, this obedience to the state seemed to me the highest ethical duty.[31]

Disobedience or resistance would have undermined the survival chances of the nation and hence would have been ethically condemnable, even if the repulsiveness of individually committed deeds was clearly recognized.

The prosecution pointed out the individual, not the state, carried the moral and legal responsibility for such deeds. Every physician had the opportunity to resign his murderous position during the Hitler regime and practice Hippocratic medicine with impunity, if not with comfort. The defendants disagreed, citing Kant's deontological argument, whereby every member of a community has to act as if his actions provided the maxim for the actions of all members. If disobedience constituted a prescriptive rule for everyone, then the community would be unable to survive, at least in its existing form. "And faced with this alternative," Fischer argued, "I saw disobedience as the worse one."[32]

The devastating results of such a Kantian interpretation have been lucidly described by Hannah Arendt in her notes on the Adolf Eichmann Trial. These results have not received sufficient attention from most other writers on the subject, who generally look more for evidence showing that National Socialists, like all fascists, endorsed any means, however brutal, that promised desired results.[33]

Arendt has pointed out that while German society cultivated a strong sense of duty based on Kant's philosophy, totalitarian-minded thinkers cannot apply it to their actions with any kind of consistency, because Kant precluded the possibility that men, who are endowed with the ability to make reasonable judgments, could prescribe acts of suppression as maxims to be observed by others.

Duty and obedience to others that violate principles of reason must therefore be rejected. But some defendants, like Fischer, had also advanced Hegel's position that the state manifests itself as the highest form of reason. Arendt suspected such philosophic arguments were mainly put forth as retroactive justifications for the their bloody acts. The manifest evil in the perpetrators was characterized more by an appalling sense of opportunism and banality than by intellectual depth. But advanced they were, and the tribunal was faced with the unenviable task of judging their appropriateness and sincerity.

At least during times of war, the defendants argued, the individuals of a community, physicians not excluded, must subordinate their own judgments to that of the whole as defined by the state. Formerly observed codes regarding medical practice and research must be reassessed to bring them in alignment with communal needs.

Doctor-patient relations were no exception, even where such relations should have enjoyed the highest trust. Hitler, for instance, discovered in 1942 that one of his generals had been treated for mental problems for two years. He gave orders that,

> physicians, practitioners, dentists are not only relieved from secrecy toward the General Commissioner Brandt, but I am now obliging them to report immediately after their diagnosis of a serious and progressive disease to a person occupying a leading and responsible position within the state, the party, and the Wehrmacht [Armed Forces], the economy, and so on, and then to inform me for my own information.

When Fischer was asked by the tribunal, "In your opinion does this request violate the oath of Hippocrates? Is something being demanded here that the physician, on the grounds of his professional ethics, should refuse?" he replied:

> In general, the physician is obliged to maintain secrecy about what he finds out in the course of his profession and not pass on any information. He is relieved from this moral law at the very moment when his knowledge implies a general danger because a physician knows that in some cases, for instance, in the case of the dangerously insane patient,

he of course is obligated to impart the knowledge which he has gained in practicing his profession and obligated to pass it on for general safety. Then the general interest exists; and it is far above the interest of the individual patient. Therefore there can be exceptions.[34]

For Gebhardt, however, the exceptions were the rule, because the physician has to place the "collective community of need" above the need of the individual, which means, "the obligation of secrecy of a physician must of necessity stop."[35] Discussions regarding the breach of traditional confidentiality between physician and patient by the defendants, and by many other physicians during the Hitler regime, did not occupy much time during the proceedings. After all, the defendants were accused of atrocities against people who in no way could be considered patients. The medical experiments performed on them were designed to help others, the "community of need," at the price of great suffering to them.

That fact led Mrugowsky to this observation:

This relation of confidence of physician to patient is fully applicable to medical ethics in the classical sense, as before, and that will certainly also hold true of all times. But all experiments which are here the subject of the indictment were not carried out on patients who put themselves into the hands of a physician with confidence; but these were inmates of concentration camps. These men were entirely healthy. . . . They were not patients of the physician in the sense of medical ethics and in reference to the concept of the relationship between the physician and patient, and therefore what we understand to be medical ethics can only conditionally by applied in this case.[36]

Under questioning by his counsel, Mrugowsky, charged with experimenting with deadly viruses on Buchenwald inmates, then argued the fate of the inmates was entirely a matter of the state, at least in times of total war.

Q. [Counsel Fleming] In your opinion, did the State have the right to dispose of the health and lives of the inmates by placing them at the disposal of medical experiments, as a result of which permanent disturbances of their health or even death could occur?
A. [Mrugowsky] In normal times the State certainly does not have that right. But the experiments which are here the subject of the indictment were carried on during the war. . . . The circumstances of total war are naturally quite unusual. Under these very unusual circumstances where the state exercises jurisdiction over its entire citizenry, I don't think the inmates of concentration camps can be excepted. Now when the State orders the performance of medical experiments because some question regarding the combating of epidemics had to be settled as quickly as possible, I would imagine that the State has the right to select persons for that special purpose because in that case the State is doing nothing else that it is not doing with its soldiers and other population.

Q. Under what circumstances would you say that the speedy settlement of any question is of highest medical importance?
A. In order to remain within the scope of the indictment, I think there is such a case when some foreign epidemic is starting, which so far was not found within the Reich

[German] territory, and where a large number of deaths is to be reckoned with, so that the speediest settlement became necessary. It is important to find out whether a certain drug or a certain vaccine can control this danger.

Q. When making these presumptions, do you think that a physician is entitled to carry out experiments on human beings using drugs or new vaccines, even if he knows that the life of the experimental subject is being endangered by that procedure?
A. I don't think that a physician is justified to do that when we are concerned with his own initiative. I think, however, that he is obliged to obey the order given by his State when the highest responsible official of the State is ordering such experiments for any specific purpose and defines expressly the circle of persons to be used. It is the duty of the State to keep its citizens free from danger as far as possible. It is the duty of the respective highest official of a State organization to take the necessary measures and to find new ways for newly appearing cases.[37]

To some degree, every defendant placed the responsibility for his ghastly deeds with the state, in a legal and ethical sense. Only Karl Brandt and Oskar Schroeder took partial responsibility for some of these deeds, Brandt for the euthanasia program and Schroeder for the seawater experiments. Brandt left no doubt about his view that he had acted out of pity for the suffering of incurably ill inmates of asylums whose "life was not worth living." Schroeder had been charged with many other experiments (high altitude, hypothermia, sulfanilamide, jaundice, typhus), which had resulted in hundreds of deaths, and taking responsibility for an experiment that had no fatality apparently was an attempt to exonerate himself of those that had.

No one admitted, despite much contrary evidence, that at least some of his experiments originated in his own mind. Only one defendant showed some sincere remorse: Fischer, for his surgical experiment on Polish women. But he was also the defendant who most adamantly insisted that he had no choice but to obey superior orders as a soldier in a situation of extreme emergency. Like all the other defendants, he also insisted that under ordinary circumstances he would not have performed these experiments and would have practiced medicine in accordance with the humane principles characteristic of peacetime.

Andrew Ivy admitted that U.S. physicians too had performed unusual experiments on prisoners to help the war effort, much to the apparent consternation of the justices on the bench, as the following exchange involving Ivy, Counselor Tipp, Prosecutor Alexander Hardy, and the Presiding Judge, Walter Beals, demonstrates:

Q. [Tipp] . . . If I understand you correctly, you said in the discussion of malaria experiments that such experiments on prisoners or COs were supposed to be for the good of the community; is that correct?

A. [Ivy] Well, now malaria experiments were not done on conscientious objectors to my knowledge, they were done on prisoners in the penitentiary.

Q. Yes, prisoners, but the results of these experiments, if I understood you correctly, were suppose to serve humanity. In other words, to express it differently, as Governor Green said according to your testimony, the State of Illinois carried out these experiments in order to help the United States win the war; is that correct?
A. Yes. In the case of the prisoners, they were motivated in order to help sick people with malaria, and in their comments they frequently referred to soldiers, or friends in the army. In the case of the conscientious objectors, their objective was to contribute to knowledge, knowledge for the prevention or alleviation of human suffering.

Q. Thus, you agree with me, Professor, that the statement can be made that the experiments were aimed at helping to win the war in these special sectors of medical research.
A. That was particularly true of the malaria experiments. It was not true of our minimum vitamin requirement experiments. There we had in mind rehabilitation of the stricken European areas. We wanted to know what food was best in relation to vitamin content, to supply people in the stricken areas, to keep them in good health. . . .

Q. (BY DR. TIPP): Professor Ivy, thus you recognize that necessities conditioned by war were a basis for experiments, do you not?
THE PRESIDENT [Beals]: I cannot see, Counsel, that these questions of cross-examination are particularly pertinent to the direct examination or the issues at present here.
DR. TIPP: If I may reply to this, Your Honor, briefly. The question of the experiments was raised, discussed repeatedly, and a number of my colleagues tried to point out that the experiments in part, or for the most part, were undertaken because of the necessities caused by wartime conditions. This point of view has so far not been recognized by the Prosecution, and I believe that the answer of the expert may clarify this matter considerably.
THE PRESIDENT: The Tribunal understands that situation. I don't know that Dr. Ivy is an expert who can testify on that subject. I think if you have no further pertinent questions, we might turn the cross-examination over to Dr. Weissgerber.
DR. TIPP: If Your Honor please, I have only one more question, since my time has been limited by the Tribunal. My question is the following: As you said, the voluntary nature of the experimental subject is the first basis for the admissibility of experiments on human beings altogether. To that extent I understood you correctly, did I not?
A. [Ivy] Yes, I think that should come first in the list of requirements.

Q. [Tipp] You stated today regarding the prerequisites for voluntary experiments on persons condemned to death that they are admissible from the ethical point of view, experiments of a nature that the condemned were given medical preparations which might have fatal consequences. Prof. Rose started this discussion: A volunteer was administered poison in this case. Is not such an experiment, however, in contradiction to the following sentence from out of Hippocrates: "I shall give no human being lethal poison, even if he asks me for it."
A. [Ivy] That, I believe, refers to the function of the physician as a therapist, not as an experimentalist, and the part that refers to the Oath of Hippocrates is that he must have respect for life and the human rights of his experimental patient.

Q. [Tipp] Thus, you believe that you have to differentiate between the physician as a therapist, that is, the curing physician, and the physician as a research worker; and thus you admit that in each of these functions different laws, different paragraphs of the Oath of Hippocrates apply.
A. [Ivy] Yes, I obviously do.
DR. TIPP: Thank you very much. In that case I have no further questions.[38]

Despite Beal's careful monitoring of Tipp's questions at the end, Tipp managed to get Ivy to concede that war-related experiments on inmates are justified and that the United States had conducted them as well, albeit on a smaller scale. However, Ivy left no doubt about his view hat no one should ever be subjected to an experiment against his will and that the defendants' unprecedented disregard for the concern of their subjects in no way could be compared to the American physicians' careful selection of volunteers.

Defense counsel Otto Nelte challenged Ivy on this point by contrasting his views with those of the prosecution's other medical expert, Werner Leibrandt.

Q. [Nelte] Professor Leibrandt was called before this Tribunal as an expert witness by the Prosecution and questions regarding professional medical ethics in the field of research were put to him. You have here testified that the prisoners' statements of consent, prisoners in American prisons, were to be regarded as volunteer statements of consent and that from the professional ethical point of view there could be no misgiving regarding such an act of consent, nor about having the experiments carried out; is that so?
A. [Ivy] Yes.

Q. I should like to put to you what the other prosecution expert witness said regarding this point before the Tribunal. He was asked: "Witness, are you of the view that a prisoner, who has been in prison for over ten years, will give his consent for an experiment if he receives no advantage from this; do you consider such consent to have been voluntarily given?" The expert witness answered: "No, according to medical ethics that is not the case, because the patient or the prisoner first of all finds himself in a state of coercion, since he is in preventive custody and secondly because he is a layman and has no way of calculating the effects of an operation on himself. As a layman, he is simply not in a position to do that."

Question: "Are you of the view that eight hundred prisoners, who are detained in various places and who give their consent for experiments do so voluntarily?"
Answer: "No."

Question: "You are not answering that in consideration of whether or not the experiment leads to lasting or only temporary injury to the prisoner?"
Answer: "Even in the last case, my answer is still no."

Question: "If such persons are inflicted with malaria, because they have declared their readiness, do you consider that possible?"
Answer: "No, because such voluntary statement of consent is not right from the point of view of medical ethics. These men, as prisoners, find themselves under a state of coercion."

Thereupon the witness was shown the magazine *Life*, 4 June 1944, and this is Document Karl Brandt no. 1. In this document, which I wish to touch on very briefly, it says that in the United States Prison in Atlanta, in the State Prison in Illinois, and in the Reform School in New Jersey, roughly 800 prisoners have declared their readiness to have themselves infected with malaria so that doctors could study the disease. And, in a further passage in this document it says that the malaria experiments in penitentiaries have shown that malaria is still a very serious medical problem and it says further on page 46 of the report: "Severe chills are the first symptoms of malaria. The above patient is an inmate of the Atlanta Penitentiary where malaria experiments were begun and developed." Then below, underneath, is the last picture under which the caption is "fever was as high as 106 degree, severe chills 20 to 60 minutes. One of the cases was allowed to proceed to a late stage before drugs were given to combat it." After the expert had seen this report, he was asked, "Please give your expert opinion on this experiment as regards medical permissibility."

Professor Leibrandt answered, "I cannot change my previously stated opinion about medical ethics involved. I am of the opinion that such experiments as these are an ill chosen form of biological thinking. And I point out particularly that when I made my testimony just now I agree with Ebermeier, the jurist, from his book *Der Arzt im Recht*, and I also pointed out that the patient when giving such approval cannot calculate the consequences of having given his consent and if on the basis of my own experience as a malaria therapeutist and as a psychiatrist, in which capacity I am accustomed to giving malaria cures to paralytics, then from this point of view I must say that malaria is a very serious disease because it has complications as a consequence, for instance severe spastic thrombosis or effects on the heart muscles that have death as a consequence. And it is my opinion that we are not dealing here with the infection of someone with a little sniffle but with a very serious disturbance which theoretically always may have death as a consequence. And in view of this, such experiments should be carried out on guinea pigs and not on human beings." Will you please say whether this attitude of Professor Leibrandt does not have an ethical foundation.

A. I do not agree with that statement of Professor Leibrandt. First, the prisoners, the experience with our prisoner volunteers in the United States is a fact showing that does not hold and, secondly, he assumes that prisoners cannot be motivated to take part in medical experiments by humanitarian incentives. This is contrary to our experience.
Mr. Hardy: Your honor, I might ask defense counsel just what he intends to prove by this examination.[39]

Nelte, of course, tried to prove the United States was in no position to point fingers, while the prosecution thought this could not even be a matter of serious discussion. When asked by his counsel what kind of experimental methods with human subjects should prevail generally, the main defendant Karl Brandt provided a summary of his views as follows:

Q. [Nelte] Witness, yesterday afternoon you were discussing your attitude toward experiments on human beings. Will you please say when such experiments in your opinion are permissible and what the guiding principles in such cases are?
A. [Brandt] I said yesterday that within medical scientific research in certain diseases and under certain conditions, in order to guarantee further developments, experiments on human beings are absolutely essential. I said there can be general reasons for this.

Of course, there can also be special reasons—I refer to the war—for special experiments and special work in certain directions.

It is a matter of course that before one undertakes a human experiment all possible animal experiments must be conducted first, and that the performance of an experiment on human beings requires all medical and human precautions.

I indicated briefly that one cannot judge retroactively from the result of an experiment its justification and that, vice versa, a negative result does not mean that the experiment as such was not justified.

If one does conduct experiments, they must be kept on as small a scale as possible and, on the other hand, must be sufficiently extensive that the results are certain. I believe there are two basic questions which one must consider if one intends to undertake a human experiment. That is the question of the "importance" and the question of the "unimportance." "Importance" is synonymous with "necessary," in the interests of humanity, which one must consider as represented by individuals.

Assuming that the experimental subject volunteers for the experiments as such is not dangerous, or is as little dangerous as is humanly possible, then I consider that such an experiment is not much disputed.

It is different when I do not say that the experiment is important, the subject is voluntary and the experiment is dangerous. If I say that the experiment is not important, a human experiment, seen from the point of view of the unimportant, is in my opinion impossible. That is, perhaps, the first point where one could actually speak of a crime. If the experiment is unimportant, the subject a volunteer, and the experiment is dangerous, this is nevertheless no justification for the execution of such an experiment, because it is in the first place unimportant.

The question becomes difficult as soon as the question of the voluntariness of the experimental subject is discussed in an experiment which is recognized as important. It is that the subject does not volunteer, even if the experiment as such is not dangerous. In such a case, the words 'not voluntary' must be defined, and one will come to different points of view.

Recently the question was discussed whether a prisoner can volunteer for an experiment. I do not want to take the definitely opposing view which was taken at the time, for I consider it quite possible that a prisoner may volunteer to have nondangerous experiments performed on his person, but from the moment when there is danger—that is, danger to the life of the experimental subject through the experiment-at that moment, the physician as such cannot alone decide whether or not to carry out the experiment. Here it is necessary that a superior authority give at least approval for such an experiment; that is, permit it.

Here the question of persons condemned to death becomes acute: whether the person condemned to death volunteers or not. I will leave that question open for the moment. The person is given an opportunity, a chance, and the decision is more or less left up to him.

These experiments will also be discussed where the importance of the experiment is recognized, the subject does not volunteer, and the experiment is dangerous, or, even if the subject volunteers, where the experiment is dangerous. It will probably be necessary to settle these questions basically, probably on an international basis, all the more because on the basis of the indications given in literature, every civilized state today—if one considers human experiments a crime—every state is guilty. I should like to say that the higher scientific research is carried, the further this development has progressed in a state, the greater would be the guilt. The purpose of an order for experiments would be given; the point of view would be established from which experiments can be conducted, and, in the third class, for the execution of the experiment itself, the necessary method would be established.[40]

As much as he avoided clear language on the most crucial point in his summary, namely the voluntariness of human subjects, he did endorse involuntary, meaning forced, dangerous experiments on human subjects, preferably on condemned prisoners, if they were deemed necessary and as long as the state would relieve the physician of any responsibility for harm inflicted on the subjects. Had he argued otherwise, i.e., had he argued with Leibrandt and Ivy that the subject's voluntariness and the physician's responsibility are untouchable essentials for any human experiment, he would have gravely incriminated himself and all of his codefendants.

One defendant, under intense questioning by the prosecution, did state the voluntariness of the subject, if not the physician's responsibility for dangerous experiments, should indeed always be such an essential element: Hermann Becker-Freyseng.

> Q. [Hardy] May it please the Tribunal, Dr. Becker-Freyseng, in the course of your direct examination you stated in regard to your position in so far as the experiments on human beings are concerned that you held three points and set forth three points which must be fulfilled prior to experimentation on human beings. As I understand it, point no. 1 was that the experiment must be necessary, that is, there is no other solution; point no. 2, the experiment must also have been well prepared and all research along these lines through animal experimentation has been exhausted, and you had perhaps model experiments and experiments on the physician himself; and no. 3, you stated medical actions. Would you kindly explain to me just what you meant by point no. 3?
> A. [Becker-Freyseng] I think my point no. 3 was that the experiments should be carried out in strict accordance with regular medical procedure.
>
> Q. Does the element of consent or the voluntary nature of the subject come into play?
> A. It does come into play and let me point out to you that when my counsel asked me this question, he explicitly said that in my answer I should leave this question of the voluntary consent of experimental subjects altogether out of my answer, and, therefore, I did not say anything at that time regarding the voluntary nature of the subjects. Later, however, I did go into the question of their consent and said I was convinced that prisoners could also be used as voluntary subjects.
>
> Q. Well then, if I understand you correctly, the ethical conditions under which you would act would be: no. 1, that the experiment must be necessary, that there is no other solution; no. 2, that it was well prepared through animal experimentation, model experiments, and self-experiments; and no. 3, that it was under the so-called medical action rule; and no. 4, the subjects must be volunteers?
> A. These are the conditions under which I consider the experimentation justified.
>
> Q. Who do you feel may volunteer for experiments?
> A. Anyone in full possession of his senses.

Q. Well, do you think somewhat along the same lines as Professor Rose, that perhaps only medical students or physicians should volunteer for experimentation?
A. No, it seems to me that any mentally normal person who can be told what the nature of the experiment is.

Q. Well, then, by that token it must be necessary for the physician to warn the experimental subject about the hazards of the experiments, is that true?
A. I should like to say that it should at least be explained to him.

Q. Then point no. 5 under Becker-Freyseng no. 1 is that the physician should advise the experimental subjects?
A. Let me point out that I had already included this condition under point 3 of my previous principles when answering questions put to me by Judge Sebring.

Q. Well now that we have your ethical principles clearly in mind, do you feel that every experiment which you instigated in the past followed these principles?
A. Since I instigated only one, namely the seawater experiment, I am convinced that what was done by me corresponds to the principles set forth.

Q. Do you feel that any experimental plan that did not comply with the ethical principles would be criminal?
A. You asked whether I believed any other experimental plan that did not meet the principles I set forth would be criminal—is that what you asked?

Q. That is what I asked, yes.
A. That I can't say because I knew nothing of my own knowledge of these plans for other experiments.
A. Well, do you think they would be unethical? Any experiments which did not meet the regulations as set forth by you here on this witness stand?
A. I can't answer that question either because to do so I should have to know all of the conditions and I don't know them.[41]

It is highly improbable that Becker-Freyseng was ignorant of everything else but the seawater experiments. He was also charged with violations in high-altitude, hypothermia, and typhus experiments, but evidence to convict him beyond reasonable doubt existed only with espect to the seawater experiments. The tribunal found that the inmate subjects had not volunteered, as he claimed.

As indicated in the prosecutor's questions to Becker-Freyseng, Gerhard Rose argued that physicians, and those studying to be physicians, should conduct human experiments only on themselves, at least during the initial dangerous phases. Such practice would resolve the question of responsibility most economically since the lay public would not be subjected to any harm and would only enjoy the research benefits. He testified self-experimentation was indeed quite common at his place of work, the Robert-Koch Institut in Berlin, and he had personally experimented with several dangerous viruses. None of the other defendants, many of whom had performed experiments on themselves as well, advanced such a strict position, which Rose nevertheless abandoned during the war, when he designed typhus experiments for inmates at the Buchenwald concentration camp.

But as much as the prosecution demonstrated the defendants, unlike the medical researchers they so frequently invoked, had shown willful and gross neglect of traditional Western codes of medical ethics, it could not dispel an emerging recognition that these codes in many respects lacked sufficient concreteness and, if anything, were in dire need of clear, universally binding and enforceable definitions.

As much as possible, the defendants tried to gain advantage of this by moving the discussion into this perceived gray zone. There can be little doubt that no interpretive stretch of any set of medical codes or discussion of ethical gray zones could justify the acts of the defendant Hoven, whose wanton killings of Buchenwald inmates, in fact, were prompted not by medical motives but by a plain desire to gain near absolute power over the inmates' lives. Unlike Sigmund Rascher and Josef Mengele, who were not sitting in the defense dock, Hoven had not even performed what Robert Jay Lifton called "medicalized killings," but had used his position as camp physician to create a fiendish system of personal terror over helpless victims of whom many ended up dead for a variety of reasons.

If the defense dock had been filled with the likes of Hoven, Mengele, and Rascher, the Medical Trial would have been a somber but morally and politically trivial exercise in expelling human madness from a society eager to reembrace sanity. But the defense dock contained men like Rose and Rostock, physicians who had shown commitment to individualistic medicine before they decided to compromise it in favor of totalitarian medicine during, and largely as a result of, the war. Rose, for instance, objected to the use of human subjects in dangerous experiments as late as May 1943, when the tide of war had turned decidedly against Germany and open criticism could be branded as defeatism and even treason.

However, at the Third Meeting of Consulting Physicians of the Armed Forces, held in Berlin in May of 1943, Rose openly protested Ding-Schuler's use of inmates for dangerous typhus experiments at Buchenwald. According to one witness, Felix Hoering, his position was unequivocal.[42] Both had been present at Ding-Schuler's presentation on his experiments with various typhus vaccines. The presentation contained no direct reference to the use of human subjects, certainly not to the forced subjection of concentration camp inmates to frequently fatal inoculations. But this practice could easily be surmised by any attentive listener and was brought to the attention of the audience by Rose.

According to Hoering:

A. [Hoering] After Dr. Ding's lecture there followed a discussion. The discussion was opened by Professor Rose. He, at first, referred briefly to the material substance of the lecture which he, by and large, recognized. He emphasized, however, that this was a question of experiments on human beings and that a number of people had lost their lives as a result. Using rather strong words, he pointed out that any such procedure was a deviation from procedures used for decades in the research of immunity. He said that this was an extremely serious matter and that the hygienists would have to maintain their old principles. Professor Rose spoke for a long time and spoke in sharp words. Naturally, I can no longer recall his words in detail, but I am sure that he voiced the substance of what I have just said. In accordance with his temperament, he did this in strong words which went beyond the customary exchange of words used during such discussions. At any rate, every participant in this meeting was well aware that this was an incident of almost sensational character. For that reason, after the end of that session and during the subsequent days, this incident was discussed among small circles and I can well remember that.

Q. [Counsel Fritz] What happened as a result of this speech by Professor Rose? I am now referring to the time of the discussion.
A. The lecturer, Dr. Ding, replied to Professor Rose and defended his experiments. He admitted that this was a question of experiments on human beings but said that the experimental subjects were criminals who had all been condemned to death. Professor Rose thereupon once more replied, saying that this didn't change anything in his criticism. He said that we were here concerned with a basic question. Thereupon the discussion was rather suddenly stopped by Professor Schreiber. Generalarzt Schreiber said that if the gentlemen wanted to discuss basic ethical questions, then they would have ample opportunity to do that after the meeting. In the printed report of the meeting which I read these discussion remarks were not printed.[43]

The report does cite the comments of one participant Kroeger who remarked "the concerns expressed by Rose, who advises against the use of mixed vaccines because of their strong side effects, cannot be shared."[44] Rose himself is cited as having warned the meeting's participants that, "since it has been established that differently produced typhus vaccines have the same effect, it is our duty to maximize efficiency and concentrate on the production of the type of vaccine that has the comperatively highest yield with the lowest cost (Aufwand) in terms of men and material, to fill the demand that still persists today."[45]

However sincere Rose's warning against "dangerous side effects" of certain vaccines and his more general concern for minimizing any harm to experimental subjects may have been, he compromised it only seven months later, when he initiated experiments with newly developed typhus vaccines himself, carried out between April and June of 1944 by Ding-Schuler on twenty-six Buchenwald inmates, of whom six died.[46]

According to his testimony at the trial, this did not mean that Rose abandoned his concerns or stopped voicing objections to inhumane treatment of human subjects in general. At a medical meeting at the Military Medical

Academy in Berlin in October of 1944, he apparently objected to the use of human subjects for influenza experiments, which, he claimed, were later carried out on German prisoners-of-war by British authorities.[47]

Asked by his own counsel why he had objected, Rose stated the following reasons. He refrained from using human subjects for his epidemiological experiments for fear of setting an irreversible precedent that could lead to an unquestioned relegation of men to the status of guinea pigs. "I know what enormous advantage a research worker would have if we were perfectly at liberty to carry out human being experiments," he explained to the court, "but here, as the advantage was evident to my reasoning, nevertheless my emotions revolted against it."[48] The least conscientious and most eager researchers, the "research fanatics," he warned, quickly move into this most volatile and important area of medicine, obviously attempting to draw a distinct line between himself and such physicians as Ding and Rascher.

The conscientious researcher may not be spared the agony of conducting dangerous human research when the reasons are sufficiently compelling, as during times of war and at the request of higher authorities. To illustrate his point, Rose referred to the initial freezing experiments Ernst Holzloehner had conducted together with Sigmund Rascher and Erwin Finke on fifty to sixty Dachau inmates, supposedly condemned volunteers, of which 15–18 died.[49] Holzloehner objected to the experiments and eventually, together with Finke, withdrew his participation, but not before reporting on them at the Freezing Conference (Aerztliche Fragen bei Seenot und Winternot) in October 1942 at Nuremberg.

"I happened to speak with Professor Holzloehner, at Nuernberg," Rose reported, " . . . and saw what an enormous spiritual burden was placed on Professor Holzloehner by having to go through this experience, because even a person condemned to death is a human being."[50] Trying to demonstrate the ethical dilemma the supposed conscientious researchers like Holzloehner and he must face when asked to weigh possible benefits of human research against calculable harm done to the subjects, especially during times of dire emergencies, Rose again tried to expose the perceived ethical dilemma of the American court that sat in judgment over German physicians for violations of principles that had gone unpunished when committed by Americans.

Rose also defended the honorable intentions and described the mental burden suffered by Richard Strong when he conducted beri-beri experiments on prison inmates in Manila forty years earlier, which had caused one fatality. "I know the man and the conditions under which he worked," Rose explained. "The driving force was alone a feeling of duty and responsibility to the millions of natives for whose health he was responsible, who were dying by the hundreds and thousands of this terrible plague and the hundreds and thousands that were suffering terrible pain from beri-beri disease."[51]

Rose, who accused his judges and prosecutors on a number of occasions of insensitivity to the difficult dilemmas medical experimenters routinely face in their research, apparently tried to place them on the ethical slippery slope he felt he himself had been on during the troubling years of the war. For example, he described his purported objection to a request made by the Reich Physician Leader Leonardo Conti in March 1942 to test typhus vaccines, which he had helped develop at the Robert-Koch Institut, on Buchenwald inmates. Realizing the high risks subjects would face, he objected and went to Conti to ask whether the experiments were absolutely necessary. At the trial Rose recalled:

> Conti said in answer that he too had had misgivings before he had decided to take this step. The seriousness of the danger of typhus, however, made extraordinary measures necessary. In the Government General, that is, in Occupied Poland, a serious typhus epidemic had already broken out. The Russian prisoners of war had, to a considerable extent, brought typhus into the Reich territory. In all posts, camps and prisons within the Reich there had already been local epidemics. How it was in the Wehrmacht [Armed Forces] I had to know better than he, he said, but he had had rather extremely disturbing news from that source too.
>
> According to the experience of the Ministry, hundreds of thousands of human lives were at stake and he, the State Secretary, and not the scientists, had the responsibility for the measures that had to be taken. In view of this emergency, he had had to subordinate his misgivings just as I had. He could not wait for epidemiological statistics, which might give a clear answer only after years or perhaps only after decades according to experience. He could not wait so long if there was a possibility, with a small cost in human lives, to learn the correct measures to protect hundreds of thousands.[52]

The analogies to Strong's beri-beri experiments are obvious. Strong too had tried to fight an epidemic by subjecting inmates to dangerous experiments, and there like here, in the eyes of Rose, the legal responsibilities for their execution rested with civil authorities, not the researcher, there with the Governor of the Philippines, here with the State Secretary. Who, Rose asked, given the larger responsibility of saving the lives of uncounted innocents, many of whom helped preserve society through personal risk and sacrifice, would decide differently, especially at times of war, and protect the interests of those who had harmed society instead? In fact, Rose argued his own resolve in facing the dilemma while trying to preserve Hippocratic principles deserved praise of the kind already given to men like Strong.

Much like Rose, most of the defendants tried to portray themselves as researchers or public health officials who had agonized over the purportedly inescapable problem of having to weigh the relative harm to be suffered by multitudes of people against that of a much smaller, supposedly less worthy group of people. Researchers had faced this situation for centuries, they argued, although never on the scale imposed by the events of World War II. Given their apocalyptic dimensions, the decisions taken could hardly have been otherwise, and the defendants expected the court to understand the compelling reasons for this tradeoff, even if the court was bent on, as they charged, victor's justice.

After all, the prosecution's chief medical expert at the trial, Andrew Ivy, in an apparent effort to defend the record of American researchers like Strong, had confirmed that in certain conditions potentially harmful medical experiments could be performed on prison inmates. This affirmation had placed Ivy on the same slippery slope on which defendants like Rose and Rostock felt they had been pulled down by the brutal demands of the war.

Karl Brandt, who accepted responsibility for the killing of tens of thousands of asylum inmates under Hitler's so-called euthanasia order, tried to take the court on his descent down the slippery slope by enlisting its empathy for his professed concern for alleviating the suffering of the hopelessly impaired and those who care for them. His initial step onto the slope was even initiated by others, months before Hitler signed the euthanasia order.

Brandt stated:

> "The father of a deformed child approached the Fuehrer and asked that this creature should be killed. Hitler turned this matter over to me and told me to go to Leipzig immediately—it had taken place in Leipzig—to confirm the fact. It was a child who was born blind, an idiot—at least it seemed to be an idiot—and it lacked one leg and part of one arm."[53]

Brandt characterized his role in the affair as that of a passive assistant.

> "He [Hitler] gave me the order to talk with the physicians who were taking care of the child and to, first of all, test the statements of the father as to their veracity. If they were correct, then in his name I was to inform the physicians that they were permitted to carry out euthanasia. . . . The physicians maintained the point of view that the keeping alive of such a child could actually not be justified, and it was pointed out in this respect that in maternity wards under circumstances by doctors themselves in such a case euthanasia would be performed without anything further being said about it."[54]

Brandt apparently hoped the predicament of the father would not leave the fathers on the judge's bench unaffected, who might even imagine his relief when "euthanasia would be performed without anything further being said about it." But everyone in the courtroom knew that only months after this isolated case, in January 1940, thousands of mental patients would be killed—first by injection, shooting, and later by gassing—under Brandt's supervision, and without the approval, and often against the express wishes of, parents and other family members. In the meantime, Hitler and his generals had started World War II, an event that more than anything else made possible this largely camouflaged mass destruction of life.

Brandt attempted to convince the court that his crucial role in this destruction manifested nothing but continuous concern for the hopelessly ill:

If anybody wants to judge the question of euthanasia he must go into an insane asylum and should stay there with the sick people for a few days. Then one can ask him two questions. The first would be whether he himself would like to live like that, and the second, whether he would ask one of his relatives to live that way—perhaps his child or his parents. The answer cannot be connected with the concept of demonic order but it will be a deeply felt gratitude for his own health and the question of whether it is more humane to help such a being to find a peaceful end or to care for it further—*this answer results without being expressed.* In this connection I have a reference to literature where it says about having a child with a hereditary brain disease kept alive for three and one-half years and that this creature screamed for three and one-half years. I see nothing particularly humane in this. [My italics].[55]

If Brandt did indeed express his true conviction on the subject of euthanasia rather than produce a carefully crafted appeal to the judge's emotions to save his neck, his slide, or rather his fall down the slippery slope of human destruction becomes disturbingly apparent. Would not the death of the screaming child be a relief, to the child as well as those who had to listen? And should not those who did not have to listen, like the judges, be subjected to the screams first before being allowed to judge? If anyone, should not the caretakers of the incurably ill and disabled be authorized to determine, Brandt poses, how "to help such a being to find a peaceful end or to care for it further"?

And if the leaders of a society decide to go to war and to subject millions of its citizens to injury and death, would this not affect quality and quantity of care for all, worsening the already intolerable lot of the incurably ill and disabled? Have acts of warfare not eroded the principles by which human beings, incurably ill and disabled included, normally treat each other? Can decisions made under such conditions to end the suffering of the incurably ill and the disabled with a "peaceful end" be judged by the principles that prevail during peacetime? For Brandt, and many of his colleagues, the answer to such rhetorical questions seemed obvious.

Once the decision had been made to end a human life for the benefit of the person whose life was taken, and for those who had to provide for his care, he had begun his descent on a very slippery slope, and the answers to the rest of the questions seemed obvious as well. It may be possible that his eventual order to apply large-scale euthanasia was not so much the result of a slow and agonizing process characterized by waging pros and cons but more the result of a sudden decision, urged perhaps by policies preparing Germany for war.

Either way, Brandt insisted throughout the trial that his intentions regarding the incurably ill were nothing but honorable. This insistence may easily be dismissed, of course, as blatant cynicism. What Brandt called incurably ill his associate Pfannmueller, for instance, called "useless eaters," and there would be enough evidence to suggest that Brandt may have thought the same. Few of the more than 60,000 asylum inmates killed at his direction were as severely ill and incurable as he generally described them, something of which he hardly could have been unaware, despite the fact that he himself did not directly select asylum inmates for euthanasia. This was done at his authorization by specially designated physicians. Many inmates were only lightly impaired. Their large-scale killing was, as it turned out, only a rehearsal for the genocide of other groups that also seemed to be a burden to the leaders of the Hitler regime.

Some later researchers, most notably Hartmut Hanauske-Abel, have rejected the slippery slope explanation, or the sudden decision argument. "The slippery slope argument," he writes fifty years after the war, "dovetails with the 'sudden subversion' concept, prevalent inside Germany and for decades aggressively promoted as the official view by the [German] Chamber of Physicians."[56] Hanauske-Abel suggests that the 1933 electoral victory of the National Socialists created new political, economic and scientific conditions that allowed opportunists of all colors to leapfrog into positions of dominance: "Instead of steady change there is a suddenly altered condition; instead of a series of intermittent states there is leapfrog transition. These observations are all qualitative descriptors for a quantum jump."[57] A quantum jump to a state of evil?

Possibly. Anyone engaged in inhuman acts such as the defendants were accused of was most likely devoid of any sense of decency and compassion. In the Hitler regime he probably owed his position to the ruthless pursuit of power. But to rule out the possibility that some men, such as Rose, Rostock and Brandt, may indeed have acted, if only in the beginning, on less execrable, and perhaps even honorable, principles deprives society of invaluable insights into human nature and possible lessons for the future. But why would these men not halt their descent down, or step off, the slope when they must have realized that it led to the pits of Dante's inferno?

Rose suggested he felt he had to stay in a system he personally detested so he could help to prevent even worse atrocities. By way of analogy, he appealed to the judges' sense of duty to uphold laws they personally may find objectionable. Referring to the assignment he received from Gildemeister to test typhus vaccines on Dachau inmates in which six persons died, he explained:

> At that moment I was in a position which perhaps corresponds to a lawyer who is perhaps a fundamental opponent of execution, or the death penalty. On occasion when he is dealing with leading members of the government, or with lawyers during public congresses or meetings, he will do everything in his power to maintain his opinion of the subject and have it put into effect. If, however, he does not succeed, he stays in his profession, and in his environment in spite of this. Under the circumstances he may perhaps even be forced to pronounce such a death sentence himself, although he is basically an opponent of such a set-up.[58]

In a different context Rose explained that relinquishing control over crucial research would only allow the less competent, generally also the politically more ambitious, person to take over, worsening the situation for all involved.

Beiglboeck, who had conducted seawater experiments on Gypsies, voiced concern for his family when responding to questions by his counsel:

> Q. [Counsel Steinbauer] Why didn't you refuse to carry out the order?
> A. [Beiglboeck] Because I had been given a military order.
>
> Q. And were you afraid that something would happen to your family, as you said in direct examination?
> A. I was afraid if I said, after I had inquired whether it was a military order, and said "I won't carry it out," I was afraid that I would be called to account for refusal to obey orders. That is customary.
>
> Q. Well now, if you had refused the order and had been brought to trial, just what would have happened to your wife and child?
> A. That depends on how the court martial turned out. It would have been possible for me to be condemned to death for refusing to obey an order and then my wife and children would have been helpless.[59]

Beiglboeck initially had objected to performing experiments on Dachau inmates but ultimately was ordered by Becker-Freyseng to proceed. His expressed fear that refusal of the order could have had adverse consequences not only for himself but also for his family may have been a matter of perception at the time, if not a retroactive justification for his acts now that he was on trial. But with the exception of possible setbacks in his military career, such consequences would have been unlikely.

There is no record of any court martial for refusal to conduct or assist in human experiments during the entire time of the Hitler regime. This suggests the experimenting physicians were likely not ordered to perform experiments, but rather they designed such experiments themselves and sought administrative approval for them later. Those whose loyalty to the regime and its professed goals may have been questionable were unlikely to be asked to participate in this gruesome work. Evidence shows even when they were asked or ordered to participate and refused, no repercussions followed.

For example, in December 1941, Weltz, Ruff, Romberg, and Rascher met to plan the first human experiments to be conducted on concentration camp inmates, the high-altitude experiments subsequently performed at Dachau. Present also were Wolfgang Lutz, an Air Force physician, and a researcher named Wendt, both staff members of Weltz's Institute for Aviation Medicine in Munich, who, apparently upon learning the true nature of their assignment, refused cooperation. Their decision was accepted and they continued their preferred experimentations on animals only. At the trial Lutz appeared as a witness for the prosecution, giving the following account of his role at the time:

> Q. [Prosecutor McHaney] Did Weltz offer you the opportunity to do high-altitude research on human beings in the Dachau concentration camp?
> A. [Lutz] Yes, Weltz asked Wendt and me whether we wanted to conduct such experiments.
>
> Q. Did you accept or refuse this offer?
> A. Both of us refused.
>
> Q. Why did you refuse?
> A. I personally primarily because I did not consider myself robust enough to conduct such experiments. . . .
>
> Q. And you state that you refused the offer of Weltz to work on human beings in Dachau because you were not ruthless enough-is that right.
> A. Yes.
>
> Q. I take it that this means that you know that brutality and ruthlessness would be required to do the work in Dachau.
> A. Yes, I mean an experiment involving a certain danger for the experimental subject, of course, to a certain extent, ruthless, shall I say?[60]

Lutz remained on Weltz' staff until the end of the war and attained the rank of Air Force captain, the same rank reached by Beiglboeck, who had not refused to conduct human experimentation, as well as Rascher, next to Josef Mengele and Erwin Ding-Schuler perhaps the most ruthless among the "human researchers." Neither does Wendt seem to have suffered adverse consequences.

Weltz, too, could have withdrawn from the Dachau experiments performed under the auspices of his institute when the involuntary nature of the human subjects and the real danger to their health and lives must have become obvious. Though an instigator of the experiments himself, he apparently had not intended to subject the Dachau inmates to forced and fatal treatment, at least not initially.

Before the war Weltz had been a lecturer of aviation medicine at the University of Munich, where he headed a small experimental department at the Physiology Institute. Because the Air Force wanted to conduct various classified research for a design of high-altitude planes, it appropriated the Institute in the summer of 1941 and renamed it the Institute for Aviation Medicine. So far, experiments had been conducted on Air Force volunteers, including Weltz himself, who claimed that he tried to continue this practice with the new assignment as well, but with little success.

Air Force volunteers apparently became scarce for two reasons. Increasing war efforts, especially along the eastern front, tied up most of the soldiers. More importantly, experiments at uncharted simulated heights increased the subjects' risks to health and life considerably. Weltz therefore eventually demanded the use of Dachau volunteers at the suggestion of his assistant Rascher. As a member of not only the Air Force but the SS as well, Rascher already had obtained support for this move from Himmler, the highest legal authority over all concentration camps. Himmler had stipulated that Rascher, who was not an expert in aviation medicine, be included in the research.

At the time, no experiments had been conducted on inmates yet, and, given the circumstances, the suggestion apparently did not seem without complete merit. At the trial, Weltz insisted he only considered the use of volunteers from among criminals condemned to death and he personally visited the Dachau camp to confirm this condition was met.

To ensure the best research results, Siegfried Ruff, the foremost German expert in aviation medicine and head of the Department for Aviation Medicine at the German Experimental Institute for Aviation, was asked to cooperate in the project. Ruff sent his principal assistant, Hans Romberg, who worked closely with Weltz's assistant Rascher. Rascher and Romberg performed the first experiments on themselves.

In low-pressure chambers they remained for many minutes at simulated altitudes above 12,000 meters, but increasing pain stopped them from ascending above 13,500 meters, i.e., below the new airplane's planed maximum altitude.[61] Their superiors, Weltz and Ruff, carried supervisory responsibilities but did not participate in these experiments themselves and apparently left their assistants to conduct them at their own discretion. Rascher and Romberg then, in accordance with the earlier determined research plan, used inmates as subjects.[62]

Rascher, in charge of conducting the experiments, quickly showed gross disregard for human life in explosive decompression and rapid-descent experiments that pushed the subjects to the threshold of physical endurance. At the trial, Romberg described his response to Rascher's first attempt to determine that threshold by terminating the life of the subject by keeping him for a fatal period of time at high altitude. Rascher operated the controls as Romberg looked on.

Q. [Prosecutor Hardy] Well now, while Rascher was operating those controls, could he himself see the electrocardiogram?
A. [Romberg] Yes, he could.

Q. Well now, could you with your arms reach out and indicate to the Tribunal how far the controls were from the electrocardiogram, how far away was he from this physically. Was he where he could look over and study it here, and just what was his position with reference to the electrocardiogram.

A. Yes, I can show you. Here [pointing] was the window where Rascher was watching the experiment, and to the left, about that far, was the machine which he had to regulate the altitude, and to the right was the electrocardiogram.

Q. Why couldn't you just reach right over there and turn that wheel and save that man's life?
A. I said to Rascher he should go down.

Q. I am asking you a question: Why couldn't you? You were standing at the electrocardiogram. You weren't ten miles away. Why couldn't you have reached over and turned that wheel and saved that man's life, you could have, couldn't you?
A. If I said that to him and he didn't do it—then I would not have been able to achieve anything by force. I would have had to beat him down, or something. . . .

Q. Well, now, after this person died, you make it ridiculous that you might well have reported him to the police for murder. Why didn't you do that? It is a logical thing to do when a man commits murder. It isn't so ridiculous to turn in a murderer.
A. It looks like murder now, and now that we know all about it we can decide that, but at the time I knew that Rascher was a Stabsarzt [medical officer with the rank of captain] of the Luftwaffe. . . .

Q. Let me ask you one question. When you saw this dead man, what did it look like then? It might look like murder now, right in this courtroom, but you saw that dead man lying there—what did it look like then?
A. It was an experiment with fatal result. Such experiments do happen in the world, and nobody says it is murder. . . .

Q. So then you reported this death and all these deaths, as a matter of fact—but you reported this first death to Ruff immediately, didn't you?
A. Yes.

Q. What did he do about it? Did he call the police?
A. No, he said himself, he did not. The police were not competent in the case of Rascher. He was a member of the Luftwaffe; Luftwaffe courts were competent. Ruff reported it to Rascher and his superior, the Chief of the Medical Service.

Q. Well, then, after the first death, how does it happen that Romberg didn't turn up his coat collar and go out to get in the tractor part of the chamber and drive it to Berlin? Why didn't you get that chamber right out there immediately? You saw deaths there. Why did you stay around?
A. We talked about that for a long time, and as Ruff mentioned that, we deliberated what we should do. It was clear that Ruff would report it; we didn't have to think about that. We also realized that we would achieve nothing with Himmler by going to him and saying Rascher performed an experiment and a person died. Himmler would have probably said, "I know, I gave him the orders. That is none of your business."
For this reason we decided that I should go back, that our experiments should be completed so that we could say the experiments had been concluded; the chamber will not be needed any more. And then, in this way, after the experiments were concluded and Rascher gave his approval and Himmler gave his approval—the chamber could be removed from Dachau to make further work impossible.[63]

But until then, at least two more deaths occurred with Romberg's purportedly reluctant participation, and perhaps ten more in experiments that Rascher conducted by himself. Eventually Ruff and Romberg dissociated themselves from Rascher, and Weltz arranged Rascher's ouster from his institute. However, a precedent had been set.

Himmler had opened the gates of the concentration camps to anyone in search of human guinea pigs, allowing, and often encouraging, such murderous designs as pursued by the likes of Rascher, Ding, and Mengele, younger members of his SS organization with all the traits of serial killers. But they were also open to reputable physicians like Rose and Beiglboeck, who apparently felt that they could justify tradeoffs between the subjection of inmates to high-risk medical experiments on the one hand and vitally needed knowledge to help perhaps thousands of others on the other. These physicians soothed their conscience with the knowledge that large-scale experiments on prison inmates had already been pioneered by American physicians, even if under less exigent circumstances. Some discontinued their human research in camps when it produced the first fatal victims, if not under the most honorable conditions, as the prosecutor showed in the case of Romberg.

Many observers will remain deeply troubled that these physicians who demonstrated some measure of human concern did descend down the slippery slope of medical ethics in a professed search for effective solutions to larger, war-related medical problems, and that at a time when the system they served had become blatantly murderous. Their testimony to the contrary notwithstanding, none of the defendants could have been ignorant of the routine mass killings at places like Auschwitz and Treblinka, whose beginnings coincided with the beginning of medical experiments on inmates not by mere chance.

Josef Mengele's twin studies, Horst Schumann's x-ray experiments and August Hirt's skeleton collection cannot be isolated from the large-scale extermination of Auschwitz inmates. Rose's insistence that he protested against dangerous human experiments all through the war and Beiglboeck's claim that he agreed to conduct such experiments to protect his family, however genuine, pale against the knowledge they must have had of the mass murder in which they were participating to various degrees. Perhaps the more appropriate question to ask is not why the defendants with a past commitment to Hippocratic principles stepped on and slid down the slippery slope of medical ethics, but why they did not immediately object to, and perhaps physically oppose, the system that slaughtered thousands of innocents on a daily basis.

When Roberk was asked by his counsel, Bernhard Vorwerk, "[a]t that time, was there any possibility in Germany to resist?" Romberg replied

"[t]here were only three types of resistance possible. First of all, for a person who was able, emigration. Second, open resistance, which meant concentration camp or death penalty and, to my knowledge, never had any success. Third, passive resistance, the apparent giving in, delaying orders, criticism among one's friends—what the writers are now calling 'inner immigration'."[64]

Romberg, like millions of others in similar circumstances, claimed to have chosen the third course. The prosecutor Alexander Hardy asked him: "You saw deaths there. Why did you stay around?" His response was that "we would achieve nothing with Himmler by going to him and saying Rascher performed an experiment and a person died. . . . [We] decided that I should go back . . . after the experiment was concluded, Rascher gave his approval and Himmler gave his approval—the chamber could be removed from Dachau to make further work impossible." That "passive resistance" cost at least twelve people's lives.

Afterward, the undaunted Rascher switched to freezing experiments, where he, with similar resistance from his new superior, Ernst Holzloehner, and his coworker, Erwin Finke, killed nearly one hundred Dachau inmates. Holzloehner and Finke concluded their experiments after, not necessarily because, at least six, and perhaps as many as eighteen, inmates had died of cold temperatures, and after they had reported on their findings at a conference in Nuremberg in October 1942.[65] Rascher then continued what he called the "terminal experiments" by himself, killing many more.

When Holzloehner presented the report of the experiments he had directed, it likely left little doubt the deaths to which it referred were hardly accidental. Becker-Freyseng was in the audience. When asked by his counsel: "Did any one of the participants in this meeting protest publicly against Holzloehner's lecture either before, during, or after the lecture?" he replied:

A. [Becker-Freyseng] No, I may say in that connection at that time I would not at all have understood any such protest had it been made. According to the Document, which is available here, fifty-five members of the Luftwaffe were present during that meeting, twelve representatives of the Army, four representatives of the Navy, four of the Waffen SS and Police, and nineteen civilians, that is, university professors and other gentlemen.

Q. [Counsel Tipp] If I may summarize briefly, witness, you are saying that you would have considered any protest senseless because you made no observations whatsoever that even could have hinted at crimes. None of the leading experts of Germany, who no doubt were present, made any such observations because no one in effect protested, is that true?
A. Yes, that is quite correct.[66]

Why the complicity of silence? Reasons included the pressure to conform, the urge to win the war, the ultimate amnesty expected to come with victory, the fear of reprisals, etc. Whatever the reasons may have been, the men in these circumstances confronted atrocities, some for the first time, and condoned them, either as individuals or as members of larger groups.

Among the lessons to be learned from the Medical Trial, one may consist in acknowledging, if not understanding, the sense of inevitability that apparently muted the judgment of many who should have known better. Most of them felt that all bridges had been burned behind them, especially with the "battle of destiny" Germany had forced upon the U.S.S.R. in June 1941, and that resistance would not change the outcome, be it victory or defeat. Most physicians who committed themselves to serving the Hitler regime adopted a collectivist form of medical ethics, which, in their mind, justified the sacrifice of the individual for the benefit of the larger community. With this they had, in varying degrees, adopted a mainstay of a fascist society in which people are either victors or vanquished. They chose to be victors, became persecutors of innocents, and helped place their whole society up on a path that ended in the calculated extermination of millions.

Romberg mused in court whether he, given the benefit of hindsight, would act differently upon witnessing the first experimental subject die if the same situation were to occur again.

> Q. [Counsel Vorwerk] . . . I would like to ask you, assuming the case you would find yourself in a similar position today, would you take the same attitude as you did then?
> A. [Romberg] That is, of course, extremely difficult because the conditions are different now. I know Rascher—I know the whole situation. I have, of course, often thought about that point. If, [given] my present knowledge, I were put in the same situation, I am certain that I would act differently. I would probably go to Berlin after the death and report it, and then would go home, get a medical certificate saying that I was sick, and write to Dachau and say that I could not come back. Whatever Rascher did then and however the experiments turned out, the main thing would be I would be out of it, then I would probably have spared myself the one and a half years in prison and the trial.
>
> Q. Is that your true opinion?
> A. If I think over what I said, one of course often imagines that, but I really don't believe I would do that because one can't act against one's inner conviction. I would probably not take the cold calculating view and let everything take its course. I would probably go back just the way I did and carry out the experiments, see to it that the chamber could be taken away. I would probably do everything just the way I did it then.[67]

All defendants shared the view they could not have acted differently, given the circumstances of the war and their commitment to ensure, as they claimed, nothing less than the survival of their threatened society. They had, by and large, accepted the do-or-die view of National Socialism and its rejection of absolute values, including medical ethical principles, save national survival itself. They had lost the war and considered the legal proceedings against them nothing more than victor's justice, an act of revenge rather than an attempt to punish violators of universally applicable principles of humanity.

Admitting otherwise would perhaps lead to a more lenient sentence, but it would legitimize the existence of the court, would acknowledge past errors in judgment, and would amount to admission of personal guilt. Instead they argued that within the scope of their experience they had acted correctly and offered themselves as legal martyrs of a selfless cause, hoping perhaps thereby to turn the tables of right and wrong.

Karl Brandt, in his last words before his execution on June 2, 1948, decried his death as an act of vengeance by a nation that had crushed its victims with the unchecked power unleashed in Hiroshima and Nagasaki. "Power rules," he said, "and power wants victims. I am such a victim."[68]

Ultimately the defendants, like millions of others who supported the Hitler regime, saw themselves as victims of the war. And the war, according to official National Socialist doctrine, had been imposed upon Germany by the victors of World War I with their unacceptable "dictate of Versailles." Seeing Germany itself as the victim of a supposed international conspiracy not only seemed to necessitate the subsequent war to save the nation but also to justify such brutal steps as those taken by the defendants.

Without the war, men like Rose and Romberg would have been unlikely to step on the slippery slope of human experimentation that lead to torture and death. But they did step on to it, and in full knowledge of the chilling consequences it had for their human subjects, despite their supposed reluctance and occasional halfhearted protests. Equally, without the war, potential mass murderers like Rascher and Mengele, who were not sitting in the dock, and Hoven and Sievers, who were sitting in the dock, could not have pursued their slaughter of camp inmates as professed biological soldiers for an envisioned Aryan empire. For all one can surmise, they would have become respectable physicians and researchers, practicing their trade within the limits of traditional Hippocratic principles, as many like them have done before and since, in Germany and everywhere else.

In fact, nearly all the physicians who were implicated in wartime atrocities-and there were thousands-quickly returned to the conventional type of medicine they generally had practiced before the war, concealing their sordid past as well as they could. Trial and imprisonment merely delayed or interrupted that transition.[69] Some, like Leonardo Conti and Hans Eppinger, committed suicide, and some, like Josef Mengele and Werner Hayde, went into hiding.

The twenty-three defendants in the Medical Trial represented the tip of the iceberg of the great number of physicians who in various ways had eagerly promoted and given active support to National Socialist medical doctrines and the many policies and projects that derived from it. The medical profession as a whole had indeed become one of the staunchest pillars of the Hitler regime.[70]

After the war, many members of the profession disseminated through medical publications the view that atrocities had been committed by only a handful of renegades. The rest supposedly had delivered the best individual and communal health care possible despite the prevailing apocalyptic conditions. In 1946 the president of the Working Association of the West German Physicians' Chambers (Arbeitsgemeinschaft der Westdeutschen Aerztekammern) asked the psychiatrist Alexander Mitscherlich, then head of the German Physicians' Committee at the First American Military Tribunal in Nuremberg, to produce a report on the forthcoming Medical Trial. He, together with his assistant Fred Mielke, finished it by the end of 1948, one year after the trial's conclusion. It contains an overwhelming number of trial documents, selected to demonstrate not merely the blatant brutality of the defendant's deeds, but also the process of dehumanization of victims that in the eyes of the authors allowed the perpetrators to insulate themselves from the horrors they inflicted on their human subjects.

Primarily meant as a warning for contemporary and future generations, the report was offered by the Working Association, which represented the German medical profession as a whole, to demonstrate to the world that medical atrocities during the war had been committed by a small misguided minority among its ranks. This should not tarnish the reputation of the rest, it was argued, who by and large had remained committed to a humanitarian practice of medicine. To that end, the Working Association included a preface, which concluded with the following message:

> The members of the committee, especially the gentlemen Dr. Alexander Mitscherlich and Fred Mielke, Heidelberg, is owed the gratitude of all physicians for the objective, conscientious and meritorious completion of their task. May their work contribute to the strengthening of the spirit of true humanity and medical commitment, and to the observance of the commands of the written and unwritten laws of medical ethics. May it further contribute, through socially and morally inviolable conduct of all German physicians, to extinguish the severe guilt incurred by a few debased members in its ranks.[71]

To show that the medical atrocities revealed at the trial were indeed the work of a "few debased members" seems to have been the prevailing sentiment of the Working Association's members and, no doubt, of the great majority of the German medical profession.

But Mitscherlich's intent had been to demonstrate the opposite, that is, to show the extent to which the whole medical profession had implicated itself in such crimes as revealed at Nuremberg. He had made his case aleady in an earlier draft of the report, entitled *Das Diktat der Menschenverachtung*, presented when the trial was still in progress. In it, he implicated, among others, such figures as the world reknown surgeon Ferdinand Sauerbruch and Wolfgang Heubner, Professor of Pharmacology at the University of Berlin. Both attended the Third Conference of Consulting Physicians in May 1943, where the use of concentration camp inmates in "terminal" experiments had become apparent. Sauerbruch and Heubner had references to their documented participation deleted from Mitscherlich's text by court order. Subsequently, Heubner and Friedrich Rein, Professor for Physiology at Goettingen, attacked Mitscherlich in the Goettingen University paper for "irresponsibility" and "defamation".[72]

The second report, entitled *Medizin ohne Menschlichkeit*, contained many changes. Unlike the first report, it was largely ignored and made unavailable. Both reports appeared in limited editions. Of the first report, 25,000 copies were printed, and of the second report, 10,000 copies. Both were meant for the benefit of the West German Physician Chambers' members. *Medizin ohne Menschlichkeit* subsequently was presented to the World Health Organization as evidence that German physicians as a whole had kept a critical distance to the Hitler regime and had upheld the traditional principles of Hippocratic medicine.

Soon thereafter German physicians were again accepted into the ranks of international organizations. Debates about the crucial roles they had played in Nazi atrocities were stifled, and reports of occasional trials against offenders were moved to the back pages of the professional journals. Those who had been fervent supporters of the system quickly shed their earlier identity, if not always their convictions, and resumed their careers less conspicuously. They apparently found comfort in one of Mitscherlich's observations, made years after the trial, according to which, "of the approximately 90,000 doctors then practicing in Germany, about 350 committed medical crimes."[73] Read out of context, it could be construed as a retroactive vindication of the entire guild.

It took forty years until this cultivated image of a generally conscientious, if sometimes misguided, community of German physicians under Hitler was effectively attacked by some of its own, albeit younger, members. In an address given in May 1986 before the Sixth World Congress of International Physicians for the Prevention of Nuclear War in Cologne, Hartmut Hanauske-Abel from the Children's Hospital of the Gutenberg University in Mainz, accused the German medical profession of encouraging a repetition of its traumatic past by hiding it. The necessary confrontation with this past, he showed, took place outside Germany.

1986 was also the year of Lifton's epochal work *The Nazi Doctors*, which was widely read and discussed in the U.S. Hanauske-Abel also pointed out that, for instance,"of 422 articles on medicine under National Socialism published worldwide between 1966 and 1979, only two originated in the Federal Republic."[74] Arguing that the German medical profession's collaboration in the Nazi Holocaust served as a precedent for the preparation of a nuclear holocaust, he urged his audience to resist the German Chamber of Physicians' support for the Federal Republic's policy of escalating global nuclear confrontation.

Hanauske-Abel was quickly branded by the head of the German Physician Chamber, Karsten Vilmar, as a non-representative outsider trying to defame the decent reputation of German medicine, because the address was delivered in English and published in *The Lancet* in Britain.[75]

Hanauske-Abel answered the charge by pointing to the conspicuous absence of any noteworthy efforts by German physicians to deal with well-known atrocities committed by members of their guild and the outright opposition to remedy this unconscionable omission at the time of his writing.[76] He asserted one major reason for this omission was the presence of known, albeit aged, offenders in controlling positions of the powerful German Physicians Chamber, who, much like Sauerbruch and Heubner, saw to it that no confrontation with the past (Vergangenheitsbewaeltigung) would take place as long as they could prevent it. Hanauske-Abel warned that ignoring lessons learned so bitterly would come back to haunt humanity.

His warnings coincided with the publication of a number of larger works by German writers outside the medical profession who exposed the role of German physicians with regards to their individual crimes, their institutional support of the Hitler regime, as well as the conspiracy of silence that followed, and did so in great detail with unrelenting clarity and irrefutable evidence.[77]

A long overdue debate on the question of guilt and responsibility resulted. It engaged scholars, media, and increasingly, physicians. As the debate continued, the need for more understanding became manifest, particularly regarding the genesis of the medical atrocities. The debate also revealed these atrocities were committed and tolerated by a larger number of people than had generally been assumed by the public and certainly much greater than has ever been acknowledged by the majority of physicians or their official organizations. The debate has by no means come to an end.

Use and Abuse of Experimental Data

AFTER THE WAR, MEMBERS of the German medical and other scientific professions remained silent not only about atrocities committed by many of their members, but also about the use of data procured from these atrocities. In this they were joined by the international community, whose condemnation of the atrocities would have sounded less sincere had it shown its willingness to benefit from their results.

For example, SS Major Wernher von Braun and his rocket scientists used their data to help the U.S. space program launch its successful shots to the moon. Although this data was procured with thousands of slave laborers, many of whom died as a result of ill treatment, no significant protest arose from the American community, despite their having viewed the war against Germany as a moral crusade.[78]

More disturbing, perhaps, may be the fact that U.S. authorities had negotiated a bargain with Japanese scientists and officials, who had conducted medical experiments on prisoners of war comparable to those of the German physicians in scope and brutality, granting legal immunity in return for experimental results.[79] As explained in an earlier part of this work, the German medical data were more easily obtained than the Japanese data, though not all were retrievable. Kurt Blome's bacteriological research results, for instance, apparently obtained from experiments on Russian prisoners, were hidden or destroyed to prevent Allied discovery.

Much of the retrieved information was put to quick use, mainly by the American Armed Forces, some even before the end of the war in the Pacific. Leo Alexander recommended in July 1945 that the results of Rascher's hypothermia experiments be adopted immediately by the U.S. Armed Forces. The U.S. military also availed itself of the expertise the defendants Siegfried Ruff, Hermann Becker-Freyseng, Konrad Schaefer, and Kurt Blome had gained through experiments on inmates, some of which were fatal, in the areas of aviation medicine, potability of seawater, and bacteriological warfare. They, like hundreds of others in similar circumstances, continued their research under government contracts arranged under Operation Paperclip, a project of the U.S. government to tap the scientific and technological resources of the conquered nation. Schaefer and Blome worked in the United States as late as 1951. If there were any ethical concerns about this practice, they were not mentioned in professional papers or discussed publically.

British observers of the trial discussed the dilemmas of using knowledge gained through the Nazi experiments in some of their journals. The views varied considerably. The *British Medical Journal* eventually concluded:

> The situation might be summed up by posing this question: If in their experiments German doctors had discovered a cure for cancer, would the rest of the world say that this information must be destroyed because of the manner in which it was obtained? To say that such information should be used would surely not be interpreted as condoning the method or as encouraging others to pursue similar methods.[80]

In other words, there was little one could do after the fact. Much of the data obtained in the murderous research became readily available in scientific journals and books without reference to their heinous origin. Some unpublished data were seized and classified by Allied powers, then submitted as evidence at the Medical Trial. Upon declassification they became a matter of public record. By this route the data were silently assimilated by the scientific community. Occasionally they were cited to substantiate scientific arguments, especially in the field of hypothermia, by researchers who may have hoped their readers would either be ignorant of, or knowingly disregard, their origin. In a few cases the origin was acknowledged, but without qualifying statements, providing Nazi experiments with an air of retrospective legitimacy, in the eyes of the victims, if not generally.[81]

The brutality inflicted on the victims to obtain these data may never be fully appreciated by Western culture, whose language has largely been shaped by historical elites insulated from the trauma inflicted on the vanquished and the helpless. These injuries remained manifest in survivors of the experiments, some of whom are still alive, only to face relegation to technical footnotes in scientific papers. It is doubtful postwar circumstances allowed many victims to ponder this dilemma to a degree that would have encouraged taking effective measures to stop this abuse. They were probably focused more on apprehending known torturers than on finding channels to control the handling of data, whose extent, encoding, dissemination, and integration into mainstream medicine must not have been transparent for many years afterward, if, indeed, it ever was fully understood by the victims at all.

The majority of victims had been Russian and Polish, and access to relevant material after the war may not have been without its hazards. In addition, Telford Taylor's words in his Nuremberg indictment speech that "the experiments were not only criminal but a scientific failure" and had "no real value to medicine" could only have encouraged the belief that not much was gained from analyzing their results anyway.

The subsequent neglect of such analysis coupled with a desire to bring living Nazi physicians to justice while time was pressing, combined with the efforts of most Germans and Austrians to establish a critical distance from Nazi atrocities and to "normalize" their lives, also closed many eyes to the deeds of dead Nazi physicians. Otherwise the elevation of Hans Eppinger to a scientist of exceptionable merit by the German Falk Foundation in 1973 could hardly have been conceivable. Eppinger, world-renowned nephrologist and hepatologist, had devised the life-threatening seawater experiment conducted on Gypsies at Dachau and had insisted on their performance over the apparently strong objections of various colleagues, most notably the defendant Konrad Schaefer, who had pointed to the negligible scientific value to be derived from the experiments. Eppinger escaped a threatening Nuremberg indictment only through suicide. His assistant Wilhelm Beiglboeck received a fifteen-year prison term for his part in the experiments.

The Falk Foundation had created an annual $5,000 Epppinger Prize for outstanding achievements in Eppinger's fields of specialization. When Howard Spiro of Yale University protested the existence of the award in 1984, it was abolished, against the advice of Hans Popper, a former associate of Eppinger and Dean of Mount Sinai School of Medicine in New York, who had awarded the prize since its inception.[82]

The Eppinger story perhaps more than any other event demonstrated to many members of the concerned, and no doubt shocked, international medical community the multifariousness of the ethical lessons that may be drawn from the Medical Trial. Eppinger's background had been impeccable, and his partly Jewish descent forced him, like so many other Jews, to leave Germany in 1933 and seek protection in his native Vienna. And yet he, much like Heydrich and Milch, became a collaborator of the Nazi regime to the bitter end, designing torturous experiments performed on Gypsies only months before the end of the war, when only fanatics anticipated victory.

Spiro, in trying to come to terms with this puzzle in 1984 offered the following reflections:

> Bringing up what must be an unpleasant and seemingly ungenerous discussion is not to accuse the dead, but to keep alive the warning that this career and complicity (as I believe) provide. I recall telling my wife and children during the Vietnam War at the time of the My Lai massacre, 'You see what THEY are doing.' And as I put the blame on 'them,' detaching myself, I felt how much I was like the 'good German' of the Nazi era. Some of them practiced 'internal migration,' condemning silently what the 'others' were doing, but they did not feel themselves responsible. I might have been no different from Eppinger and that is the reason to repeat his story.[83]

This event certainly helped to alert the scientific community as well as the general public to the ethical dilemma that had lurked, largely unnoticed, in many parts of medical literature and discourse for nearly forty years. Also in 1984, the first detailed study on the use of Nazi experimental data appeared.[84]

This coincided with the survivors of Mengele's genetic experiments on twins in Auschwitz, performed largely on Gypsies and Jews, forming a U.S.-based organization entitled Children of Auschwitz Nazi Deadly Lab Experiments Survivors (acronym CANDLES). Its purpose: "to reunite the survivors of the twin experiments; to research the experiments and their effects on the twins; to bring Dr. Mengele to trial for his crimes."[85] A mock trial of Mengele was held the following year in Jerusalem, finally drawing worldwide attention to the crucial role victims of Nazi experiments who are still alive must play in determining the use of medical data procured through their agony while they still have the power to do so.[86] Indeed, victims of Mengele's experiments have participated in the two major conferences dealing with the ethical implications of Nazi experiments held since then. Both were held in 1989 in the United States, one at the University of Minnesota, one at Boston University.[87]

What can happen in a society without sufficient concern for the plight of victims of the Nazis and clear guidelines for the use of knowledge acquired through their victimization became apparent in 1988 when the U.S. Environmental Protection Agency (EPA) utilized studies based on data from deadly phosgene experiments performed on inmates at the Natzweiler concentration camp. The data, supplied by a consulting firm, were deemed useful in determining pollution control standards for phosgene gas, which many industries routinely emit into the environment at dangerously high levels. Determined protests by some of the agency's scientists eventually persuaded its director to order his staff to disregard this information. This in turn spurred a widening controversy about the benefits and detriments of such a restrictive policy.[88]

Scientists at the EPA who questioned the policy pointed to the agency's responsibility to protect the public from a potentially severe environmental threat, even if it meant using data whose abominable origin was undeniable, when those data were otherwise unobtainable. Those whose protest had prompted the enactment of the policy argued that any use of the data would openly condone unconscionable trade-offs, a practice that in the future could be advanced again to justify the taking of lives by claiming to save lives.

They found the data not only ethically reprehensible but scientifically unsound as well. The phosgene experiments, like all Nazi experiments, were performed on maltreated concentration camp inmates, a group of people hardly representative of the largely well-nourished American citizens to which the data were applied. The data's reliability was further impaired by the researchers' subscribing to a political ideology whose doctrines promoted anything but objective scientific thinking or incorruptible commitment to scientific truth. In other words, self-serving and destructive politics and ethics invariably produce skewed science, whose results should not be trusted even when appearing valid. The declaration of some EPA scientists that no comparable data were available for the task at hand in the end paled by comparison. The prohibition against use of the data by the head of the EPA remained final.

The EPA case revealed to the general public the profound moral and scientific issues scientists and administrators, and not only they, must face when confronted with practical tasks involving the use of medical data from the Nazi's victims or, for that matter, from anyone else subjected to willfully inflicted, brutal and involuntary treatment.

For the most part, however, debates on the subject have remained academic. They have focused on revealing the use of tainted information in scholarly discourse and exposing authors connected with inhumane treatment of subjects in their care. Most of the actual and potential users of the Nazi data may not be medical researchers and may see no compelling reason to ponder their origin, more than fifty years after the experiments. Such a user might be an emergency physician at a small hospital who resuscitates a hypothermic patient with the rapid rewarming method developed on Dachau inmates. Scientists engaged in the relevant research, on the other hand, are only too aware of the data's origin, and those who use them defend their decision in various ways.

One critic reported "many of the scientists I spoke to regard the Nazi data as useful and necessary to their work. Typical was the comment by John S. Hayward of the University of Victoria in British Columbia, who uses the Nazi measurements of the rate of body cooling in cold water: 'I don't want to have to use this data, but there is no other and will be no other in an ethical world. I've rationalized it a little bit. But to not use it would be equally bad. I'm trying to make something constructive out of it. I use it with my guard up, but it's useful.' Much of his hypothermia research involves testing cold-water survival suits that are put on fishing boats in Canada's frigid ocean waters."[89]

Like the EPA case, this case demonstrates how researchers and others may perceive themselves as caught in a double bind, either giving some measure of retroactive justification to Nazi experiments by demonstrating they produced something of value after all, or withholding possible help from people to prevent any upgrading of the experimenters' reputation and consequent degrading of their victims' humanity. Extending such help may also lower the threshold of ethical permissibility for human experimentation in the future by allowing open speculation on how much damage may be inflicted on some, predictably more helpless, subjects for the benefit of others. The fact that knowledge, especially after it has been absorbed by a larger population, cannot be unlearned or easily ignored intensifies the dilemma.

How, for instance, can an emergency room physician be persuaded to forget or ignore a rapid heating method that may save the life of a hypothermia accident victim or, more accurately, to forget or ignore only those data about hypothermia that come from Nazi physicians? Since such data have become an integral part of generally available knowledge, to separate them out again would seem close to impossible. And there would be other data derived from unethical experiments as well, which should be excluded too.

This, according to one ethicist, would have crippling consequences. With respect to medical research, he argues: "If you exclude from use all the experiments now viewed as unethical, you'd have to tear up half the medical textbooks."[90] Hardly anyone, inside or outside the medical profession, could be expected to accept such exclusion, even if the ratio were much lower. But neither could anyone expect the victims of such experiments to tolerate the prevailing sense of embarrassed helplessness that seems to emerge from such revelations, or expect society at large to countenance continued abuse of human beings for medical purposes.

One effective way of solving this dilemma is to resume and broaden the public discourse initiated earlier by victims of Nazi experiments and groups like the dissenting scientists at the EPA. Encouraging greater participation by all members of the medical community, preferably including actual and suspected offenders, and society at large, would likely produce a wider consensus on how to handle data questionably or criminally obtained in the past and how best to avoid medical victimization of human beings in the future. To be sure, excellent contributions to the debate do exist and have left their mark in literature.

Still reeling from the echoes of the Nuremberg Medical Trial, Henry Beecher in the 1960s remained unequivocal about the lesson he learned regarding the propagation of data obtained in unconscionable experiments.

> The question rises, then, about valuable data that have been improperly obtained. It is my view that such material should not be published. There is a practical aspect to this matter: failure to obtain publication would discourage unethical experimentation. How many would carry out such experimentation if they KNEW its results would never be published? Even though suppression of such data (by not publishing it) would constitute a loss to medicine, in a specific localized sense, this loss, it seems, would be less important than the far reaching moral loss to medicine if the data obtained were to be published. Admittedly, there is room for debate. Others believe that such data, because of their intrinsic value, obtained at great risk or damage to the subjects, should not be wasted but should be published with stern editorial comments. This would have to be done with exceptional skill, to avoid an odor of hypocricy.[91]

Beecher's words have been heeded, and today no reputable journal knowingly publishes material containing references to unethically obtained data of any kind, not merely tainted Nazi data. In 1975, the World Health Organization adopted a revised version of the 1964 Declaration of Helsinki, a document that declared the principles of the Nuremberg Code, in a slightly amended version, to be a universal standard. The 1975 version contained, among others, the following addition: "Reports on experimentation not in accordance with the principles laid down in this Declaration should not be accepted for publication."[92] Since then, most editors of professional journals have developed a consensus not to publish data of ethically dubious origin.

Willard Gaylin, the president of The Hastings Center, with respect to the data obtained from concentration camp victims stated unequivocally: "We cannot cite these atrocities. To use this data is to become an onlooker, and beyond that, an accomplice."[93] Stephen Post of Case Western Reserve University demanded:

> "(a) that as a prima facie duty, unethically obtained data should never be used, (b) that such data should be expunged from published works insofar as possible, (c) that the editors of all journals that have in the past published Nazi data without a statement of moral condemnation should print such a statement now, and (d) that science should at a moral minimum be sensitive to the emotions of the victims from whom it has pillaged data."[94]

Such scholars as Benno Mueller-Hill and William Seidelmann have made similar statements. Howard Spiro, who admitted that "I might have been no different from Eppinger," also stated in the same breath that "I would have

burned the data from the concentration camps."[95] But that, according to Velvl
Greene from the Ben Gurion University in Israel, would have put him on a slippery slope different from the one Eppinger chose, but going down hill
nevertheless:

> [T]o paraphrase Heine's immortal warning about burning books and burning people,
> a society that burns Nazi data will soon go on to burn other data that will be deemed
> in the future as equally excoriable. What will be next after Rascher's notes and Mengele's
> report? South African medical journals look like good candidates."[96]

As convincing as this argument may sound to some, it should be juxtaposed
with the views of the victims, as firmly expressed by Eva Mozes Kor, a survivor
of Mengele's twin experiments and founding member of CANDLES. Her
words echo those of Spiro:

> Regarding the Nazi data: I am appalled by anyone who seemingly is justifying the means
> by using the results of the Nazi experiments. In Auschwitz we were treated like a com-
> modity; the hair was used for mattresses; the fat was used for soap; the skin for lamp-
> shades; the gold collected from the teeth of the dead went into the Nazi treasury, and
> many of us were used as guinea pigs. Today some doctors want to use the only thing
> left by these victims. They are like vultures waiting for the corpses to cool so they could
> devour every consumable part. To use the Nazi data is obscene and sick. One can always
> rationalize that it would save human lives, the questions should be asked, at what
> cost."[97]

Telford Taylor's assertion before the Nuremberg tribunal that these "experiments revealed nothing which civilized medicine can use," hence nothing that
needed to be burned, may have done much to avoid the moral quandary that
emerged when actual practice eventually proved him wrong. His assertion
affirmed a generally held assumption that no one capable of the heinous cruelty shown by the defendants could possess the kind of commitment to truth
that would guarantee faithful adherence to scientific method and correctness
of experimental results. Lack of ethical principles, in fact, meant lack of principles in every human domain, and therewith untrustworthiness in general.
Despite the largely unadmitted use of some of the Nazi data in the years following World War II, the point that bad ethics make bad science seemed to be
in no need of belaboring.

However, in an evaluation of the Nazi experiments published in 1984,
Mueller-Hill wrote of the experimenters that they "often, knowingly, brought
about the death of those whom they were investigating. But even their investigations could not have been judged 'bad science' if they had been carried out
on mice."[98] The fact that, by then, various experimental results were applied
and acknowledged by members of the medical community supported his
observation. Arthur Caplan observed, "the force of the question 'Should the
data be used?' is diminished not only because there are reasons to doubt the

reliability and exclusivity of the data but also because the question has already been answered: Nazi data have been used by many scientists from many nations."[99] Taylor's assumption, therefore, at the very least should be subjected to a critical probe.

The view that bad ethics generally will produce bad science, and good ethics good science, may be traced back to classical philosophy. Socrates' logical demonstration that goodness and truth and even beauty, are one and the same has found considerable acceptance throughout Western history. The ramifications were manifold. To the degree that a person adhered to principles of goodness he was judged to possess knowledge of truth as well. Lack of such adherence meant ignorance, or pursuit of falsehood, and vice versa. Ignorance of true, logically verifiable, knowledge and pursuit of false, logically nonverifiable, knowledge revealed a morally impaired mind that, furthermore, showed little appreciation of beauty.

The latter, to various degrees, constituted the multitude of populations in the form of mean laborers, unintegrated citizens and outsiders, violators of public rules, and, most recognizably, slaves. Because such people possessed little or no truth and goodness, they possessed little or no humanity, since truth and goodness also constituted humanity. Slaves, for instance, were little more than animals in human guise, who could be treated accordingly when necessary or desired. Especially during the Hellenistic and Roman period, many physicians, trained in Hippocratic medicine, would not find it contradictory to subject humans who in their view lacked humanity to the same torturous and fatal experiments generally performed on animals, including vivisection.[100]

For all we know today, the scientific procedures did not vary. Men had come to see other men as research animals, whose suffering apparently evoked little more response than the suffering of mice, and they were able to do so only within the context of the prevailing view of humanity. It was this view of humanity that allowed them to pursue their murderous activity with unrestrained scientific efficiency.

The classic view of humanity eventually was replaced by the Judeo-Christian view, which endowed every individual with equal moral value, whatever his formal knowledge of worldly and other matters. St. Augustine assured wary Christians that ignorance could only enhance an individual's moral stature, because it signified the presence of innocence uncorrupted by the pride of knowledge. The Renaissance, the scientific revolution, and the Enlightenment subsequently restored much of the classic spirit in Western culture, and with it a renewed confidence that a person's moral value and intellectual performance can be mutually enhancing.

This confidence was shattered with the appearance of Immanuel Kant's *Critiques* at the end of the Eighteenth Century. Trying to rescue faith and freedom from the deterministic logic of classic philosophy and its empirical consequences as found in the writings of David Hume, Kant demonstrated that man's scientific, moral, and esthetic faculties abide by different ontological and epistemological principles, which work independent of each other. An exceptionally gifted scientist, for example, could possess a satanic disposition, and a highly virtuous individual could scorn scientific knowledge. It meant that a person's moral, scientific, and esthetic achievements could be fully appreciated only if assessed separately, even if human reason could draw certain connections.

This view finally was overshadowed by Hegelian and Marxian arguments, which, much like classic philosophy, tried to reestablish principles by which to judge individuals, and societies, in their entirety.

Hegelian and Marxian arguments, respectively, became the principal bases for subsequent totalitarian thinking on the political right and left in Western society and elsewhere. Kant's liberalizing proclamation that individuals are ends in themselves largely gave way to Hegel's and Marx's proclamations that individuals are means to higher ends: the self-fulfillment, or self-realization, of a wold idea in one case, and the establishment of a scarcity-free material society in the other.

Fascists of all colors later came to identify human will, manifested individually as well as collectively, as the chief agent in Hegel's self-fulfilling process, which the National Socialists identified as a process toward the political and cultural domination of Europe by the Nordic race. With selected arguments from such philosophers as Schopenhauer and Nietzsche, they tried to show that the level of contribution to this collective goal determined individual moral value, true knowledge, and esthetic understanding. Rejection of and work toward the prevention of the goal's realization determined the level of individual worthlessness, ignorance, and esthetic repulsiveness, all to a comparable degree.

The ramifications again were manifold. Knowing one aspect of a person's life allowed the rest to be inferred. People could judge other people with relative certainty despite a lack of relevant information, often on the basis of mere appearance. National Socialists espoused theories that correlated physical characteristics commonly used to identify anthropological groups (Germanic people, Latins, Gypsies, Jews, Slavs, etc.) with moral characteristics along a sliding scale. Germanic people, on the whole, were inherently more courageous and idealistic than others; Jews were the most selfish and materialistic, and so on. Physical and moral characteristics also correlated with esthetic characteristics. The physical characteristics of Germanic people were elevated to typical standards of beauty, contrasted with physical characteristics of other groups, particularly Jews and Slavs, defined mostly as unattractive and even repulsive. Possession of Germanic characteristics, or at the very least acceptance of their idealized version, denoted the possession of the kind of mental faculties that alone could guarantee the acquisition of true knowledge and virtuous living, and therewith humanity. Their absence or rejection meant the opposite and, consequently, showed lack of humanity.

This standard ultimately led the National Socialists to deny humanity to whole segments of the European population, which they subsequently destroyed, along with a rich cultural heritage, a feat forever associated with images of book burnings and death camps. Achievements of scientists, artists, and writers who lacked sufficient commitment to National Socialist views, or who opposed them, deserved condemnation, not scrutiny. Einstein's theory of relativity, for instance, was discarded as Jewish gimmickry, Schoenberg's music as decadent noise, and Brecht's plays as Bolshevik propaganda. Ascribing value to them merely demonstrated lack of humanity, and their promotion provided grounds for confinement. Ultimately, millions were so confined in specially built camps, looked upon by their jailors as human scum selected for destruction, and in many cases as mice for medical experiments.

The researchers often lived lives of exemplary civility, a fact that has puzzled many a person trying to come to terms with this dark chapter in human history. How was it possible for humans to inflict upon other humans the tortures described earlier in this work? It was possible precisely because humans have the ability to relegate other humans to the level of mice without apparent damage to their particular conception of humanity. Human history is too replete with evidence to deny this conclusion. In fact, denial can only be a hindrance in the quest for a vision of humanity that will make such a division impossible in the future.

To be sure, there are many world views whose advocates firmly believe they embody principles that lack even the potential to dehumanize a person. But most, if not all, have failed the test of time. It is, for instance, very difficult to imagine that those who endured a dehumanized existence under the Hitler regime would not feel the urge to deny any sense of humanity to their torturers, and it is equally difficult to imagine that anyone but those torturers would fail to show sympathy for this feeling. But those sentiments too attest to the apparent universality of a perceived less-than-human characteristic of the human race. Perhaps Gandhi's vision may hold out the best, if not the only, hope for the species to make the world more humane despite itself.

For any vision of humanity to hold out optimism in this respect, at the very least it must debunk the claim that any correlations between a person's moral values and quality of knowledge are fixed. To the degree that their relation is ill understood, it should be subject to more research. Again, it is difficult to imagine that anyone but the defendants in the Medical Trial, and those sharing their views, would object to Telford Taylor's assessment at the time that the "moral shortcomings of the defendants and the precipitous case with which they decided to commit murder in quest of 'scientific results' dulled also that scientific hesitancy, that thorough thinking-through, that responsible weighing of every single step which alone can insure scientifically valid results."[101]

But today this statement should be examined to show whether and to what extent it may give credence to a view that formed an essential part of the ideology Taylor denounced. It is in this area that the discussion has been most hesitant, primarily, no doubt, to spare surviving victims the final indignity of facing uncomfortable comments about the treatment suffered at the hands of their torturers. As a result, contributions to the discussion by and large have echoed Taylor's earlier condemnation.

But this view gives unwitting support to those who would like to dismiss discussions about ethics and science all together. According to Benno Mueller-Hill, their number is growing, and they consider discussions about linkages between science and ethics to be mere impediments in their quest for ever greater control over physical nature. Mueller-Hill leaves no doubt about his view that the ensuing consequences for society will be devastating. "Verdun, Auschwitz and Hiroshima," he writes, "were only the first signs of things to come. This will be so if science and nothing but science is valued."[102] The main culprits are the scientists themselves: "Scientists are no heroes, it is true. But I believe it is worse than that: the more you understand of science, the less you (want to) understand of the rest of the world."[103]

This vision of a dehumanized world in which science, good or bad, reigns supreme is sustained by fears that too many scientists are always tempted to drive a Faustian bargain, to sell their soul for knowledge and power, much like the Nazi physicians had done. The best antidote to this destructive vision may have found its most powerful expression in the simple words of a Nazi victim:

> I, Eva Mozes Kor, a survivor of the Nazi medical and genetic experiments, appeal to all scientists and doctors to make a pledge to do the following things:
> 1. Take a moral commitment never to violate anyone's human rights and human dignity.
> 2. To promote a universal idea that says: 'Treat the subjects of your experiments in the manner that you would want to be treated if you were in their place.'
> 3. To do your scientific work, but please, never stop being a human being. The moment you do, you are becoming a scientist for the sake of science alone, and you are becoming the Mengele of today.[104]

Epilogue

WHETHER THE INCREASING PASSAGE of time since the horrors of the Hitler regime will help or hurt efforts to understand and avoid their recurrence remains to be seen. As the warning voices of eyewitnesses will turn silent in the new century, the crimes of the old century may not seem so heinous or relevant anymore. Fear of this reality surely helped spur the creation of the many memorials and museums toward the close of this past century. The lasting legacy of the Nuremberg Medical Trial, most people would agree, is the Nuremberg Medical Code. Initially ignored as an instrument designed to restrain abusive physicians in Germany, it eventually became accepted globally as a moral, if not legal, foundation to protect the interests and dignity of human medical subjects.

In September of 1947, soon after the American Military Tribunal passed judgment on the twenty-three defendants, the newly formed World Medical Association (WMA) met in Geneva, condemned the criminals' actions, and endorsed a modernized version of the ancient Hippocratic Oath.[1] In 1954, the WMA adopted the Resolution on Human Experimentation. It contained the principles enumerated in the Nuremberg Code.[2] Increasingly sophisticated medical technology and growing concern about subjects' ability to give fully informed consent has prompted the WMA to make periodic revisions. Its 1964 Declaration of Helsinki allowed legal guardians to provide consent if the subject is physically or legally unable to do so himself or herself. Further revisions in 1975, 1983, and 1989 distinguished more closely between therapeutic and nontherapeutic research and required the inclusion of ethical review committees in all human experiments.[3] In its efforts to balance necessary freedom of research for the investigator with maximum protection for the subjects the WMA has worked closely with other organizations, notably the World Health Organization (WHO) and the Council for International Organizations of Medical Sciences (IOMS).

Together these organizations developed a set of guidelines, first endorsed in 1981, to protect particularly vulnerable groups of people from abusive medical research so often promoted by large corporations to maximize profits. These vulnerable groups included children, pregnant women, the mentally ill, uninformed populations of developing nations, etc. Finally, in 1998 the International Criminal Court decreed that medical experiments performed on unwilling individuals during and in connection with armed conflict constitute war crimes, even if the conflict is considered a domestic issue under international law.[4] Additional protective measures may be expected in the future, both on the national and international level, hopefully in the area of enforcement as well.

As impressive as these efforts may look to some, there are critics who have pointed to some disturbing faults. Henry Beecher's lament that, especially in the United States, the Nuremberg Code was ignored for too long and as a result did not stop dangerous and fatal experiments on, among others, African-Americans and impaired children until the 1960's may be the most familiar case.[5]

Some critics in Europe, especially France, in fact, have rejected the code itself, charging that it represents a successful attempt by American physicians and institutions to distance themselves from the atrocious Nazi experiments while creating a legal and ethical basis for continuing their own condemnable, nontherapeutic experiments at home.[6] Others have heralded the code as a breakthrough in the evolution of human rights which, regrettably in their view, was marginalized as soon as it was formulated.[7]

No one argues the Nuremberg Code, and the developments it subsequently promoted, had no merit at all, and most critics overwhelmingly agree the code has given human experiments, and the practice of medicine in general, a sense of security and dignity unimaginable a century earlier. But does this alone guarantee the Nazi experiments will never be repeated? Hardly.

The Nazi experiments were possible only in the context of the Holocaust. The camps in which they were performed had become places from which the Nazis had removed all sense of humanity. The will of the inmates to assert as much of their humanity as possible despite the Nazis was often crushed. Perhaps nobody has evoked this experience of degradation as vividly as Eli Wiesel did in his writings. For the Nazis, the inmates had become subhumans, indistinguishable and unworthy of life. And for the experimentors, they were potential guinea pigs. It is difficult to imagine that the experiments suffered by the victims could have been performed outside the context of the Holocaust. But the Holocaust itself was possible only in the context of the war that started in September of 1939, when Germany marched into Poland.

It has been a matter of much debate when precisely Nazi leaders had firmed up their resolve to exterminate marked segments of the European population, especially Jews, when, in other words, they decided that "elimination" did not mean removal and segregation but physical destruction. But there can be little disagreement that many felt that the time had come with the outbreak of the war. Hitler certainly did.

Under cover of war, a "final solution" was implemented in relative secrecy in the newly acquired territories of Eastern Europe, mainly Poland. Nazi leaders figured correctly that during times of war, especially when casualty figures are numbingly high, people's preoccupation with their own welfare reduces concerns for the welfare of others, especially if those others are deemed to be responsible for the diminished welfare to begin with. And the Nazis had left no doubt that they thought the major responsibility for the deterioration of life experienced in Germany and elsewhere following World War I, especially during the Great Depression, rested mainly with communists and Jews.

The situation was not much different in other European countries, or the U.S. For instance, the eugenics movement that gave Nazis scientific support for their racist ideology had a strong following in Britain and the U.S. But here it did not lead to the devastating consequences observed in Germany. Comparing the eugenics movements in the U.S. and Germany, the biologist Garland Allen argues, "[t]he severity of the German outcome compared to our own lies not with abstract differences in 'national character' or the tradition of Prussian authoritaranism, but rather in the very concrete differences in the degree of economic and social chaos between the two countries in the interwar period." [8] The politial chaos in Germany at the time was much greater than that experienced in the U.S. To save Germany from it, the Nazis ultimately imposed a war on the world that provided them with the conditions and rational for their extermination policy. And the extermination policy provided the conditions and rational for the medical experiments.

As a prosperous Western society starts the new millennium, even those who personally experienced the horrors of the war and the Holocaust often seem to think of them as surreal, hopefully never to be seen again. We now witness a world where a survivor of Mengele's murderous twin experiments, the very same Eva Mozes Kor quoted at the end of the previous chapter, finds the strength to reach out to one of Mengele's colleagues at Auschwitz, Hans Muench. She forgave him for his crimes, at the very spot where she was reduced to a human guinea pig fifty years earlier and where he, in his own words, "could make experiments on people otherwise possible only on rabbits."[9]

One of the messages presumably given in this gesture is that we all have to leave that surreal world behind us and somehow get on with our lives. And fear that such a world may revisit us is subsiding. Martin Walser's insistence that a repetition of Auschwitz, an avowedly unique event, is inconceivable today, especially in Germany, seems to echo the thoughts of most people. Still, one should not forget the words of the defendant Hans Romberg when asked how he would act under circumstances similar to those prevailing during the days of Hitler. "I would probably do everything just the way I did it then," he replied. While this reply more than anything demonstrates Romberg's personal failings, it also shows the most effective way to ensure a future free of the types of crimes the Nazis committed rests in making sure that we, all of us, do not tolerate, anywhere, the kind of circumstances he found when growing up in war-torn Europe.

Illustrations

Fig 1: The defendants in the dock, National Archives, Washington, D.C.

Fig 2: Karl Brandt: Gruppenfuehrer in the SS, personal physician to Chancellor Adolf Hitler, Reich Commissioner for Health and Sanitation, National Archives, Washington, D.C.

Fig 3: Siegfried Handloser: Lieutenant General, Medical Services, Chief of the Medical Services of the Armed Forces, National Archives, Washington, D.C.

Fig 4: Paul Rostock: Chief of the Office of Medical Science and Research, Surgical Advisor to the Army, National Archives, Washington, D.C.

Fig 5: Oskar Schroeder: Lieutenant General, Medical Service, Chief of Staff of the Inspectorate of the Medical Service of the Air Force, National Archives, Washington, D.C.

Fig 6: Karl Genzken: Gruppenfuehrer in the SS, Chief of the Medical Department of the Waffen SS (Combat SS), National Archives, Washington, D.C.

Fig 7: Karl Gebhardt: Gruppenfuehrer in the SS, personal physician to the head of the SS, Heinrich Himmler, Chief Clinician of the SS and Police, President of the German Red Cross, National Archives, Washington, D.C.

Fig 8: Kurt Blome: Deputy Reich Health Leader, National Archives, Washington, D.C.

Fig 9: Rudolf Brandt: Colonel in the SS, personal administrative officer to Heinrich Himmler, Chief of the Ministerial Office of the Ministry of the Interior

Fig 10: Joachim Mrugowsky: Senior Colonel in the Waffen SS, Chief Hygienist of the SS and Police, Chief of Hygiene Institute of Waffen SS, National Archives, Washington, D.C.

Fig 11: Helmut Poppendick: Senior Colonel in the SS, Chief of the Personal Staff of the Reich Physician SS and Police, National Archives, Washington, D.C.

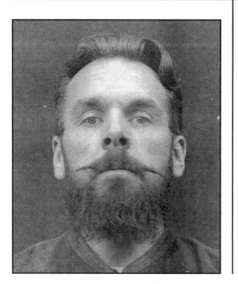

Fig 12: Wolfram Sievers: Colonel in the SS, Manager of the Cultural Heritage Society, Director of the Institute for Military Scientific Research, National Archives, Washington, D.C.

Fig 13: Gerhard Rose: Brigadier General of the Air Force, Hygiene Advisor for the Tropical Medicine to the Chief of the Medical Service of the Air Force, Chief of the Department for Tropical Medicine at the Robert Koch Institute, National Archives, Washington, D.C.

Fig 14: Siegfried Ruff: Director of the Department for Aviation Medicine at the German Experimental Institute for Aviation, National Archives, Washington, D.C.

Fig 15: Hans Wolfgang Romberg: Physician on the Staff of the Department for Aviation Medicine at the German Experimental Institute for Aviation, National Archives, Washington, D.C.

Fig 16: Victor Brack: Senior Colonel in the SS, Chief Administrative Officer in the Chancellery of Adolf Hitler, National Archives, Washington, D.C.

Fig 17: Hermann Becker-Freyseng: Captain, Medical Services, Chief of the Department of Aviation Medicine of the Medical Inspectorate of the Air Force, National Archives, Washington, D.C.

Fig 18: Georg August Weltz: Lieutenant Colonel, Medical Services, Chief of the Institute for Aviation Medicine (Munich), National Archives, Washington, D.C.

Fig 19: Konrad Schaefer: Physician on the Staff of the Institute for Aviation Medicine (Berlin), National Archives, Washington, D.C.

Fig 20: Waldemar Hoven: Captain in the SS, Chief Physician of the Buchenwald Concentration Camp, National Archives, Washington, D.C.

Fig 21: Wilhelm Beiglboeck: Consulting physician to the Air Force, National Archives, Washington, D.C.

Fig 22: Adolf Pokorny: Physician, specialist in skin and venereal diseases, National Archives, Washington, D.C.

Fig 23: Herta Oberhauser: Physician at the Ravensbrueck Concentration Camp, National Archives, Washington, D.C.

Fig 24: Fritz Fischer: Major in the Waffen SS, Assistant Physician to Defendant Karl Gebhardt, National Archives, Washington, D.C.

178   *The Nuremberg Medical Trial*

Fig 25: The Judges (from left to right): Harold Sebring, Walter Beals (presiding), Johnson Crawford, Victor Swearingen, National Archives, Washington, D.C.

Fig 26: Telford Taylor, Chief Council for the Prosecution, delivering opening remarks, National Archives, Washington, D.C.

Fig 27: Palace of Justice, Nuremberg, site of the trial, National Archives, Washington, D.C.

Fig 28: Palace of Justice, front view, National Archives, Washington, D.C.

Fig 29: General view of the courtroom, National Archives, Washington, D.C.

Fig 30: Andrew Ivy, U.S. medical expert, being
sworn in, National Archives, Washington, D.C.

Fig 31: Walter Leibrandt, German medical expert, giving testimony, National Archives, Washington, D.C.

Fig 32: U.S. medical expert Leo Alexander points to the leg injuries of the Polish victim Jadwiga Dzido, National Archives, Washington, D.C.

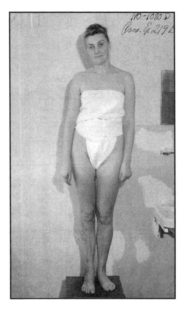

Fig 33: Victim showing her leg injuries sustained in forced experiments to control infections, conducted by defendants Fritz Fischer and Herta Oberhauser, National Archives, Washington, D.C.

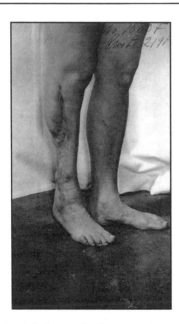 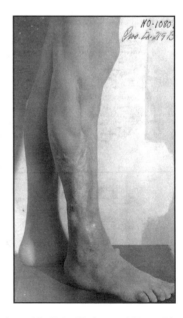

Fig 34: Leg injuries sustained on experiments conducted by Fritz Fischer and Herta Oberhauser, National Archives, Washington, D.C.

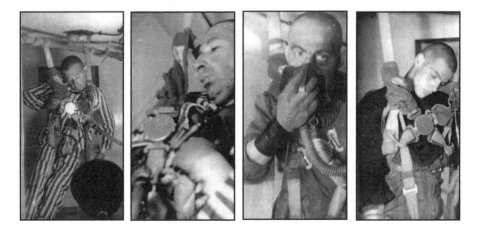

Figs 35–42: Inmates of Dachau Concentration camp were forced to be subjects in the often-fatal high altitude experiments of the defendants Siegfried Ruff, Hans Romberg, and Hermann Becker-Freyseng, National Archives, Washington, D.C.

Fig 43: Main defendant Karl Brandt giving testimony, National Archives, Washington, D.C.

Fig 44: Defendant Gerhard Rose giving testimony, National Archives, Washington, D.C.

Fig 45: Defendant Karl Gebhardt receiving the death sentence, National Archives, Washington, D.C.

Notes

Introduction

1. Ron Rosenbaum, *Explaining Hitler: The Search for the Origin of Evil* (New York: Random House, 1998), p. 261.

2. *Ibid.*, pp. 251–66.

3. Quoted by Hayden White in, "Historical Emplotment and the Problem of Truth," *Probing the Limits of Representation: Nazism and the "Final Solution"* (Cambridge: Harvard Univ. Press, 1992), p. 43.

4. Martin Walser, *Erfahrungen beim Verfassen einer Sonntagsrede* (Frankfurt a/M: Edition Suhrkamp, 1998), pp. 17–18. Author's translation.

5. Bernhard Schlinck, "Auf dem Eis," *Der Spiegel*, No. 19 (May 7, 2001), pp. 82–86.

6. Arthur Caplan, "How Did Medicine go so Wrong?" *When Medicine Went Mad* (Totowa, NJ: Humana Press, 1992), p. 78.

7. Robert Jay Lifton, *The Nazi Doctors: Medical Killing and the Psychology of Genocide* (New York: Basic Books, 1986).

8. Norman Ravitch, "Reflections on Robert Jay Lifton's 'The Nazi Doctors'," *The Psychohistory Review*, 16, No. 1 (Fall 1987): 7.

9. Thomas A. Kohut, "Empathizing with the Nazis: Reflections on Robert Jay Lifton's 'The Nazi Doctors'," *The Psychohistory Review*, 16, No. 1 (Fall 1987): 45–46.

10. Bruno Bettelheim, "Their Specialty was Murder," *The New York Times Book Review* (Oct. 15, 1986), p. 62.

11. Robert Jay Lifton, "On Investigating Nazi Doctors: Further Thoughts," *The Psychohistory Review*, 16, No. 1 (Fall 1987): 51–66.

12. Benno Mueller-Hill, *Murderous Science* (Oxford: Oxford Univ. Press, 1988).

13. George J. Annas and Michael A. Grodin, *The Nazi Doctors and the Nuremberg Code: Human Rights in Human Experimentation* (Oxford: Oxford Univ. Press, 1992), Francis R. Nicosia and Jonathan Huener, *Medicine and Medical Ethics in Nazi Germany* (New York: Berghahn Books, 2002), and Angelika Ebbinghaus and Klaus Doerner, eds., *Vernichten und Heilen* (Berlin: Aufbau-Verlag, 2001).

14. Caplan, *When Medicine Went Mad,* p. 59.

Chapter One

1. Jay Kantz and Alexander Capron, *Experimentation with Human Beings* (New York: Russell Sage Foundation, 1972), p. n287.

2. See James H. Jones, *Bad Blood* (New York: Free Press, 1981).

3. Dom Peter Flood, ed. *Medical Experimentation on Man* (Cork, Ireland: Mercier Press, 1955), p. 18.

4. Albert Moll, *Aerztliche Ethik: Die Pflichten des Arztes in allen Beziehungen seiner Taetigkeit* (Stuttgart: F. Enke, 1904), pp. 533–34. Author's translation.

5. *Ibid.,* p. 535.

6. *Ibid.,* p. 505.

7. *Ibid.,* p. 578.

8. *Ibid.,* p. 556.

9. For a detailed account of the directive, see Michael A. Grodin, "Historical Origins of the Nuremberg Code," *The Nazi Doctors and the Nuremberg Code,* by George J. Annas and Michael A. Grodin (Oxford: Oxford Univ. Press, 1992), pp. 121–144.

10. William B. Bean, "Walter Reed and Yellow Fever," *JAMA,* Vol. 250, No. 5 (Aug. 5, 1983): 659–662.

11. "Deaths Associated with Yellow Fever," *JAMA,* Vol. 249, No. 9 (March 4, 1983): 1150–51. .

12. Richard P. Strong, "Vaccination Against Plague," *The Philippine Journal of Science,* Vol. I (1906): 181–190.

13. Richard P. Strong, The Investigation Carried on by the Biological Laboratory in Relation to the Suppression of the Recent Cholera Outbreak in Manila," *The Philippine Journal of Science,* Vol. II (1907): 422.

14. Richard P. Strong and B.C. Crowell, "The Etiology of Beriberi," *The Philippine Journal of Science,* Vol. VII B, No. 4 (1912): 291.

15. A very thorough account of this event can be found in Elizabeth W. Etheridge's *The Butterfly Cast: A Social History of Pellagra in the South* (Westport, CT: Greenwood Publishing C., 1972).

16. Gert H. Brieger, "Human Experimentation: History," *Encyclopedia of Bioethics,* 2 (New York: Free Press, 1978), pp. 684–692.

17. In 1903, the Social Democratic Labor Party of Russia split in two factions, the Bolsheviks (majority) and the Mensheviks (minority) over the issue of how to transform Russia's semifeudal society into an industrial socialist society. The Mensheviks adopted a long-range strategy, arguing that Russia had to go through a stage of laissez-faire capitalism first. The

Bolsheviks adopted a short-range strategy that substituted the laissez-faire stage with state capitalism. This required a "revolutionary vanguard party" with highly effective leadership qualities.

18. Carl Zuckmayer, *A Part of Myself* (New York: Harcourt Brace, 1970), p. 145.

19. Quoted in Heinz Peter Schmiedebach, "Sozialdarwinismus, Biologismus, Pazifismus-Aerztestimmen zum Ersten Weltkrieg," *Medizin und Krieg*, J. Bleker and H.-P. Schmiedebach, eds. (Frankfurt: Fischer Verlag, 1987), p. 114. Author's translation.

20. Benno Mueller-Hill, *Murderous Science* (Oxford: Oxford Univ. Press, 1988, p. 10.

21. Philip R. Reilly, "Involuntary Sterilization in the United States: A Surgical Solution," *The Quarterly Review of Biology*, 62, No. 2 (June 1987): 160.

22. *Ibid.*, p. 162.

23. Konrad Lorenz, "Durch Domestikation verursachte Stoerungen arteigenen Verhaltens," *Zeitschrift fuer Angewandte Psychologie und Characterkunde*, 59, Nos. 1,2 (June 1940): 75. Author's translation.

24. Records of the United States Nuernberg War Crimes Trials, United States vs. Karl Brandt et al. (Case 1, Medical Case). National Archives Microfilm Publications, Washington, D.C., Publications M887, Proceedings, pp. 63–64.

25. The United States vs. Karl Brandt, Document No. 220.

26. Proceedings, pp. 8850–8982.

27. Document No. 861.

28. Document No. 198.

29. Document No. 2210.

30. Testimony of Witness Ferdinand Hall, Proceedings, p. 1056.

31. Document No. 1852.

32. Document No. 409.

33. Document No. 861.

34. Witness Sofia Maczka, Proceedings, pp. 1448–49.

35. Proceedings, p. 6196.

36. Alexander Mitscherlich and Fred Mielke, *Doctors of Infamy: The Story of the Nazi Medical Crimes* (New York: Henry Schuman, 1949), p. 46, table.

37. See Guenter Schwarberg, *Der SS-Arzt und die Kinder vom Bullenhuser Damm* (Goettingen: Steidl Verlag, 1988).

38. "German Medical War Crimes," United Nations War Crimes Commission, World Medical Association, British Medical Association House, London, 1949: pp. 12–13.

39. *Ibid.*, p. 11.

40. *Ibid.*, p. 12.

41. Joachim Mrugowsky, Proceedings, pp. 5210–11.

42. Yandell Henderson, *Adventures in Respiration* (Baltimore: The Williams and Wilkins Co., 1938), pp. 152–53.

43. Document No. 035.

44. Document No. 205.

45. Document No. 089.

46. Document No. 212.

47. Document No. 203.

48. *Ibid.*

49. *Ibid.*

50. Proceedings, pp. 5277–78, 5602–04.

51. Document No. 085.

52. See Victor von Weizsaecker, *"Euthanasie" und Menschenversuche* (Heidelberg: Verlag Lambert Schneider, 1947).

53. "Medicine in Germany," *The Lancet* (January 12, 1946): 62.

54. "Scientific Results of German Medical War Crimes: Report of an Enquiry by a Committee under the Chairmanship of Lord Moran" (London: Her Majesty's Stationary Office, 1949), p. 4.

55. Eugen Kogon, *The Theory and Practice of Hell* (New York: Octagon Books, 1976), p. 146.

56. Proceedings, p. 71.

57. 'The Treatment of Shock From Prolonged Exposure to Cold, Especially in Water," Combined Intelligence Objectives Sub-Committee, G-2 Div., SHAEP (Rear), (Washington, D.C.: Office of the Publication Board, n.d.), p. 68.

58. Linda Hunt, "U.S. Coverup of Nazi Scientists," *Bulletin of the Atomic Scientist*, 41, No. 4 (April 1985): 16–24.

59. Kristine Moe, "Should Nazi Research Data Be Cited?" *The Hastings Center Report* (December 1984): 5.

60. See William Seidelman, "Mengele Medicus: Mengele's Nazi Heritage," *Milbank Quarterly*, 66, No. 2 (1988): 221–39.

61. *The New York Times*, March 23, 1988, p. A1.

62. Mueller-Hill, *Murderous Science*, p. 100.

63. Robert L. Berger, "Nazi Science-The Dachau Hypothermia Experiments," *The New England Journal of Medicine*, 322, No. 20 (May 17, 1990): 1435–40.

Chapter Two

1. George J. Annas and Michael Grodin, *The Nazi Doctors and the Nuremberg Code* (Oxford: Oxford Univ. Press, 1992), p. 8.

2. W. Paul Burman, ed., *The first German War Crimes Trial: Chief Judge Walter B. Beals' Desk Notebook of the Doctors' Trial, Held in Nuernberg, Germany, December 1945 to August 1947* (Chapel Hill, NC: Documentary Publications, 1985), p. 14.

3. Bradley F. Smith, *Reaching Judgment at Nuremberg* (New York: Basic Books, 1977), p. 18.

4. See Bradley Smith's formulation of the problem in *Reaching Judgment at Nuremberg*.

5. *Reaching Judgment*, p. 16.

6. *Ibid.*, p. 14.

7. W. Paul Burman, ed., *The First German War Crimes Trial*, p. 15.

8. August Wimmer, "Die Bestrafung von Humanitaetsverbrechen und der Grundsatz 'nullum crimen sine lege'," *Sueddeutsche Juristenzeitung* II (Sondernummer, March 1947): 123–32.

9. "An Inquiry into the Juridicial Basis for the Nuernberg War Crimes Trial," *Minnesota Law Review*, 30, No. 5 (April 1946): 329.

10. W. Paul Burman, ed. *The First German War Crimes Trial*, p. 13.

11. *Ibid.*, p. 14.

12. *Ibid.*, p. 31.

13. "Biomedical Ethics and the Shadow of Nazism: A Conference on the Proper Use of the Nazi Analogy in Ethical Debate," *The Hastings Center Report*, Special Supplement (August 1976): 4.

14. Laws were extended accordingly. On the basis of Control Council Law No. 10, the U.S. Military Government in Germany decreed Ordinance No. 7, allowing for the establishment of military tribunals to try and punish suspected war criminals in the American Zone of occupation.

15. Proceedings, pp. 63–64.

16. François Bayle, *Croix Gammee Contre Caducee: Les Experiences Humaines en Allemagne Pendent la Deuxieme Guerre Mondiale* (L'Office Militaire de Securite, 1950).

17. Rebecca West, *A Train of Powder* (Chicago: Ivan R. Dee, n.d.), p. 28.

18. Proceedings, p. 01.

19. *Ibid.*, p. 04.

20. *Ibid.*, p. 11.

21. *Ibid.*, p. 03.

22. Proceedings, Closing Argument of Prosecution, p. 20.

23. *Ibid.*, p. 29.

24. Proceedings, p. 7896.

25. *Ibid.*, p. 8161.

26. See Trial Brief for the Military Tribunal I, II and III, Nuernberg, concerning the Conspiracy for the Joint Commission of War Crimes and Crimes Against Humanity, submitted by Carl Hansel, Nuernberg, June 30, 1947. Proceedings, pp. 1512–55.

27. Arguments of General Taylor on the Conspiracy Count, presented before the Joint Session of Tribunals I, II, III, IV and V, July 9, 1947. Proceedings, pp. 1600–1617.

28. Order, Case No. 1, Defendants' Motion Against Count I of the Indictment, July 14, 1947. Proceedings, p. 1618.

29. Proceedings, p. 06.

30. Document No. 520.

31. Proceedings, p. 4186.

32. *Ibid.*, pp. 4188–89.

33. *Ibid.*, pp. 4331–32.

34. *Ibid.*, pp. 2606–07.

35. Michael Grodin, "Historical Origins of the Nuremberg Medical Code," *The Nazi Doctors and the Nuremberg Code*, George J. Annas and Michael A. Grodin, eds. (Oxford: Oxford Univ. Press, 1992), pp. 127–32.

36. Proceedings, p. 4650–51.

37. *Ibid.*, pp. 9029–9324.

38. Alexander Mitscherlich, *Doctors of Infamy: The Story of the Nazi Medical Crimes* (New York: Henry Schuman, 1949), pp. 5–6.

39. Alexander Mitscherlich and Fred Mielke, Medizin ohne Menschlichkeit: Dokumente des

Nuernberger Aerzteprozesses (Frankfurt a/M: Fischer Taschenbuch Verlag, 1985), p. 24. Author's translation.

40. Mitscherlich, Doctors of Infamy, p. 12

41. Mitscherlich and Mielke, *Medizin ohne Menschlichkeit*, p. 26. Author's translation.

42. *The Theory and Practice of Hell* (New York: Octagon Books), pp. 143–44.

43. *Ibid.*, p. 158.

44. Proceedings, p. 9851.

45. *Ibid.*, p. 5500.

46. Document No. 1189.

47. Proceedings, p. 4243.

48. *Ibid.*, p. 4214.

49. *Ibid.*, p. 7202.

50. Proceedings, Judgment, pp. 216–17.

51. *Ibid.*, p. 280.

52. *Ibid.*, p. 274.

53. *Ibid.*, p. 279.

54. Document No. 179.

55. Proceedings, Closing Brief for U.S. against Beiglboeck, p. 21.

56. *Ibid.*, p. 10.

57. Proceedings, p. 8705.

58. *Ibid.*, pp. 8711–12.

59. *Ibid.*, p. 8706.

60. Proceedings, Judgment, p. 237.

61. Proceedings, p. 7729.

62. Proceedings, Closing Argument of the Prosecution, pp. 58–59.

63. *Ibid.*, p. 69.

64. *Ibid.*, p. 71.

65. See Robert N. Proctor, *Racial Hygiene: Medicine Under the Nazis* (Cambridge: Harvard Univ. Press, 1988).

66. See Michael Kater, *Doctors Under Hitler* (Chapel Hill: University of North Carolina Press, 1989).

67. Proceedings, Indictment, p. 013.

68. Proceedings, Judgment, p. 156.

69. *Ibid.*, pp. 160–61.

70. *Ibid.*, p. 161.

71. Trial of Major War Criminals before the International Military Tribunal, 42 vols., Judgment (Nuremberg: 1947), p. 16930.

72. *Ibid.*, p. 16930.

73. Proceedings, Judgment, p. 180.

74. Burman, *The First War Crimes Trial*, p. 241.

75. Proceedings, p. 2622.

76. Karl Jaspers, "The Significance of the Nuremberg Trials for Germany in the World," *Notre Dame Lawyer*, 22 (January 1947), p. 157.

77. Proceedings, Judgment, pp. 25–26.

78. *Ibid.*, pp. 3–4.

79. Control Council Law No. 10, Art. III, 1d.

80. Proceedings, p. 13.

81. This argument was advanced very forcefully by Hodo von Hodenberg in "Zur Anwendung des Kontrollratsgesetzes Nr. 10 durch deutsche Gerichte," *Sueddeutsche Juristen-Zeitung*, Sondernummer (March 1947): 114–124.

82. For a discussion of these points see August Wimmer, "Die Bestrafung von Humanitaetsverbrechen und der Grundsatz 'nullum crimen sine lege'," and Gustav Radbruch, "Zur Discussion ueber die Verbrechen gegen die Menschlichkeit," *Sueddeutsche Juristen-Zeitung*, Sondernummer (March 1947): 124–136.

83. Article 3 of the Charter reads: "Neither the Tribunal, its members nor their alternatives can be challenged by the Prosecution or by the Defendants or their Counsel."

84. Nathan April, "An Inquiry into the Juridicial Basis for the Nuernberg War Crimes Trial," *Minnesota Law Review*, 30, No. 5 (April 1946): 319.

85. Proceedings, p. 9091.

86. *Ibid.*, p. 6492.

87. *Ibid.*, p. 7011.

88. See Peter Williams and David Wallace, *Unit 731: Japan's Secret Biological Warfare in World War II* (New York: Free Press, 1989).

89. *Ibid.*, p. 210.

90. Proceedings, p. 13.

91. *Ibid.*, p. 4002.

92. *Ibid.*, p. 8970.

93. *Ibid.*, pp. 9085–87.

94. *Ibid.*, p. 9094.

95. *Ibid.*, pp. 9201–3.

96. *Ibid.*, pp. 9254–67.

97. William B. Bean, Walter Read and Yellow Fever, "*JAMA*, 250, No. 5 (Aug. 5, 1983): 659–662.

98. Richard P. Strong and B.C. Crowell, "The Etiology of Beriberi," *The Philippine Journal of Science*, VII, No. 4 (1912): 291.

99. There was a lengthy report about the general nature of the experiments in *Life* (June 14, 1945): 43–45.

100. Jon M. Harkness, "*Nuremberg and the Issue of Wartime Experiments on the U.S. Prisoners: The Green Committee,*" JAMA, 276, No. 20 (November 27, 1996): 1672–76.

101. Proceedings, pp. 9029–9324.

102. Michael A. Grodin, "Historical Origins of the Nuremberg Code," *The Nazi Doctors and the Nuremberg Code*, pp. 121–44.

103. Only some pictures of the defendants were shown on page one. The report appeared on page two: "Nicht zu heilen, sonder zu vernichten war ihr Ziel," *Nuernberger Nachrichten*, Vol. 2 (Dec. 11, 1946).

104. "7 Todesurteile-7 Freispruehe im Aerzteprozess," Nuernberger Nachrichten, Vol. 3 (Aug. 23, 1947).

105. "Sieben Todesurteile in Nuernberg," *Berliner Zeitung*, Vol. 3, No. 193 (Aug. 21, 1947, and "Schuldsprueche im Aerzteprozess," *Neues Deutschland*, Vol. 3, No. 193 (Aug. 20, 1947).

106. Alexander Mitscherlich and Fred Mielke, *Das Diktat der Menschenverachtung* (Heidelberg: Verlag Lambert Schneider, 1947).

107. David J. Rothman, *Strangers at the Bedside: A History of How Law and Bioethics Transformed Medical Decision Making* (New York: Basic Books, 1994), p. 62.

108. *Ibid.*, pp. 62–63.

Chapter Three

1. Robert A. Birt, "The Suppressed Legacy of Nuremberg," *The Hastings Center Report*, 26, No. 5 (Sept./Oct. 1996): 30–34.

2. Arthur L. Caplan, "The Doctors' Trial and Analogies to the Holocaust in Contemporary Bioethical Debates," *The Nazi Doctors and the Nuremberg Code*, George J. Annas and Michael A. Grodin, eds. (Oxford: Oxford Univ. Press, 1992), pp. 258–59.

3. Daniel J. Goldhagen, *Hitler's Willing Executioners: Ordinary Germans and the Holocaust* (New York: Alfred A. Kopf, 1996).

4. See especially "Aus der Geschichte lernen-How to Learn from History," mit Reden von Juergen Habermas, Jan Philipp Reemtsma, Daniel Goldhagen, *edition Blaetter* 2 (Bonn: Blaetter Verl.-Ges., 1997).

5. See Hayden White, *Metahistory: The Historical Imagination in Nineteenth-Century Europe* (Baltimore: The Johns Hopkins University Press, 1973).

6. Proceedings, pp. 2571–72.

7. *Ibid.*, pp. 4280–81.

8. *Ibid.*, p. 3967.

9. *Ibid.*, pp. 2803, 4067.

10. Leo Alexander, "Medical Science Under Dictatorship," *The New England Journal of Medicine*, 241, No. 2 (July 14, 1949): 37.

11. Proceedings, pp. 9245–46.

12. *Ibid.*, p. 6382.

13. *Ibid.*, p. 9166.

14. G.E.R. Lloyd, ed. *Hippocratic Writings* (New York: Penguin, 1983), p. 67.

15. Proceedings, p. 1969.

16. *Ibid.*, pp. 3472–73.

17. *Ibid.*, p. 3950.

18. *Ibid.*, pp. 1989–90.

19. *Das aerztliche Ethos: Christoph Wilhelm Hufelands Vermaechtnis einer Fuenfzigjaehrigen Erfahrung* (Berlin: J.F. Lehmanns Verlag, n.d.).

20. Proceedings, p. 1991.

21. See Ludwig Edelstein, "The Hippocratic Oath: Text, Translation and Interpretation," *Bulletin of the History of Medicine*, Supplement No. 1, 1943, pp. 1–64.

22. See Chauncey D. Leake, "Theories of Ethics and Medical Practice," *JAMA*, 208 (1969): 842–47.

23. Proceedings, p. 7133.

24. *Ibid.*, p. 7131.

25. *Ibid.*, p. 7802.

26. *Ibid.*, p. 9148.

27. *Ibid.*, pp. 9251–52.

28. See Lloyd, ed., *Hippocratic Writings.*

29. *Ibid.*, p. 11.

30. Proceedings, p. 9147.

31. *Ibid.*, pp. 4330–31.

32. *Ibid.*, p. 4332.

33. See Hannah Arendt, *Eichmann in Jerusalem* (New York: Penguin Books, 1985).

34. Proceedings., pp. 2656–57.

35. *Ibid.*, p. 3949.

36. *Ibid.*, p. 5028.

37. *Ibid.*, pp. 5030–31.

38. *Ibid.*, pp. 9314–17.

39. *Ibid.*, pp. 9239–42.

40. *Ibid.*, pp. 2378–80.

41. *Ibid.*, pp. 8085–87.

42. The witness Felix Hoering attended the meeting as an active officer of the German Army and delivered a lecture on yellow fever. A colleague of Rose, his testimony for the defense naturally was very favorable.

43. Proceedings, pp. 6035–36.

44. Abschriften aus dem Bericht ueber die 3. Arbeitstagung Ost der Beratenden Fachaerzte vom 24.-26. Mai 1943 in der Militaerischen Akademie Berlin, Rose Document No. 38, Exhibit 10, pp. 42–43. Also see Rose testimony, Proceedings, pp. 6168–70.

45. *Ibid.*, pp. 43–44.

46. Document Nos. 1186, 265.

47. Proceedings, pp. 6172–78.

48. *Ibid.*, p. 6181.

49. *Ibid.*, p. 672.

50. *Ibid.*, p. 6182.

51. *Ibid.*, p. 6187.

52. *Ibid.*, pp. 6155–56.

53. *Ibid.*, p. 2398.

54. *Ibid.*, p. 2399.

55. *Ibid.*, p. 2437.

56. Hartmut M. Hanauske-Abel, "Not a slippery slope or sudden subversion: German medicine and National Socialism in 1933," *British Medical Journal*, 313 (Dec. 7, 1996): 1454.

57. *Ibid.*, p. 1461.

58. Proceedings, p. 6567.

59. *Ibid.*, pp. 8829–30.

60. *Ibid.*, pp. 268–70.

61. Document No. 402.

62. For the method selecting the subjects see Chapter II, C) Count Two: War Crimes.

63. Proceedings, pp. 6928–32.

64. *Ibid.*, pp. 6840–41.

65. Aerztliche Fragen bei Seenot und Winternot. The report mentioned six deaths. Document No. 428. The Witness Walter Neff, one of Rascher's inmate assistants, mentions fifteen to eighteen. Proceedings, p. 672.

66. Proceedings, pp. 7914–15.

67. *Ibid.*, pp. 6843–44.

68. Francois Bayle, *Croix Gammee Contre Caducee: Les Experiences en Allemagne Pendant la Deuxieme Guerre Mondiale* (L'Office Militaire de Securite, 1950), p. 70. Author's translation.

69. See Ernst Klee, *Was sie Taten-Was Sie wurden: Aerzte, Juristen und andere Beteiligte am Kranken- oder Judenmord* (Frankfurt a/M: Fischer Taschenbuch Verlag, 1986).

70. See Michael H. Kater, *Doctors Under Hitler* (Chapel Hill: Univ. of North Carolina Press, 1989).

71. Alexander Mitscherlich and Fred Mielke, Medizin ohne Menschlichkeit: Dokumente des Nuernberger Aerzteprozesses (Frankfurt a/M: Fischer Taschenbuch Verlag, 1978), p. 15.

72. Christian Pross and Goetz Aly, eds., *Der Wert des Menschen: Medizin in Deutschland 1918–1945* (Berlin: Edition Hentrich, 1989), p. 376.

73. Mitscherlich and Mielke, *Medizin ohne Menschlichkeit*, p. 13.

74. Hartmut M. Hanauske-Abel, "From Nazi Holocaust to Nuclear Holocaust: A Lesson to Learn?" *The Lancet* (Aug. 2, 1986): 271.

75. Ibid., pp. 271–73, and the rejoinder: Karsten Vilmar, "Die 'Vergangenheitsbewaeltigung' darf nicht kolletiv die Aerzte diffamieren," Deutsches Aerzteblatt, 84, No. 18 (April 30, 1987): B847–49.

76. Hartmut M. Hanauske-Abel, "Die Unfaehigkeit zu Trauern: Erziehungsziel fuer Junge Deutsche Aerzte," Rundbrief, Sondernummer, November 1987, pp. 2545.

77. See in particular Benno Mueller-Hill, *Toedliche Wissenschaft* (Reinbeck bei Hamburg: Rowohlt Taschenbuch Verlag, 1984), Ernst Klee, *Euthanasie im SS-Staat* (Frankfurt a/M: Fischer Taschenbuch Verlag, 1985), Fridolf Kudlien et al., *Aerzte im Nationalsozialismus* (Koeln: Kiepheuser and Witsch, 1985), Goetz Aly et al., *Aussonderung und Tod: Die Klinische Hinrichtung der Unbrauchbaren* (Berlin: Rotbuch Verlag, 1985), and Johanna Bleker and Heinz-Peter Schmiedebach, eds., *Medizin und Krieg* (Frankfurt a/m:Fischer Taschenbuch Verlag, 1987).

78. See Linda Hunt, "U.S. Coverup of Nazi Scientists, " *Bulletin of the Atomic Scientists*, 41, No. 4 (April 1985): 16–24.

79. See "U.S. Role Alleged in Cover-up of Researchers Guilty of War Crimes," *Nature*, 335 (Oct. 6, 1988): 481, and Peter Williams and David Wallace, *Unit 731: Japan's Secret Biological Warfare in World War II* (New York: Free Press, 1989).

80. "Doctors on Trial,*" British Medical Journal* (Jan. 25, 1947): 143.

81. See Kristine Moe, "Should Nazi Research Data Be Cited?" *The Hastings Center Report*, 14, No. 6 (December 1984), and Berhard Dixon, "Citations of Shame," *New Scientist* (Feb. 28, 1985).

82. "What's in a Name? The Eppinger Prize and Nazi Experiments," *The Hastings Center Report*, 14, No. 6 (December 1984): 3–4.

83. Howard M. Spiro, "Eppinger of Vienna: Scientist and Villain?" *Journal of Clinical Gastroenterology*, 6 (1984): 493–97.

84. Moe, "Should Nazi Data Be Cited?"

85. "The Nazi Doctors and the Nuremberg Medical Code: Relevance for Modern Medical Research," Law, Medicine and Ethics Program, Boston University School of Medicine and Public Health, December 4–5, 1989, University Publications, pp. 140–41.

86. Dixon, "Citations of Shame."

87. "Nazi Scientists and Ethics of Today," The New York Times (May 21, 1989): 34 for the Minnesota Conference, and "The Nazi Doctors and the Nuremberg Code," Boston University.

88. Philip Shaecoff, "Head of E.P.A. Bars Nazi Data in Study on Gas," *The New York Times* (March 23, 1988): 1, and Marjorie Sun, "EPA Bars Use of Nazi Data," *Science*, 240, No. 4848 (April 1, 1988): 21.

89. Moe, "Should Nazi Data Be Cited?", p. 5.

90. *Ibid.*, p. 7.

91. Henry Beecher, "Ethics and Clinical Research," *The New England Journal of Medicine*, 274, No. 24 (June 16, 1966): 1360.

92. Annas and Grodin, *The Nazi Doctors*, p. 281.

93. "Commentary," *Hastings Center Report*, 19 (July/August 1989): 18.

94. Stephen G. Post, "The Echo of Nuremberg: Nazi Data and Ethics," *Journal of Medical Ethics*, 17 (1991): 42.

95. Spiro, "Eppinger in Vienna," pp. 495, 497.

96. "Can Scientists Use Information Derived from the Concentration Camps?" *When Medicine Went Mad: Bioethics and the Holocaust*, Arthur L. Caplan, ed. (Totowa, N.J.: Humana Press, 1992), p. 162.

97. Eva Mozes Kor, "Nazi Experiments as Viewed by a Survivor of Mengele's Experiments," *When Medicine Went Mad*, p. 7.

98. Benno Mueller-Hill, *Murderous Science: Elimination by Scientific Selection of Jews, Gypsies and Others, Germany 1933–1945* (Oxford: Oxford Univ. Press, 1988), p. 100.

99. Caplan, *When Medicine Went Mad*, p. 70.

100. G.E.R. Lloyd, *Greek Science After Aristotle* (New York: W.W. Norton, 1973), pp. 75–90.

101. Proceedings, pp. 71–72.

102. Benno Mueller-Hill, "Genetics After Auschwitz," *Holocaust and Genocide Studies*, 2, No. 1 (1987): 17.

103. *Ibid.*, p. 15.

104. "Nazi Experiments as Viewed by a Survivor of Mengele's Experiments," *When Medicine Went Mad*, pp. 7–8.

Epilogue

1. George J. Annas and Michael A. Grodin, *The Nazi Doctors and the Nuremberg Medical Code* (Oxford: Oxford Univ. Press, 1992), p. 154.

2. *Ibid.*, p. 155.

3. *Ibid.*, p. 160.

4. Roy Gutman and David Rieff, eds., *Crimes of War* (New York: W.W. Norton, 1999), p. 242.

5. Henry Beecher, "Ethics and Clinical Research," *The New England Journal of Medicine*, 274 (1966): 1354–60.

6. Giovanni Maio, "Das Humanexperiment vor und nach Nuernberg," *Medizin und Ethik im Zeichen von Auschwitz: 50 Jahre Nuernberger Aerzteprozess,* Claudia Wieseman und Andreas Frewer, eds. (Erlangen: Verlag Palm und Enke, 1996), pp. 45–78.

7. Evelyne Shuster, "The Nuremberg Code: Hippocratic Ethics and Human Rights," *The Lancet*, 351, No. 9107 (March 28, 1998): 974–78.

8. Garland E. Allen, "The Ideology of Elimination: American and German Eugenics, 1900–1945," *Medicine and Medical Ethics in Nazi Germany*, Frances R. Nicosia and Jonathan Huener, eds. (New York: Berghahn Books, 2002), pp. 13–39.

9. Bruno Schirra, "Die Erinnerung der Taeter," *Der Spiegel*, No. 40 (Sept. 28, 1998): 91.

Bibliography

Aly, Goetz; Chroust, Peter and Pross, Christian, *Cleansing the Fatherland: Nazi Medicine and Racial Hygiene* (Baltimore: The Johns Hopkins University Press, 1994).

Alexander, Leo, "Medical Science Under Dictatorship," *The New England Journal of Medicine*, 241, No. 2 (July 14, 1949): 39–47.

Alexander, Leo, "War Crimes: Their Socio-Psychological Aspects." *American Journal of Psychiatry*, 105 (1948): 170–77.

Angell, Marcia, "The Nazi Hypothermia Experiments and Unethical Research Today," *The New England Journal of Medicine*, 322, No. 20 (May 17, 1990): 1462–64.

Annas, George J., and Grodin, Michael A., *The Nazi Doctors and the Nuremberg Code: Human Rights in Human Experimentation* (Oxford: Oxford University Press, 1992).

April, Nathan, "An Inquiry into the Juridical Basis for the Nuernberg War Crimes Trial," *Minnesota Law Review*, 30, No. 5 (April 1946): 313–31.

Arendt, Hannah, *Eichmann in Jerusalem* (New York: Penguin Books, 1985).

Ascherson, Neal, "The Death Doctors," Review of R.J. Lifton's "The Nazi Doctors," *The New York Review of Books* (May 28, 1987): 29–34

"Aus der Geschichte lernen-How to Learn from History: Verleihung des Blaetter-Demokratiepreises 1997," mit Reden von Juergen Habermas, Jan Philipp Reemtsma, Daniel Goldhagen, *edition Blaetter* 2 (Bonn: Blaetter Verlagsgesellschaft, 1997).

Baader, Gerhard, and Schulz, Ulrich, eds., *Medizin und Nationalsozialismus: Tabuisierte Vergangenheit-Ungebrochene Tradition?* (Berlin: Verlagsgesellschaft Gesundheit, 1980).

Bayle, Francois, *Croix Gammee Contre Caducee: Les Experiences en Allemagne Pendant la Deuxieme Guerre Mondiale* (L'Office Militaire de Securite, 1950).

Barondess, Jeremiah, "Medicine Against Society: Lessons From the Third Reich," *The Journal of the American Medical Association*, 276, No. 20 (November 27, 1996): 1657–61.

Bean, William B., "Walter Reed and Yellow Fever," *The Journal of the American Medical Association*, 250, No. 5 (August 5, 1983): 659–662.

Beecher, Henry K., "Ethics and Clinical Research," *The New England Journal of Medicine*, 274, No. 24 (June 16, 1966): 1354–60.

Begley, Sharon, and King, Patricia, "The Deadliest Kind of Cold: Exploring Hypothermia, *Newsweek* (March 9, 1987): 63.

Berger, Robert L., "Nazi Science: The Dachau Hypothermia Experiments," *New England Journal of Medicine*, 322, No. 20 (May 17, 1990): 1435–40.

Bettelheim, Bruno, "Their Specialty was Murder," *The New York Times Book Review* (October 15, 1986): 62

"Biomedical Ethics and the Shadow of Nazism: A Conference on the Proper Use of the Nazi Analogy in Ethical Debate, April 8, 1976," *The Hastings Center Report*, 6, Special Supplement (August 1976): 1–19.

Birt, Robert A., "The Suppressed Legacy of Nuremberg," *The Hastings Center Report*, 26, No. 5 (September/October 1996).

Bleker, Johanna and Jachertz, Norbert, eds., *Medizin im Dritten Reich* (Koeln: Deutscher Aerzte-Verlag, 1989).

Bleker, Johanna and Schmiedebach, Heinz-Peter, *Medizin und Krieg: Vom Dilemma der Heilberufe* 1865–1985 (Frankfurt a/M: Fischer Taschenbuch Velag, 1987).

Blome, Kurt, *Arzt im Kampf: Erlebnisse und Gedanken* (Leipzig: J.A. Barth Verlag, 1942).

Burleigh, Michael, *Death and Deliverance: "Euthanasia" in Germany* c. 1900–1945 (Cambridge: Cambridge University Press, 1994).

Boozer, Jack S., Children of Hippocrates: Doctors in Nazi Germany," *Annals of the American Academy of Political and Social Science*, 450 (July 1980): 83–97.

Brieger, Gert H., "Human Experimentation: History," *Encyclopedia of Bioethics*, 2 (New York: Free Press, 1978).

Burman, W. Paul, *The First German War Crimes Trial: Chief Judge Walter BB. Beals's Desk Notebook of the Doctors' Trial, Held in Nuernberg, Germany, December, 1945 to August, 1947* (Chapel Hill, N.C.: Documentary Publications, 1985).

Burt, Robert A., "The Suppressed Legacy of Nuremberg," *The Hastings Center Report*, 26, No. 5 (September/October 1996): 30–33.

Campbell, Courtney S., ed. "Nazi Data: Dissociation From Evil," *The Hastings Center Report*, 19 (July/August 1989): 16–19.

Caplan, Arthur L., ed., *When Medicine Went Mad: Bioethics and the Holocaust* (Totowa, N.J.: Humana Press, 1992).

Crum, Gary E., "Nazi Bioethics and a Doctor's Defense," *The Human Life Review*, 8 (1982): 55–69.

"Deaths Associated with Yellow Fever," *The Journal of the American Medical Association*, 249, No. 9 (March 4, 1983): 1150–51.

Deichmann, Ute, *Biologists Under Hitler* (Cambridge: Harvard University Press, 1996).

Dickman, Steven, "US role alleged in cover-up of researchers guilty of war crimes," *Nature*, 335 (October 6, 1988): 481.

Dixon, Bernard, "Citations of Shame," *New Scientist* (February 28, 1985): 31.

Ebbinghaus, Angelika and Doerner, Klaus, eds., *Vernichten und Heilen: Der Nuernberger Aerzteprozess und seine Folgen* (Berlin: Aufbau-Verlag, 2001).

Edelstein, Ludwig, *The Hippocratic Oath: Text, Translation and Interpretation* (Baltimore: The Johns Hopkins Press, 1943).

Elkeles, Barbara, "Medizinische Menschenversuche gegen Ende des 19. Jahrhunderts und der Fall Neisser," *Medizinhistorisches Journal*, 20 (1988): 135–48.

Engelhardt, H. Tristram, *The Foundations of Bioethics* (Oxford: Oxford University Press, 1986).

Etheridge, Elizabeth W., *The Butterfly Cast: A Social History of Pellagra in the South* (Westport, CT: Greenwood Publishing C., 1972).

Faden, Ruth R., and Beauchamp, Tom L., *A History and Theory of Informed Consent* (Oxford: Oxford University Press, 1986).

Faden, Ruth; Lederer Susan; Moreno, Jonathan, "US Medical Researchers, the Nuremberg Doctors Trial, and the Nuremberg Code," *The Journal of the American Medical Association*, 276, No. 20 (November 27, 1996): 1667–71.

Flood, Dom Peter, ed., *Medical Experimentation on Man* (Cork, Ireland: Mercier Press, 1955).

Friedlander, Saul, ed., *Probing the Limits of Representation: Nazism and the "Final Solution,"* (Cambridge: Harvard University Press, 1992).

German Aviation Medicine: World War II, 2 Vols., (Washington, D.C.: Dept. of the Air Force, 1950).

"German Medical War Crimes," United Nations War Crimes Commission, World Medical Association, British Medical Association House, London, 1949, pp. 12–13.

Goldhagen, Daniel Jonah, *Hitler's Willing Executioners: Ordinary Germans and the Holocaust* (New York: Alfred A. Knopf, 1996).

Grotjahn, Alfred, *Soziale Pathologie: Versuch einer Lehre von den sozialen Beziehungen der menschlichen Krankheiten als Grundlage der sozialen Medizin und der sozialen Hygiene* (Berlin: Verlag A. Hirschwald, 1912).

Gutman, Roy and Rieff, David, *Crimes of War: What the Public Should Know* (New York: W.W. Norton, 1999). Habermas, Juergen et al., *edition Blaetter* 2 (Bonn: Blaetter Verl.-Ges., 1997).

Hackethal, Julius, *Der Meineid des Hippokrates: Von der Verschwoerung der Aerzte zur Selbstbestimmung des Patienten* (Bergisch Gladbach: Gustav Luebbe Verlag, 1992).

Hanauske-Abel, Hartmut M., "From Nazi Holocaust to Nuclear Holocaust," *The Lancet* (August 2, 1986): 271–73.

Hanauske-Abel, Hartmut M., "Not a Slippery Slope or Sudden Conversion: German Medicine and National Socialism in 1933," *British Medical Journal*, 313 (December 7, 1996): 1453–63.

Harkness, Jon M., "Nuremberg and the Issue of Wartime Experiments on US Prisoners: The Green Committee," *The Journal of the American Medical Association*, 276, No. 20 (November 27, 1996): 1672–75.

Henderson, Yandell, *Adventures in Respiration: Methods of Asphyxiation and Methods of Resuscitation* (Baltimore: The Williams and Wilkins Co., 1938).

Hodenberg, Hodo von, "Zur Anwendung des Kontollratsgesetzes Nr. 10 durch deutsche Gerichte," *Sueddeutsche Juristen-Zeitung*, Sondernummer (March 1947): 114–124.

Hoedeman, Paul, *Hitler or Hippocrates: Medical Experiments and Euthanasia in the Third Reich* (Sussex, England: The Book Guild, 1991).

Hunt, Linda, "U.S. coverup of Nazi scientists," *Bulletin of the Atomic Scientists*, 41, No. 4 (April 1985): 16–24.

Ivy, Andrew C., "The History and Ethics of the Use of Human Subjects in Medical Experiments," *Science*, 108 (July 2, 1948): 1–5.

Jaspers, Karl, "The Significance of the Nuernberg Trials for Germany and the World," *Notre Dame Lawyer*, 22 (January 1947): 150–160.

Jones, James H. *Bad Blood: The Tuskegee Syphilis Experiment-A Tragedy of Race and Medicine* (New York: Free Press, 1981).

Kater, Michael H., *Das "Ahnenerbe" der SS 1935–1945: Ein Beitrag zur Kulturpolitik des Dritten Reiches* (Stuttgart: Deutsche Verlags-Anstalt, 1974).

Kater, Michael H., *Doctors Under Hitler* (Chapel Hill, N.C.: University of North Carolina Press, 1989).

Katz, Jay, and Capron, Alexander, *Experimentation with Human Beings* (New York: Russell Sage Foundation, 1972).

Katz, Jay, "The Nuremberg Code and the Nuremberg Trial: A Reappraisal," *The Journal of the American Medical Association*, 276, No. 20 (November 27, 1996): 1662–66.

Klee, Ernst, *Auschwitz, die NS-Medizin und Ihre Opfer* (Frankfurt a/M: S. Fischer Verlag, 1997).

Klee, Ernst, *"Euthanasie" im NS-Staat: Die "Vernichtung lebensunwerten Lebens,"* (Frankfurt a/M: Fischer Taschenbuch Verlag, 1985).

Klee, Ernst, *Was sie taten-Was sie wurden: Aerzte, Juristen und andere Beteiligte am Kranken- oder Judenmord* (Frankfurt a/M: Fischer Taschenbuch Verlag, 1986)

Kochavi, Arieh J., *Prelude to Nuremberg: Allied War Crimes Policy and the Question of Punishment* (Chapel Hill, N.C.: University of North Carolina Press, 1998).

Kogon, Eugen; Langbein, Hermann; Rueckerl, Adelbert, et al., eds, *Nationalsozialistische Massentoetungen durch Giftgas: Eine Dokumentation* (Frankfurt a/M: Fischer Taschenbuch Verlag, 1986).

Kogon, Eugen, *The Theory and Practice of Hell* (New York: Octagon Books, 1976).

Kohut, Thomas, "Empathizing With Nazis: Reflections on Robert Jay Lifton's 'The Nazi Doctors'," *Psychohistory Review*, 16, No. 1 (Fall 1987): 33;50.

Kruif, Paul de, *Hunger Fighters* (New York: Harcourt, Brace and Co., 1928).

Kudlien, Fridolf, *Aerzte im Nationalsozialismus* (Koeln: Kiepenheuer and Witsch, 1985).

Kudlien, Fridolf, "Medical Ethics and Popular Ethics in Greece and Rome," *Clio Medica*, 5 (1970): 91–121.

Kuehl, Stefan, *The Nazi Connection: Eugenics, American Racism, and German National Socialism* (Oxford: Oxford University Press, 1994).

Leake, Chauncey D., "Theories and Ethics of Medical Practice," *The Journal of the American Medical Association*, 208 (1969): 842–47.

Lederer, Susan E., *Subjected to Science: Human Experimentation in America Before the Second World War* (Baltimore: The Johns Hopkins University Press, 1995).

Lerner, Barron H., and Rothman, David J., Medicine and the Holocaust: Learning More of the Lessons," *Annals of Internal Medicine*, 122, No. 10 (May 15, 1995): 793–94.

Liek, Erwin, *Der Arzt und seine Sendung* (Muenchen: J.F. Lehmanns Verlag, 1927).

Lifton, Robert Jay, *The Nazi Doctors: Medical Killing and the Psychology of Genocide* (New York: Basic Books, 1986).

Lifton, Robert Jay, "On Investigating Nazi Doctors: Further Thoughts," *Psychohistory Review,* 16, No. 1 (Fall 1987): 51–66.

Lloyd, G.E.R., ed., *Hippocratic Writings* (New York: Penguin, 1983).

Lock, Stephen, "Research Ethics: A Brief Historical Review to 1965," *Journal of Internal Medicine,* 238, No. 6 (December 1995): 513–20.

Lorenz, Konrad, "Durch Domestikation verursachte Stoerungen arteigenen Verhaltens," *Zeitschrift fuer Angewandte Psychologie und Characterkunde,* 59, No. 12 (June 1940).

Maio, Giovanni, "Das Humanexperiment vor und nach Nuernberg," *Medizin und Ethik im Zeichen von Auschwitz: 50 Jahre Nuernberger Aerzteprozess,* Claudia Wiesmann and Andreas Frewer, eds. (Erlangen: Verlag Palm and Enke, 1996), pp. 45–78.

Martini, Paul, "Eroeffnungsansprache des Vorsitzenden," *Verhandlungen der deutschen Gesellschaft fuer Innere Medizin,* 54 (1948): 1–11.

Mellanby, Kenneth, *Human Guinea Pigs* (London: Merlin Press, 1973).

Michalczyk, John J., ed., *Medicine, Ethics, and the Third Reich: Historical and Contemporary Issues* (Kansas City: Sheed and Ward, 1994).

Mitscherlich, Alexander, and Mielke, Fred, *Doctors of Infamy: The Story of the Nazi Medical Crimes* (New York: Henry Schuman, 1949).

Mitscherlich, Alexander and Mielke, Fred, eds., *Medizin ohne Menschlichkeit: Dokumente des Nuernberge Aerzteprozesses* (Frankfurt a/M: Fischer Taschenbuch Verlag, 1985).

Moe, Kristine, "Should Nazi Research Data be Cited?" *The Hastings Center Report,* 14, No. 6 (December 1984): 5–7.

Moll, Albert, *Aerztliche Ethik: Die Pflichten des Arztes in allen Beziehungen seiner Taetigkeit* (Stuttgart: F. Enke, 1904).

Mrugowsky, Joachim, *Das aerztliche Ethos: Christoph Wilhelm Hufelands Vermaechtnis einer fuenfzigjaehrigen Erfahrung* (Berlin: J.F. Lehmanns Verlag, n.d.).

Mueller-Hill, Benno, "Genetics After Auschwitz," *Holocaust and Genocide Studies,* 2, No. 1 (1987): 3–20.

Mueller-Hill, Benno, *Murderous Science: Elimination by Scientific Selection of Jews, Gypsies and Others: Germany 1933–1945* (Oxford: Oxford University Press, 1988).

"Nazi Scientists and Ethics of Today," *The New York Times* (May 21, 1989), p. 34.

"Nicht zu heilen, sondern zu vernichten war ihr Ziel," *Nuernberger Nachrichten,* 2 (December 11, 1946).

Nicosia, Francis R., and Huener, Jonathan, eds., *Medicine and Medical Ethics in Nazi Germany: Origins, Practices, Legacies* (New York: Berghahn Books 2002)

Nyiszli, Miklos, *Auschwitz: A Doctor's Eyewitness Account* (Greenwich, CT.: Fawcett Publication, 1960).

Platen-Hallermund, Alice, *Die Toetung Geisteskranker in Deutschland* (Frankfurt a/M: Verlag der Frankfurter Hefte, 1948).

Post, Stephen G., "The Echo of Nuremberg: Nazi Data and Ethics," *Journal of Medical Ethics,* 17 (1991): 42–44.

Proctor, Robert N., *Racial Hygiene: Medicine Under the Nazis* (Cambridge: Harvard University Press, 1988).

Pross, Christian, Breaking Through the Postwar Coverup of Nazi Doctors in Germany," *Journal of Medical Ethics,* 17, No. 4 (December 1991): 13–16

Pross, Christian and Aly, Goetz, eds. *Der Wert des Menschen: Medizin in Deutschland 1918–1945* (Berlin: Edition Hentrich, 1989).

Pross, Christian, *Paying for the Past: The Struggle over Reparations for Surviving Victims of the Nazi Terror* (Baltimore: Johns Hopkins University Press, 1998).

Radbruch, Gustav, "Zur Diskussion ueber die Verbrechen gegen die Menschlichkeit," *Sueddeutsche Juristen-Zeitung*, Sondernummer (March 1947): 124–136.

Ravitch, Norman, "Reflections on Robert Jay Lifton's 'The Nazi Doctors'," *Psychohistory Review*, 16, No. 1 (Fall 1987): 3–14.

Records of the United States Nuernberg War Crimes Trials, United States of America vs. Karl Brandt et al. (Case 1, Medical Case), National Archives Microfilm Publications, Washington, D.C. Publications M887.

Reilly, Philip R., "Involuntary Sterilization in the United States: A Surgical Solution," *The Quarterly Review of Biology*, 62, No. 2 (June 1987): 160.

Reilly, Philip R., *The Surgical Solution: A History of Involuntary Sterilization in the United States* (Baltimore: The Johns Hopkins University Press, 1991).

Reisman, W. Michael and Antoniou, Chris T., eds., *The Laws of War: A Comprehensive Collection of Primary Documents on International Laws Governing Armed Conflict* (New York: Vintage Books, 1994).

Rosenbaum, Ron, *Explaining Hitler: The Search for the Origins of His Evil* (New York: Random House, 1998).

Rothman, David J., *Strangers at the Bedside* (New York: Basic Books, 1994).

Sass, Hans-Martin; Rothman, David J.; Katz, Jay, "The Nuremberg Code, German Law, and Prominent Physician Thinkers," *The Journal of the American Medical Association*, 277, No. 9 (March 5, 1997): 709–10.

Sass, Hans-Martin, "Reichsrundschreiben 1931: Pre-Nuremberg German Regulations Concerning New Therapy and Human Experimentation," *Journal of Medicine and Philosophy*, 8 (1983): 99–111.

Schirra, Bruno, "Die Erinnerung der Taeter," *Der Spiegel*, No. 40 (September 28, 1998): 90–100.

Schirrmacher, Frank, ed., *Die Walser-Bubis Debate: Eine Dokumentation* (Frankfurt a/M: Suurkamp Verlag, 1999).

Schlinck, Berhhard, "Auf dem Eis," *Der Spiegel*, No. 19 (May 7, 2001): 82–86.

"Scientific Results of German Medical War Crimes: Report of an Enquiry by a Committee under the Chairmanship of Lord Moran" (London: Her Majesty's Stationary Office, 1949).

Schmuhl, Hans-Walter, *Rassenhygiene, Nationalsozialismus, Euthanasie* (Goettingen: Vandenhoeck and Ruprecht, 1987).

Schneider, Ulrich and Stein, Harry, "IG Farben, Buchenwald, Menschenversuche: Ein dokumentarischer Bericht," *Buchenwald*, Heft 26 (Weimar: Nationale Mahn- und Gedenkstaette Buchenwald, 1986).

"Schuldsprueche im Aerzteprozess," *Neues Deutschland*, 3, No. 193 (August 20, 1947).

Schwarberg, Guenther, *Der SS-Arzt und die Kinder vom Bullenhuser Damm* (Goettingen: Steidl Verlag, 1988).

Seidelman, William E., "Mengele Medicus: Medicine's Nazi Heritage," *Milbank Quarterly*, 66, No. 2 (1988): 221–239.

Seidelman, William E., "Nuremberg Lamentation: For the Forgotten Victims of Medical Science," *British Medical Journal*, 313, No. 7070 (December 7, 1996): 1463–67.

Shaecoff, Philip, "Head of E.P.A. Bars Nazi Data in Study of Gas," The New York Times (March 23, 1988): 1.

Shelley, Lore, ed., *Criminal Experiments on Human Beings in Auschwitz and War Research Laboratories: Twenty Women Prisoners' Accounts* (San Francisco: Mellen Research University Press, 1991).

Shuster, Evelyne, "Fifty Years After: The Significance of the Nuremberg Code," *The New England Journal of Medicine*, 337, No. 20 (November 13, 1997): 1436–40.

Shuster, Evelyne, "The Nuremberg Code: Hippocratic Ethics and Human Rights," *The Lancet*, 351, No. 9107 (March 28, 1998): 974–77.

"Sieben Todesurteile in Nuernberg," *Berliner Zeitung*, 3, No. 193 (August 21, 1947).

Smith, Bradley F., *Reaching Judgment at Nuremberg* (New York: Basic Books, 1977).

Spiro, Howard M., "Eppinger of Vienna: Scientist and Villain," *Journal of Clinical Gastroenterology*, 6 (December 1984): 493–97.

Strong, Richard P. "The Investigation Carried on by the Biological Laboratory in Relation to the Suppression of the Recent Cholera Outbreak in Manila," *The Philippine Journal of Science*, 2 (1907): 422.

Strong, Richard P. "Vaccination Against Plague," *The Philippine Journal of Science*, 1 (1906): 181–190.

Strong, Richard P. and Crowell, B.C., "The Etiology of Beriberi," *The Philippine Journal of Science*, 7B, No. 4 (1912): 291.

Sun, Marjorie, "EPA Bars Use of Nazi Data," *Science*, 240, No. 4848 (April 1, 1988): 21.

Taylor, Telford, *The Anatomy of the Nuremberg Trials* (New York: Little, Brown and Co., 1992).

"The Treatment of Shock From Prolonged Exposure to Cold, Especially in Water," Combined Intelligence Objectives Sub-Committee, G-2 Div., SHAEP (Rear), (Washington, D.C.: Office of the Publication Board, n.d.).

Veatch, Robert M., "Nazis and Hippocratists: Searching for the Moral Relation," *Psychohistory Review*, 16, No. 1 (Fall 1987): 15–31.

Walser, Martin, *Erfahrungen beim Verfassen einer Sonntagsrede* (Frankfurt a/M: Edition Suhrkamp, 1998).

Walzer, Michael, *Just and Unjust Wars: A Moral Argument With Historical Illustrations* (New York: Basic Books, 1992).

Weindling, Paul, "Human Guinea Pigs and the Ethics of Experimentation: The BMJ's Correspondent at the Nuremberg Medical Trial," *British Medical Journal*, 313, No. 7070 (December 7, 1996): 1467–70.

Weizsaecker, Viktor von, *"Euthanasie" und Menschenversuche* (Heidelberg: Verlag Lambert Schneider, 1947).

Wyers, Wolfgang, *Death of Medicine in Nazi Germany* (New York: Ardor Scribendi, 1998).

"What's in a Name? The Eppinger Prize and Nazi Experiments," *The Hastings Center Report*, 14, No. 6 (December 1984): 3–4.

White, Hayden, *Metahistory: The Historical Imagination in Nineteenth-Century Europe* (Baltimore: The Johns Hopkins University Press, 1973).

Wiesemann, Claudia, and Frewer, Andreas, eds., *Medizin und Ethik im Zeichen von Auschwitz: 50 Jahre Nuernberger Aerzteprozess* (Erlangen: Verlag Palme und Enke, 1996).

Williams, Peter, and Wallace, David, *Unit 731: Japan's Secret Biological Warfare in World War II* (New York: Free Press, 1989).

Wimmer, August, "Die Bestrafung von Humanitaetsverbrechen und der Grundsatz 'nullum crimen sine lege'," *Sueddeutsche Juristen-Zeitung* II, Sondernummer (March 1947): 123–32.

Zuckmayer, Carl, *A Part of Myself* (New York: Harcourt Brace Janovich, 1970).

"7 Todesurteile-7 Freisprueche im Aerzteprozess," *Nuernberger Nachrichten*, 3 (August 23, 1947).

Index

Studies in Modern European History

The monographs in this series focus upon aspects of the political, social, economic, cultural, and religious history of Europe from the Renaissance to the present. Emphasis is placed on the states of Western Europe, especially Great Britain, France, Italy, and Germany. While some of the volumes treat internal developments, others deal with movements such as liberalism, socialism, and industrialization, which transcend a particular country.

The series editor is:

Frank J. Coppa
Director, Doctor of Arts Program
in Modern World History
Department of History
St. John's University
Jamaica, New York 11439

To order other books in this series, please contact our Customer Service Department:

(800) 770-LANG (within the U.S.)
(212) 647-7706 (outside the U.S.)
(212) 647-7707 FAX

or browse online by series at:
WWW.PETERLANGUSA.COM